Poses for Artists Series, Volume 7 by Justin R. Martin
www.PoseMuse.com for details and links

Introduction

The poses included in the Pose for Artists Book Series were first available online to encourage all artists to create. The purpose of sharing the poses is to help artists get over 'artist's block' that occurs at the very beginning of a new drawing. Staring at that blank page can be daunting. These poses are here to jump-start the whole process.

If you draw, you know the fear of wasting energy starting at a blank page. Use these poses to side-step the problem, and get drawing.

These books are not step-by-step drawing tutorials. There are PLENTY of those available. Here is a "middle step" not a "step by step" to get you moving forward quickly on your new art.

Thank you for supporting our project by purchasing this book. Keep drawing. Share your work often so others may be inspired, by YOU.

PoseMuse
PO Box 2105
Edwards, CO 81632 USA
www.PoseMuse.com
posemuse@gmail.com

Ordering Information:
Available on Amazon.com in paperback or Kindle formats, and Gumroad.com in pdf format via PoseMuse.com. All ebook formats available on SmashWords.com. Special discounts are available on quantity purchases by businesses, corporations, associations, and others. For details, contact PoseMuse above.

Publisher's Cataloging-in-Publication Data:
Martin, Justin R.
Poses for Artists Volume 6: An essential reference for figure drawing and the human form. Inspiring Art and Artists
Series/ Justin R. Martin
1. Nonfiction - Art - Techniques - Drawing
2. Nonfiction - Art - Reference
3. Nonfiction - Art - Illustration

First Edition, First Printing 2022
ISBN: 978-1-7377937-1-7
Imprint: Independently Published
14 13 12 11 10 9 8 7 6 5 4 3 2 1

TABLE OF CONTENTS

This book contains illustrations of faces drawn in a way to make them easily understandable. The next time you need a reference for a face, keep this book in mind.

We create these poses to help artists make new art. Think of them as a jumpstart to your next drawing.

No need to give attribution to POSEmuse we created the poses to make things easy, not difficult.

A final word of advice, DRAW EVERY DAY. If you want to get better, draw more.

- Justin Martin, August 2022

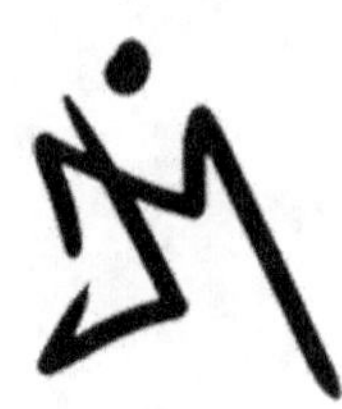

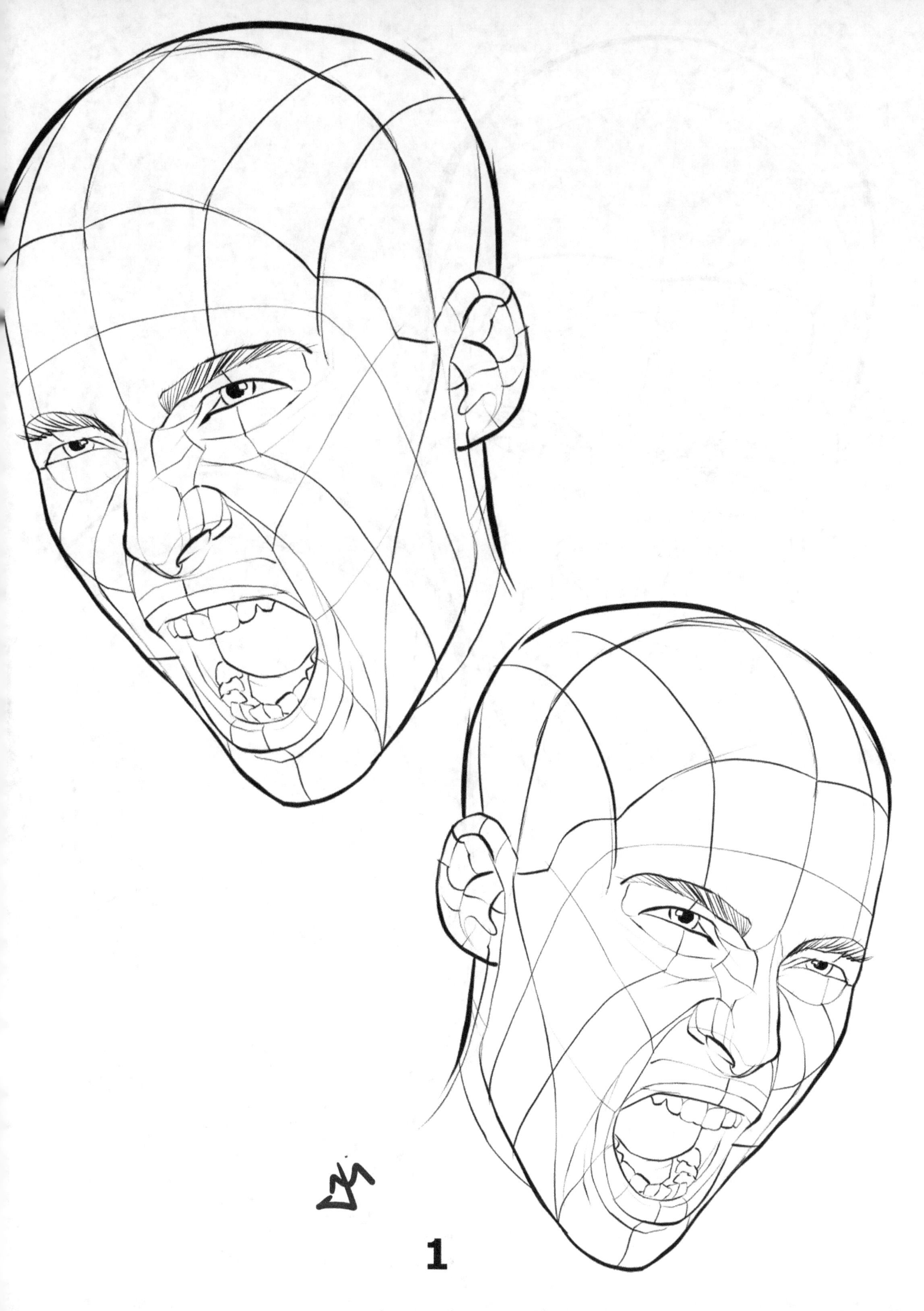

1

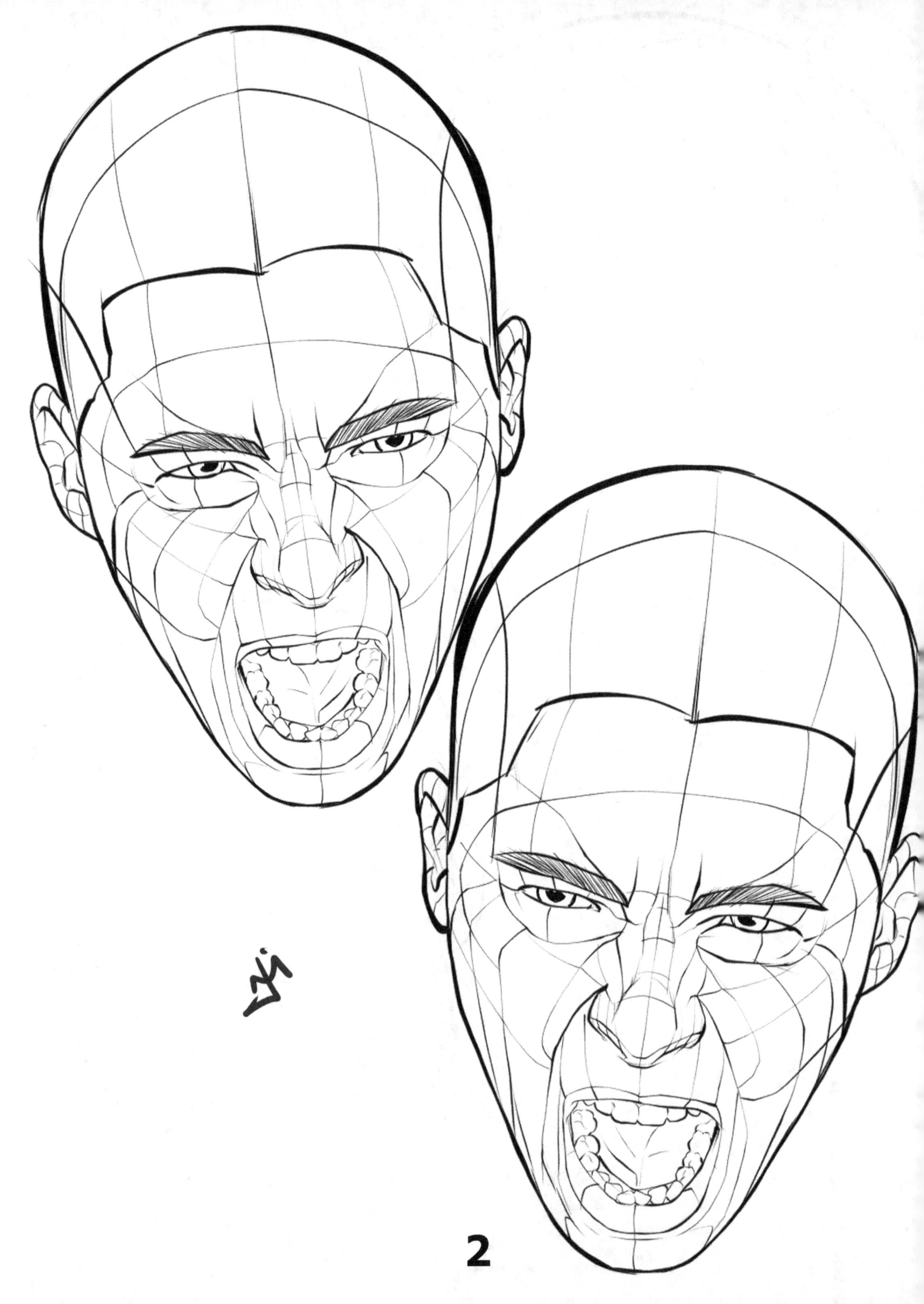

2

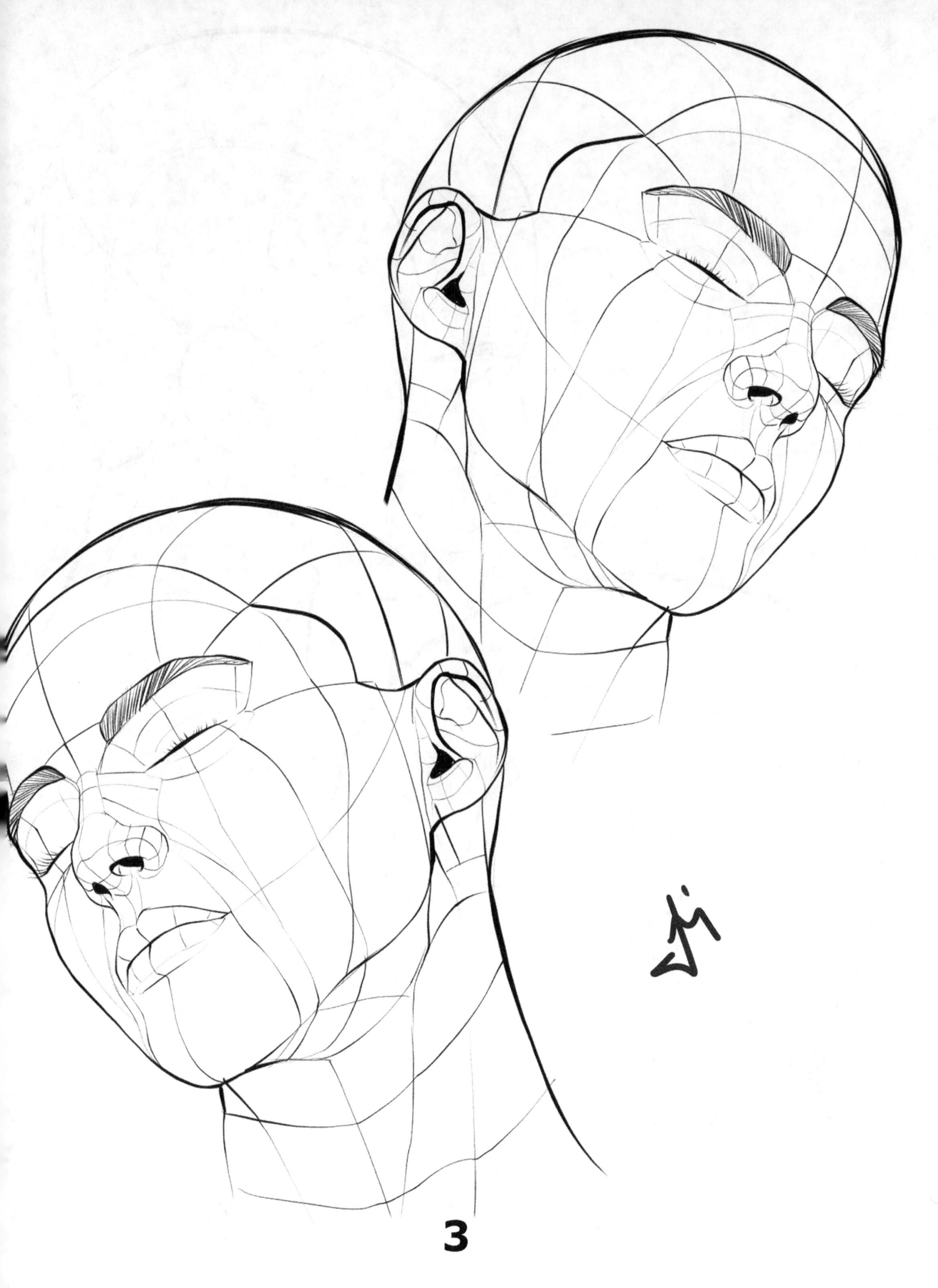

3

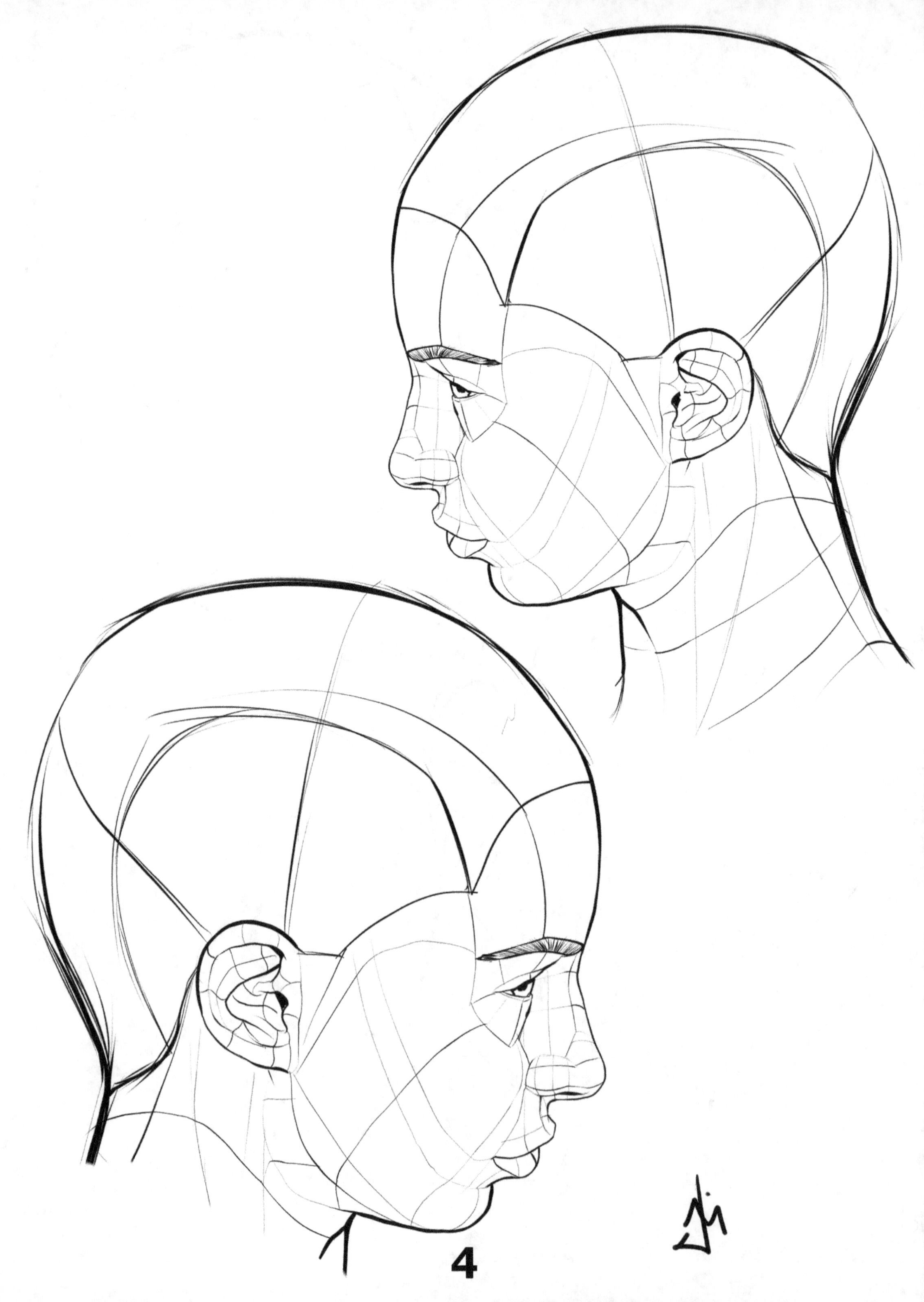

4

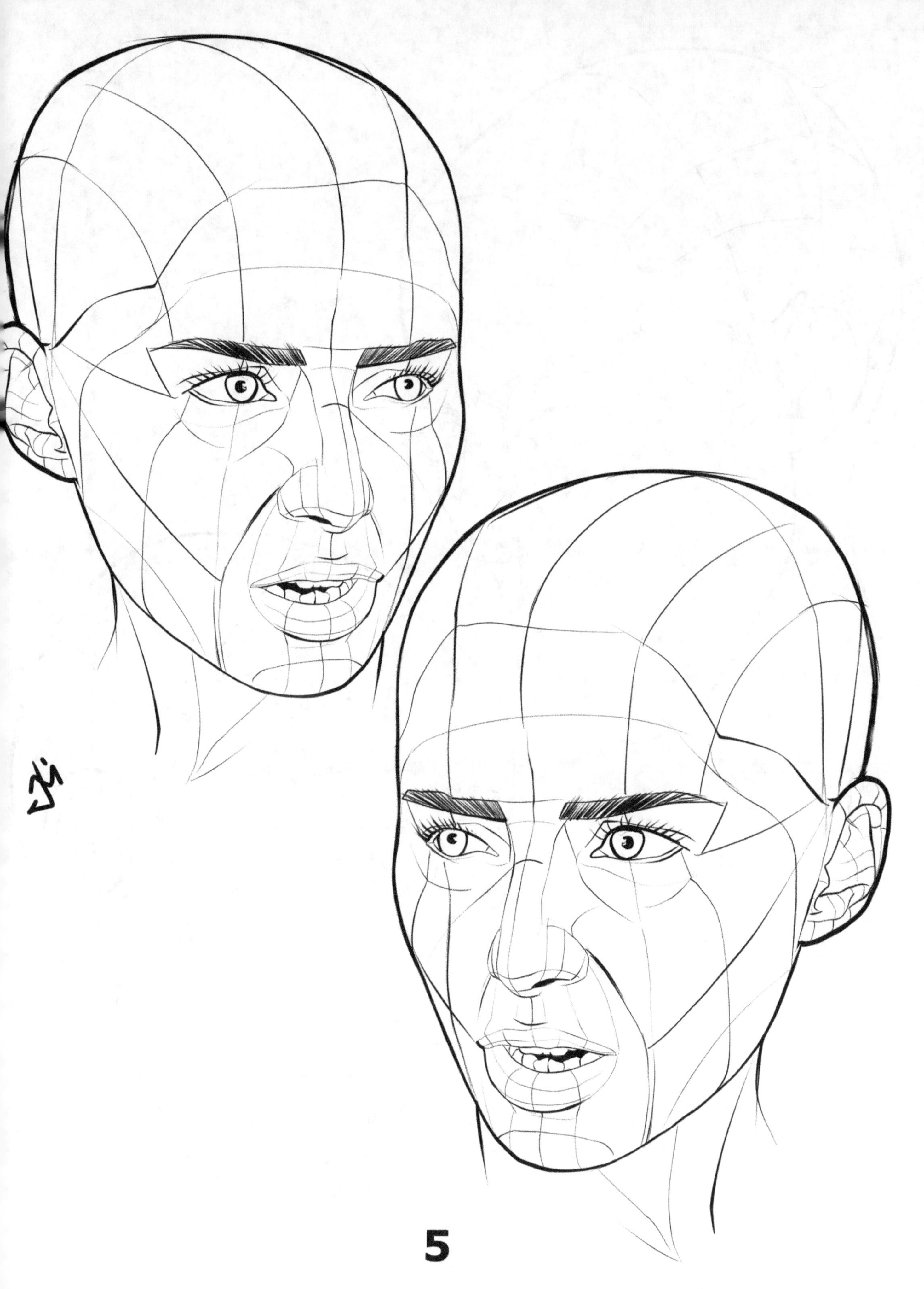

5

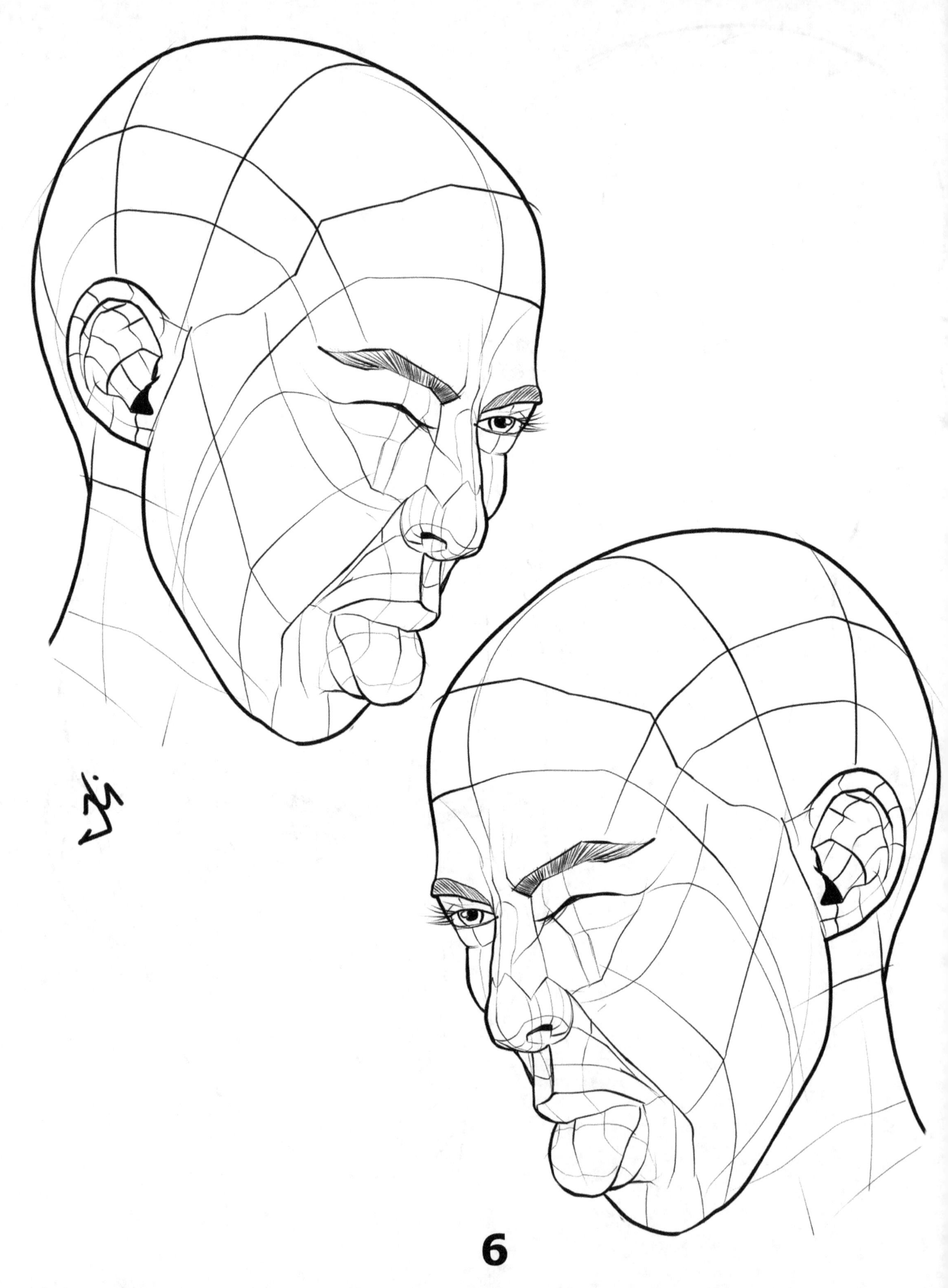

6

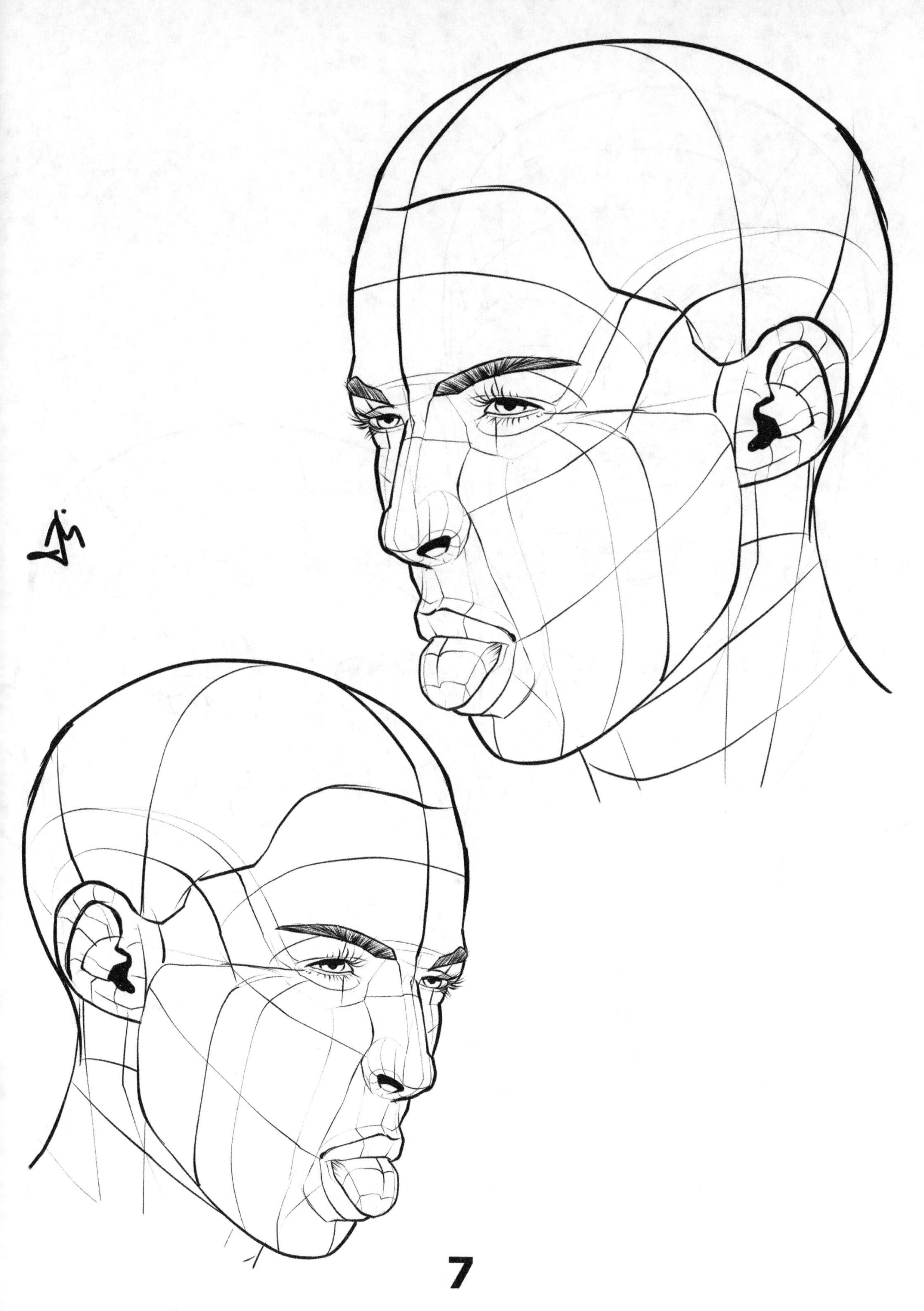

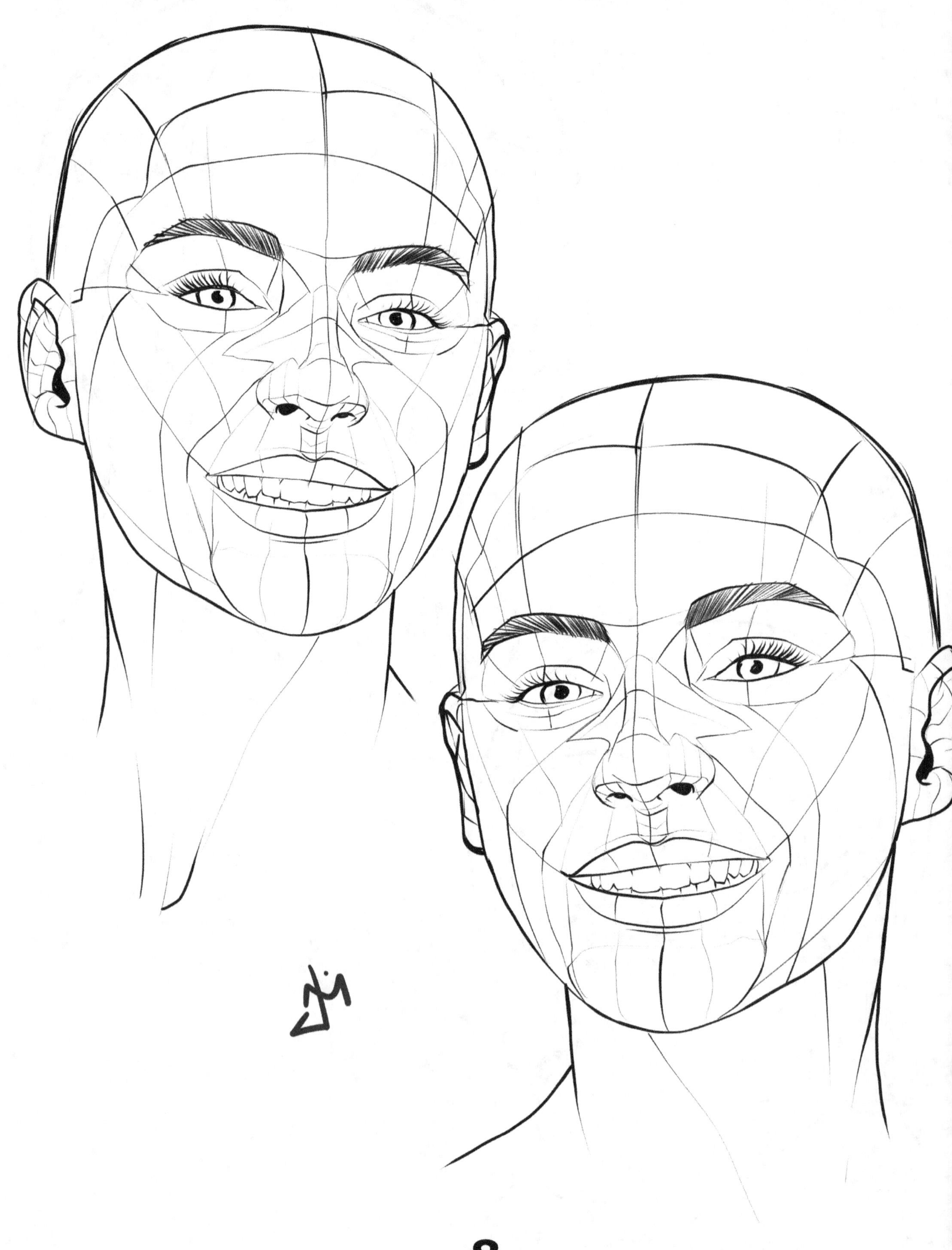

8

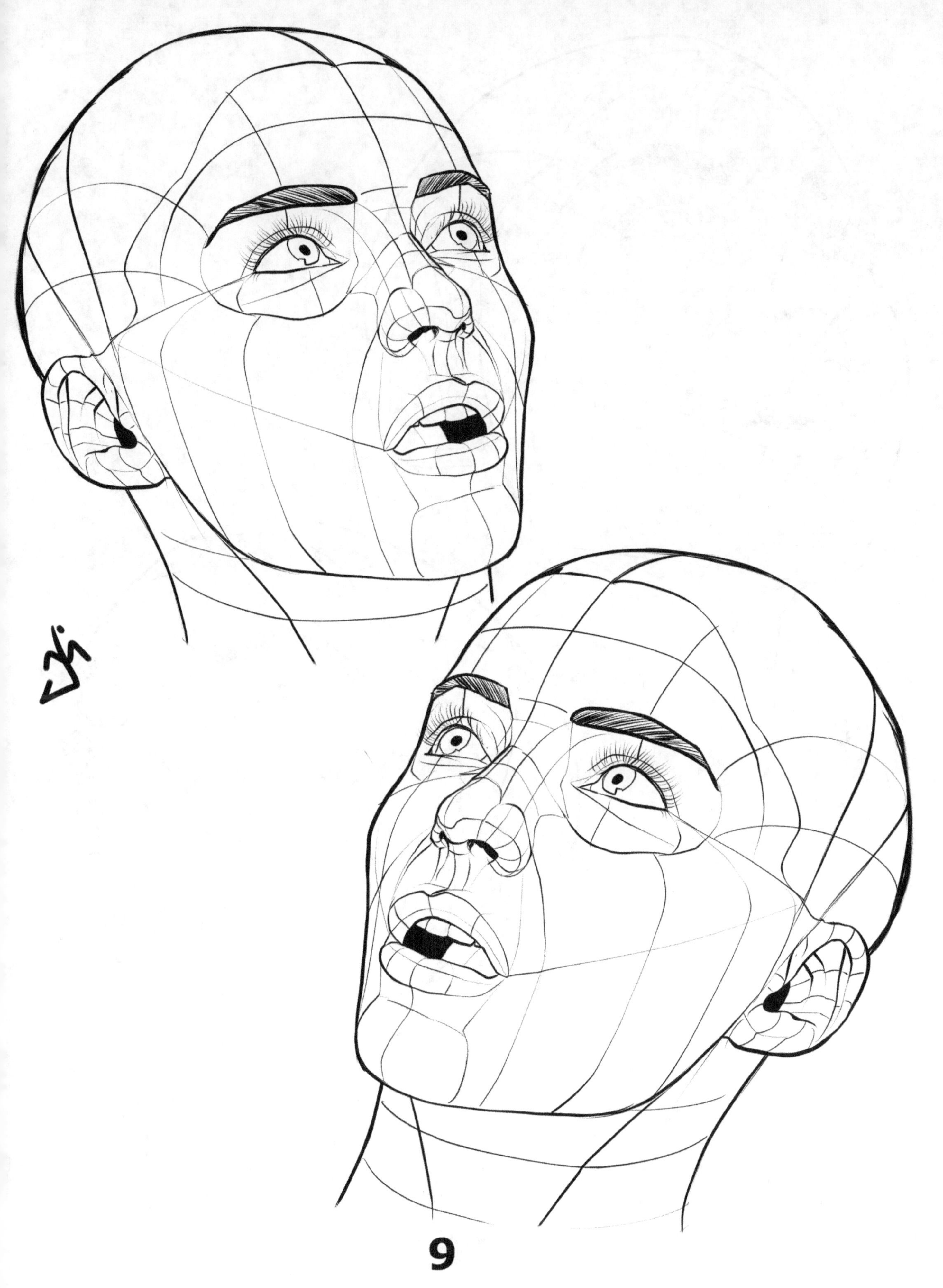

9

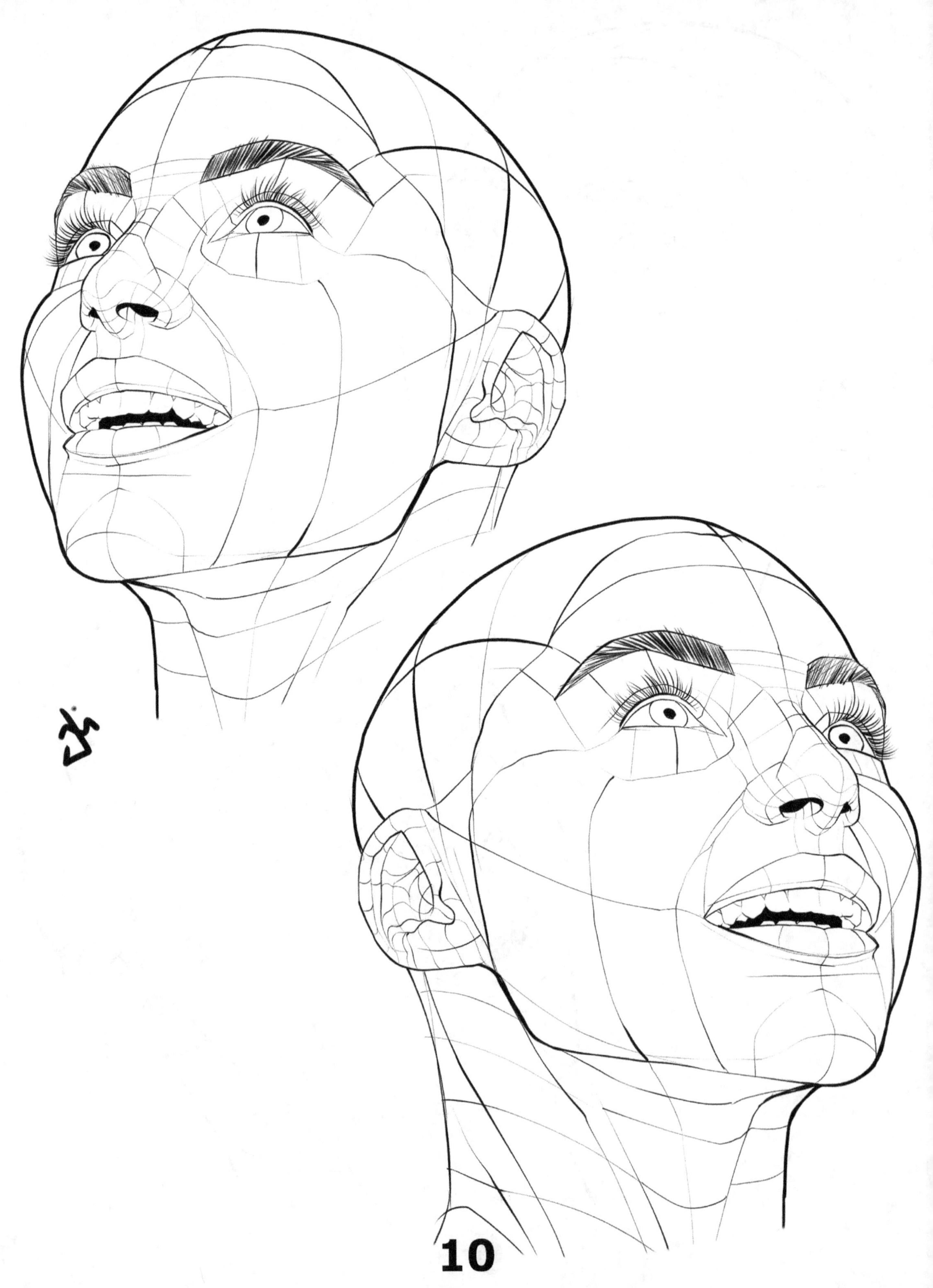

10

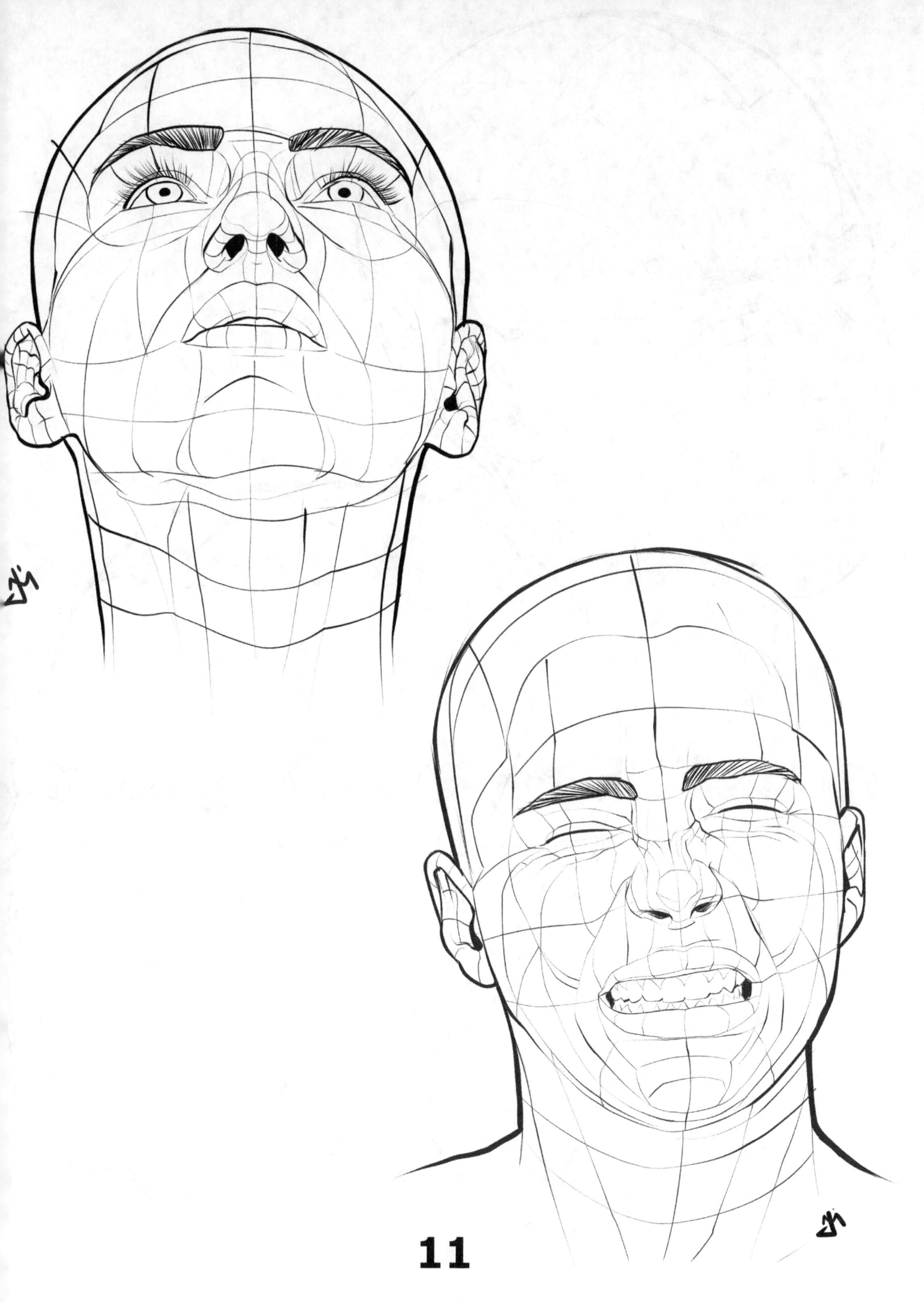

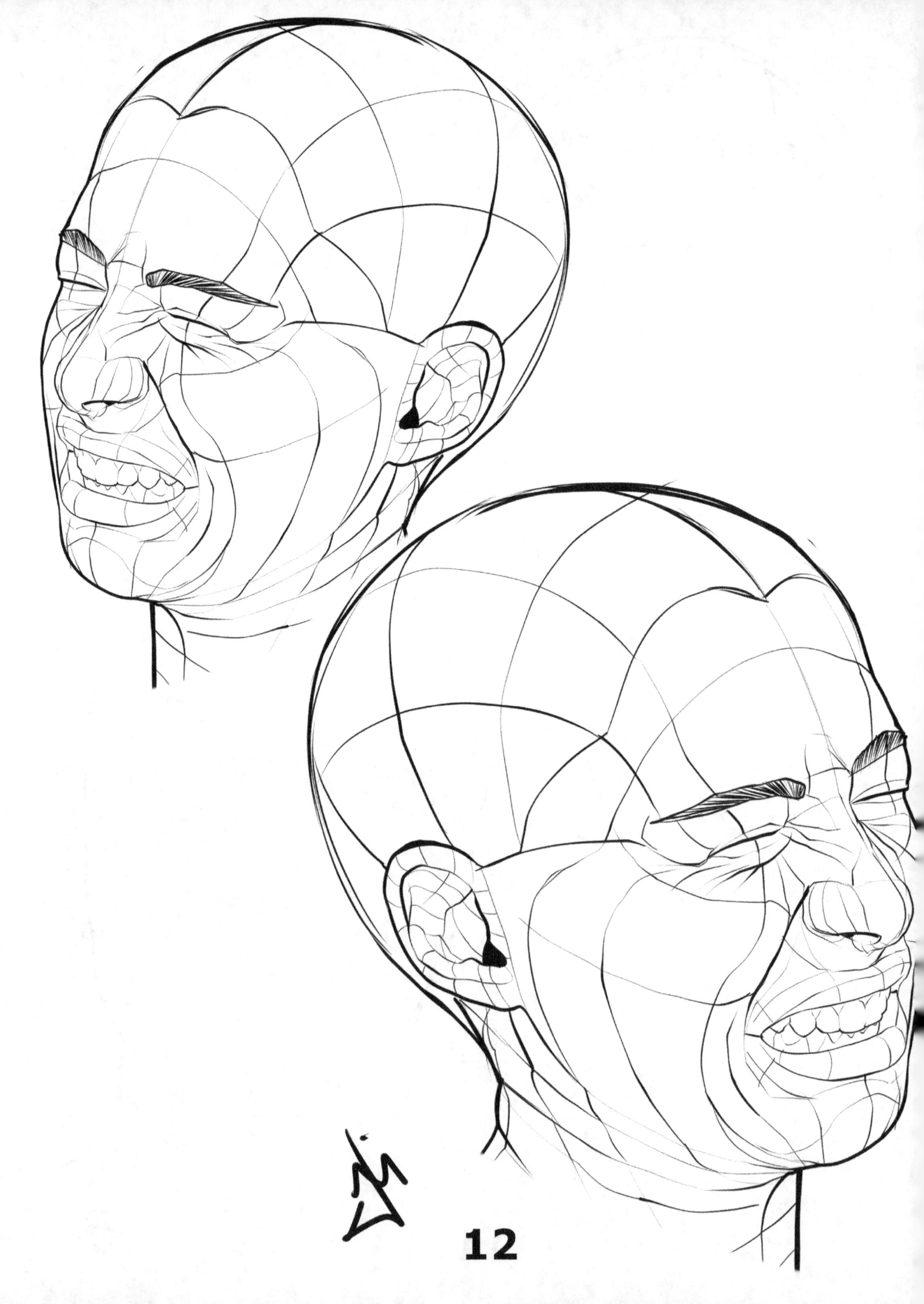

12

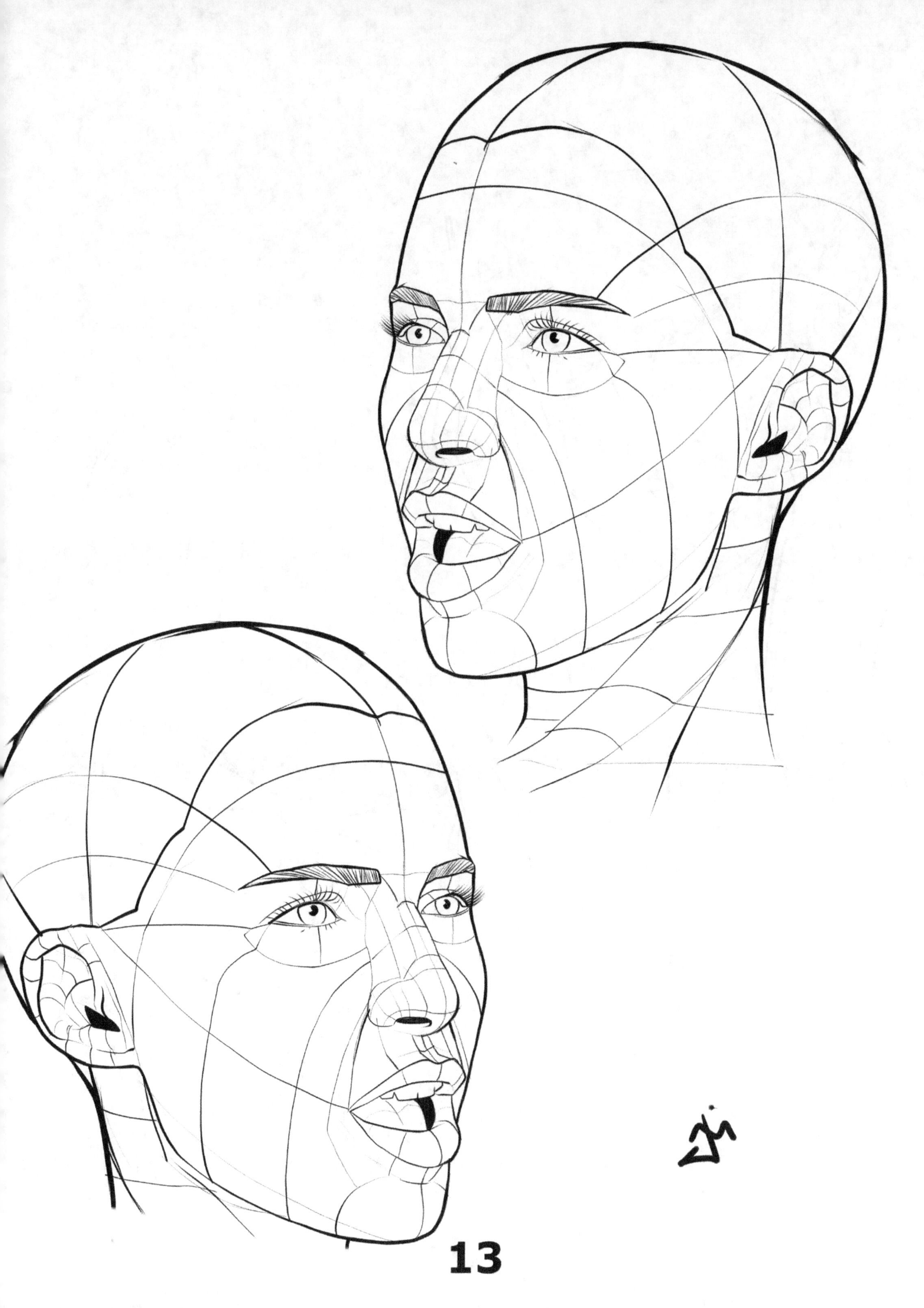

13

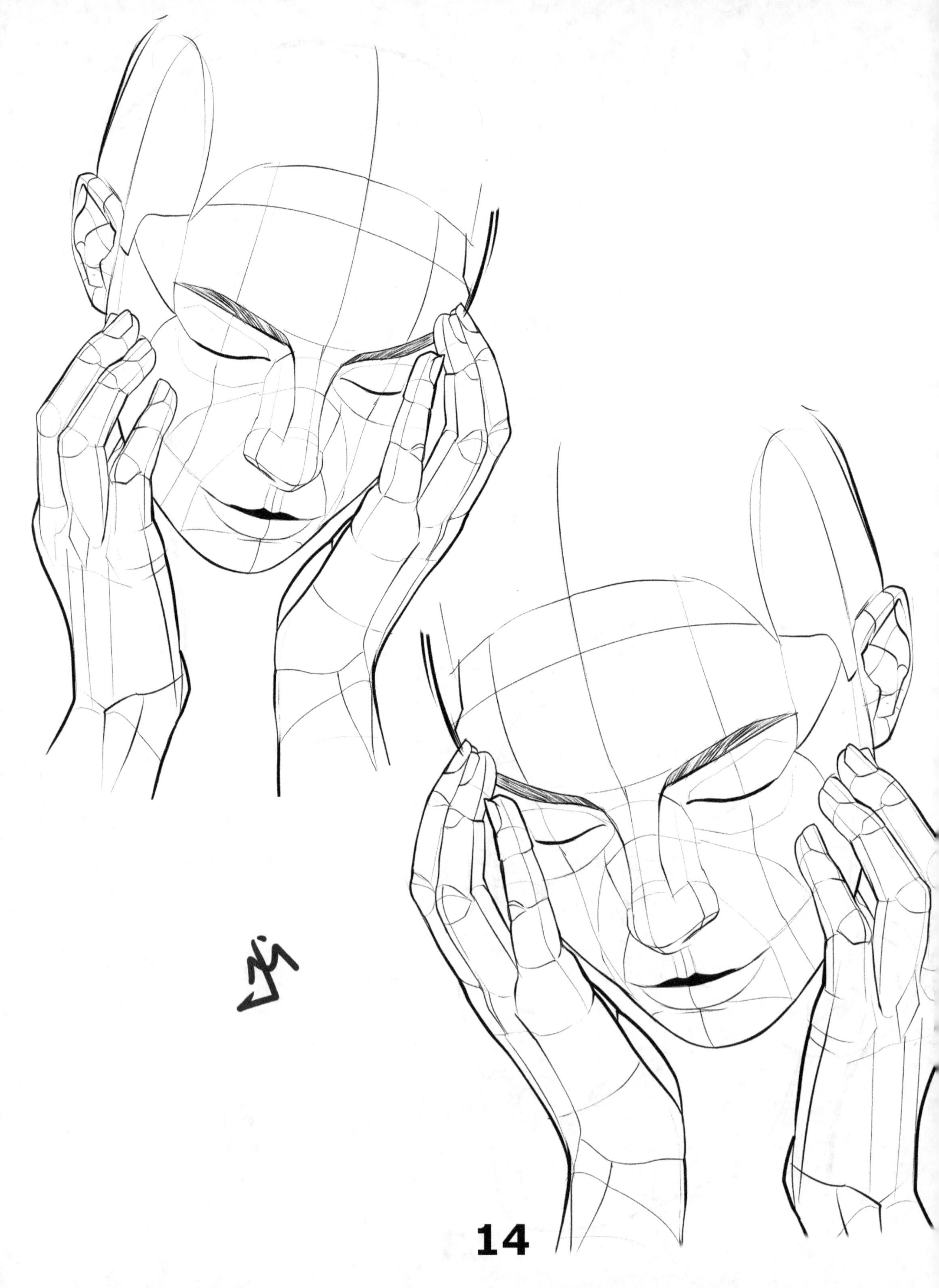

14

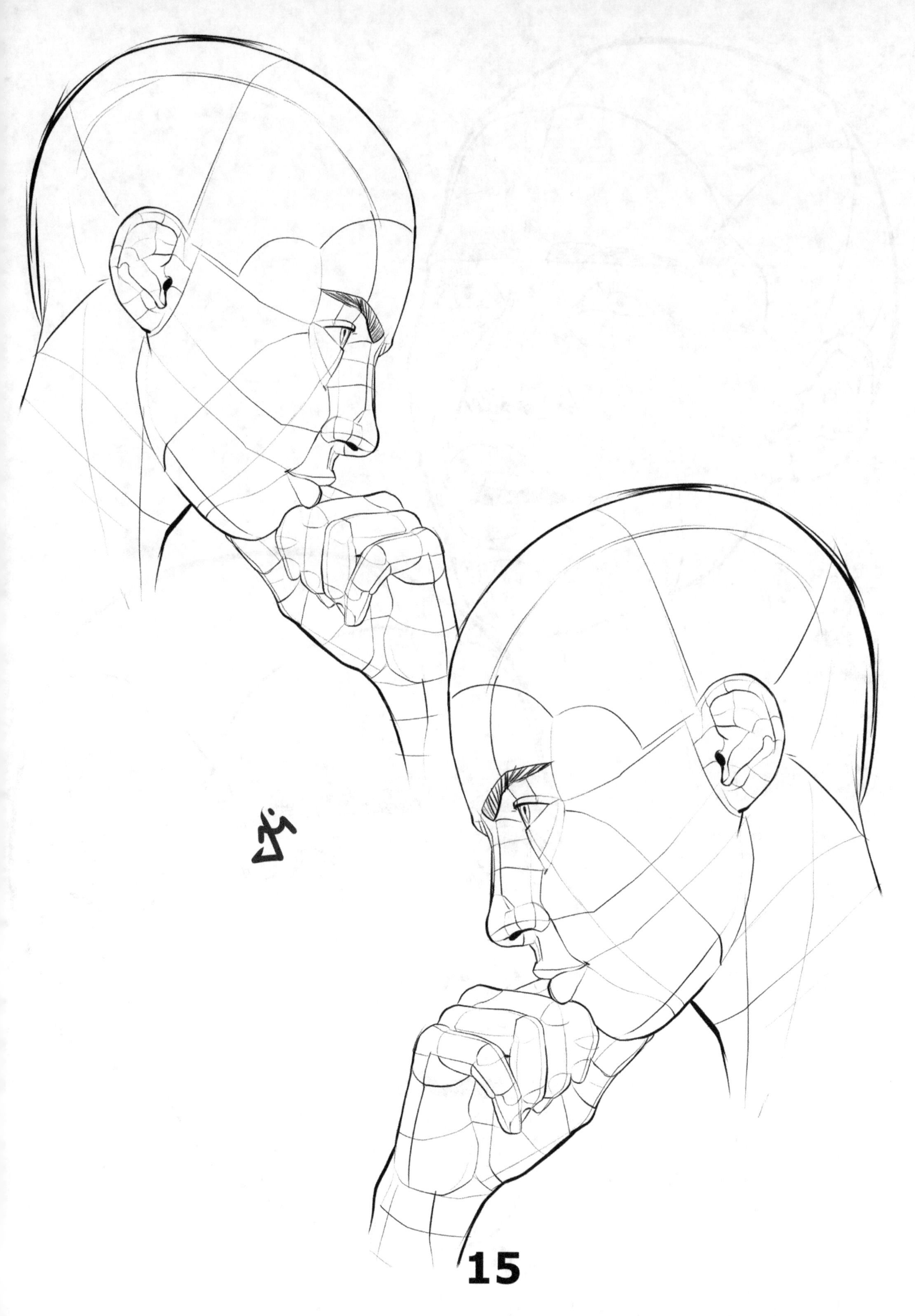

15

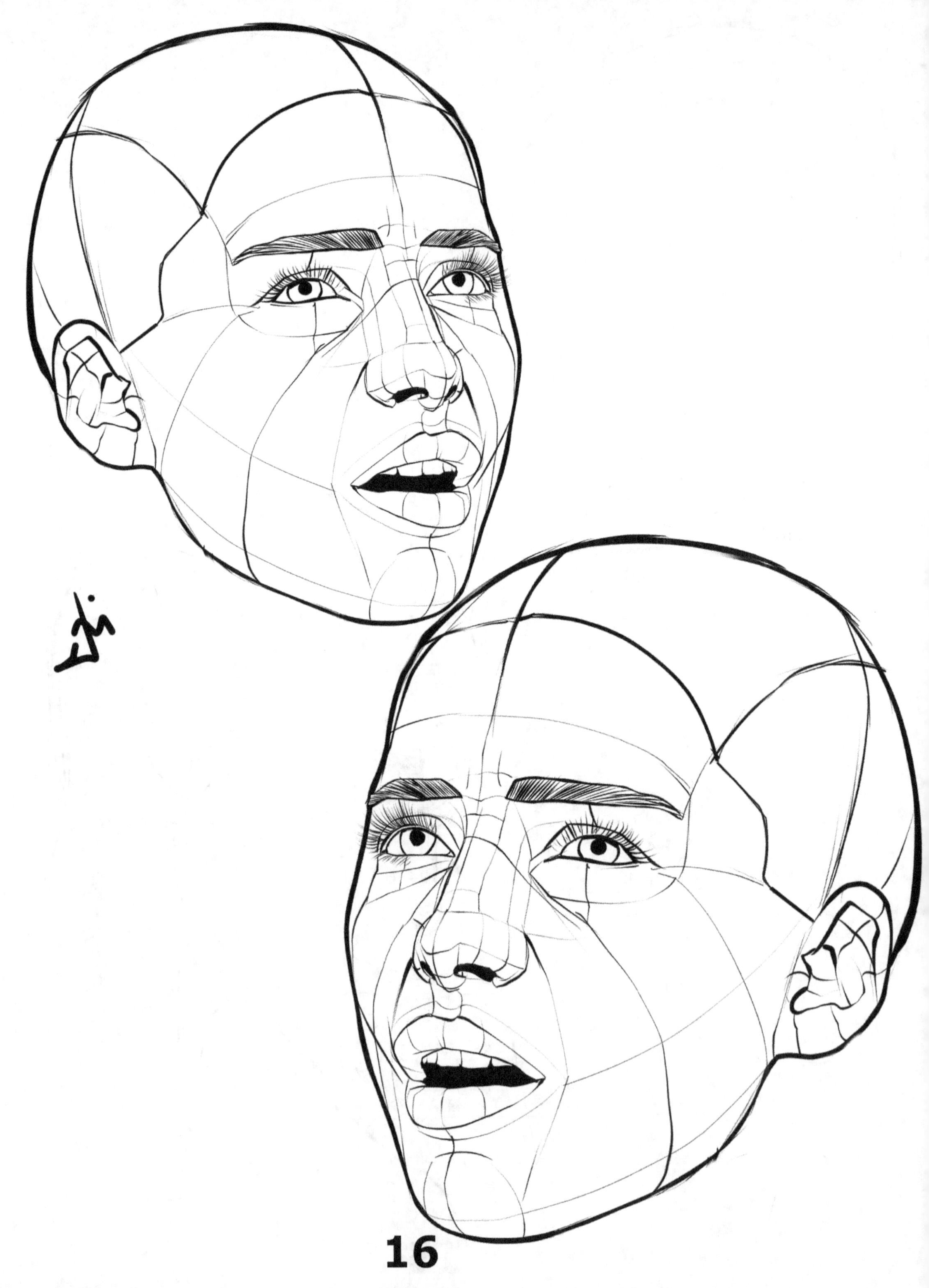

16

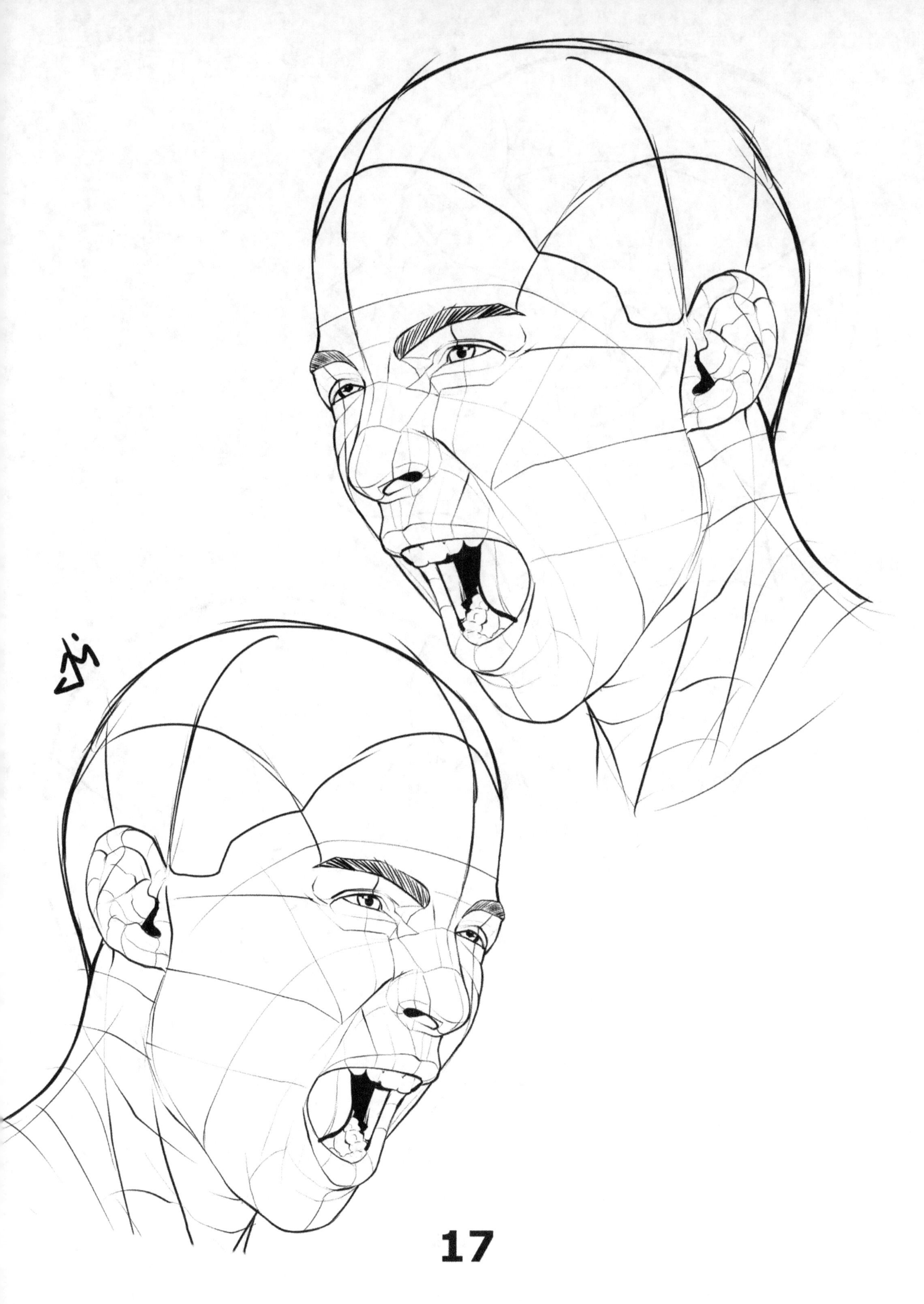

17

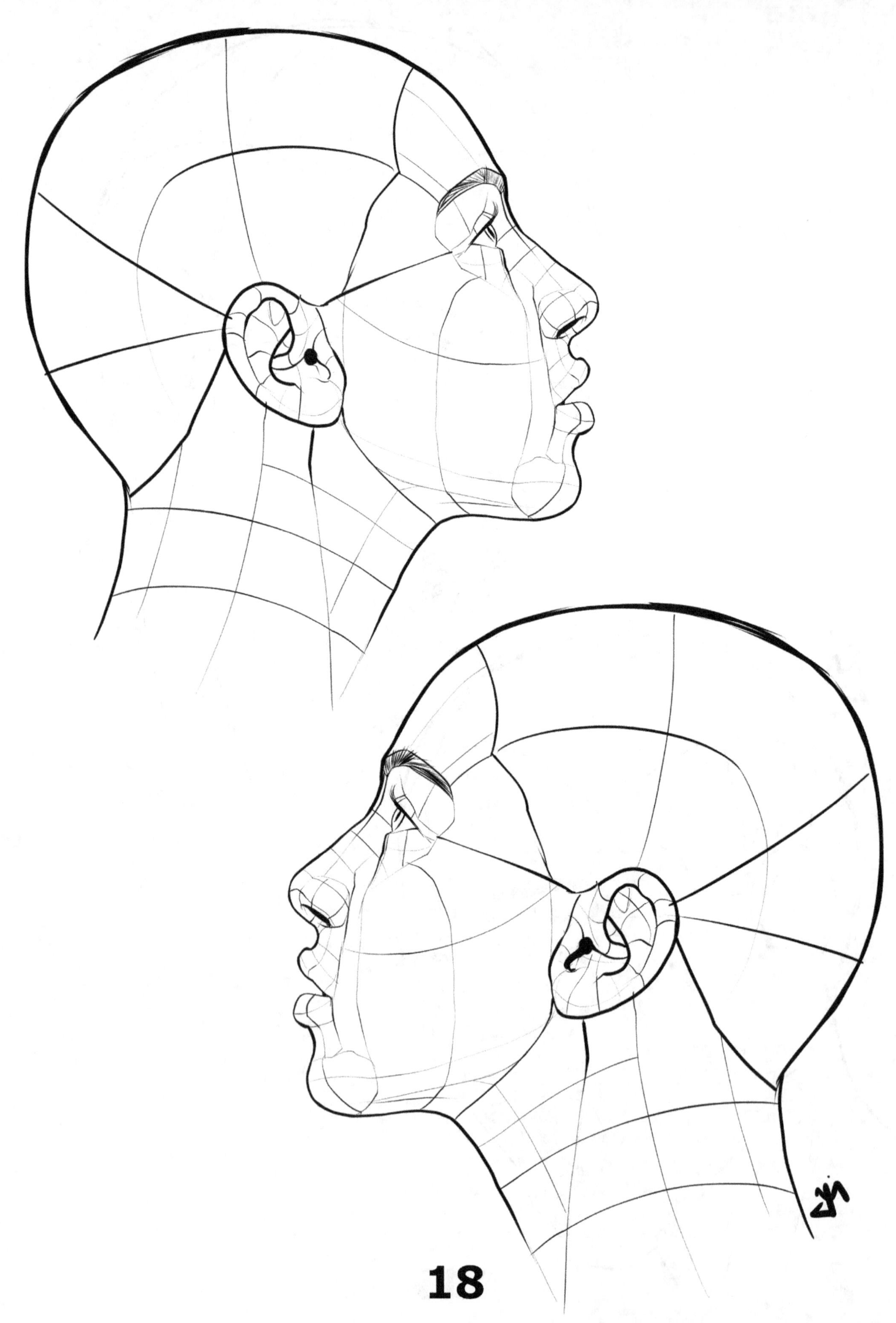

18

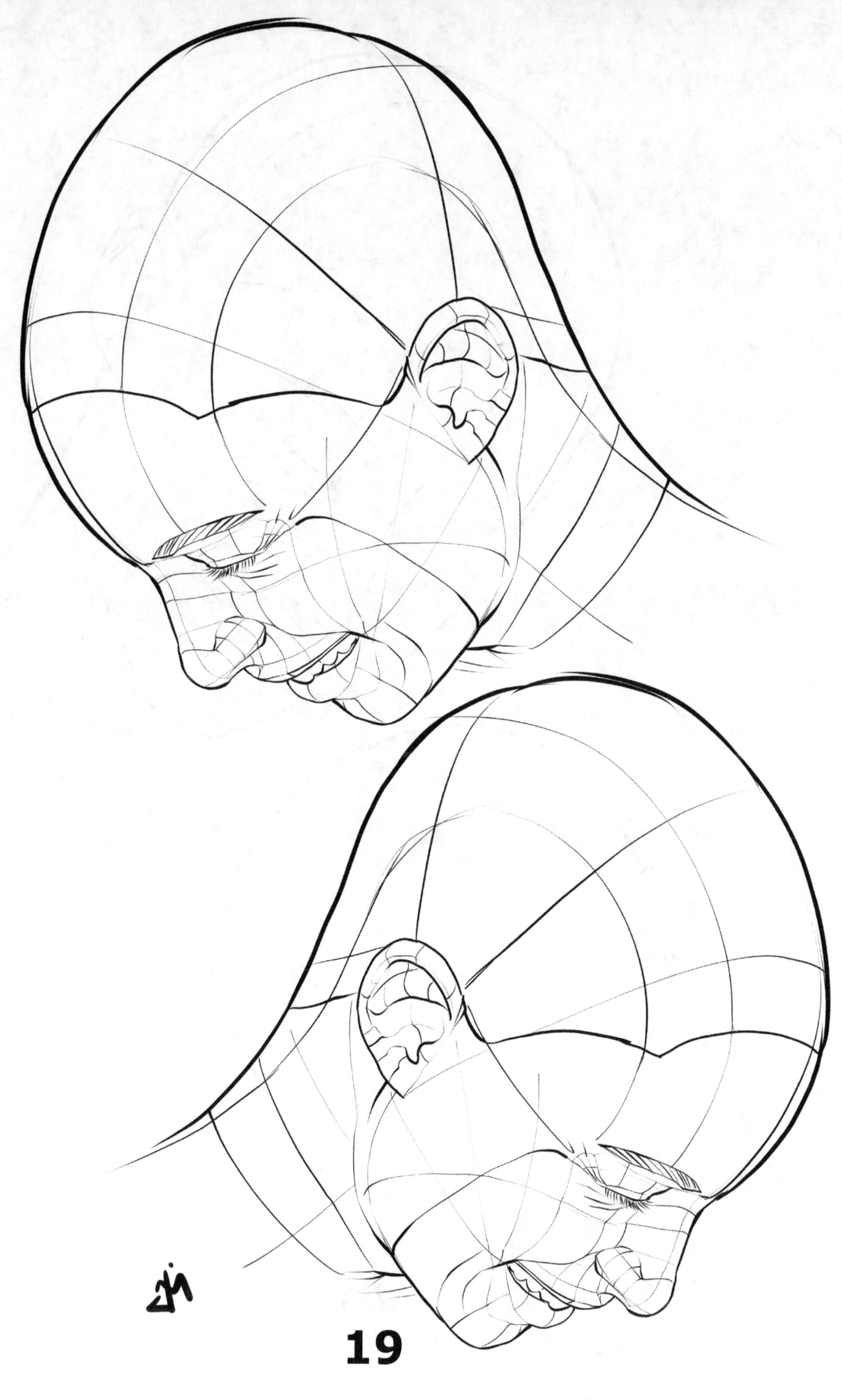

19

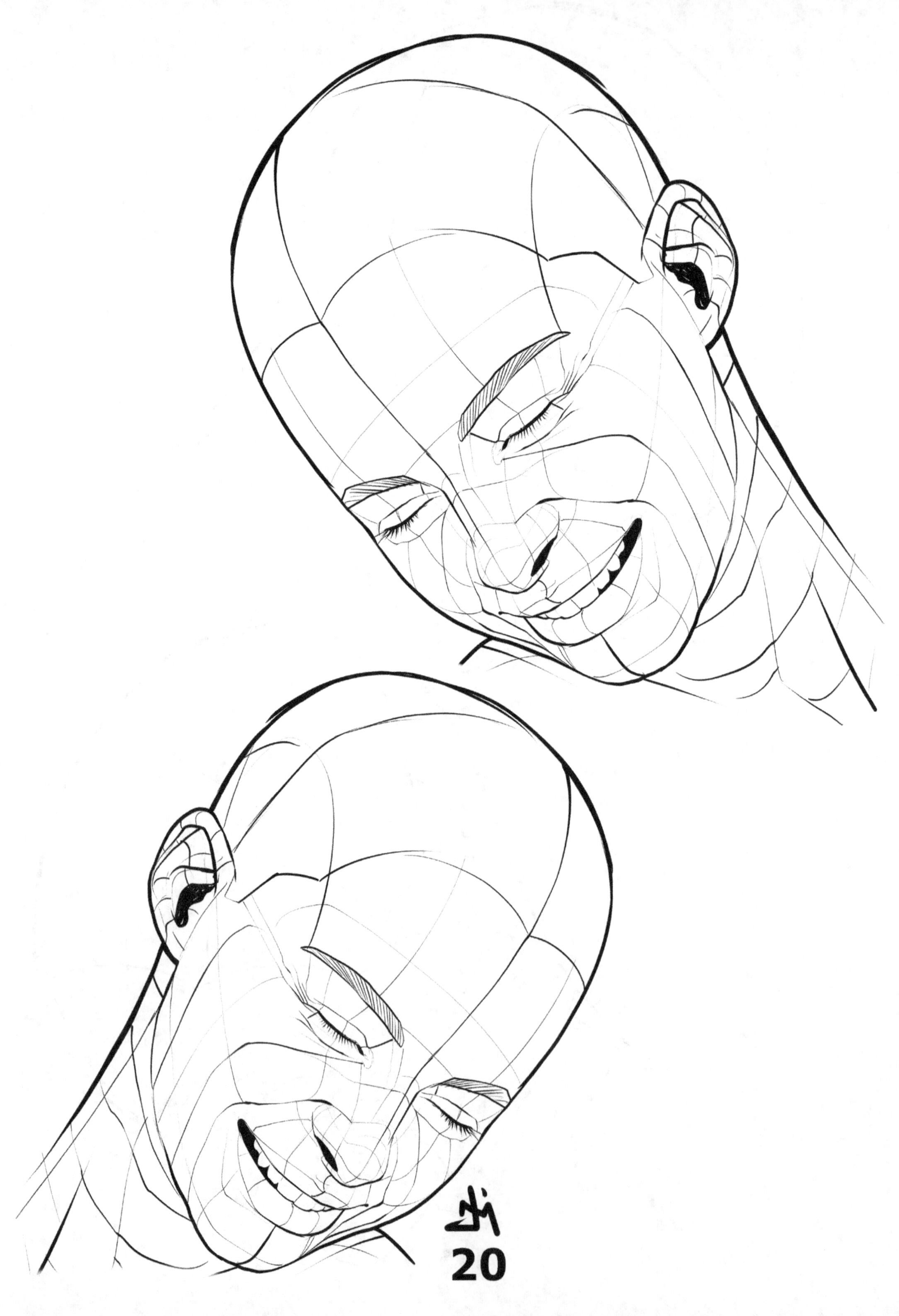

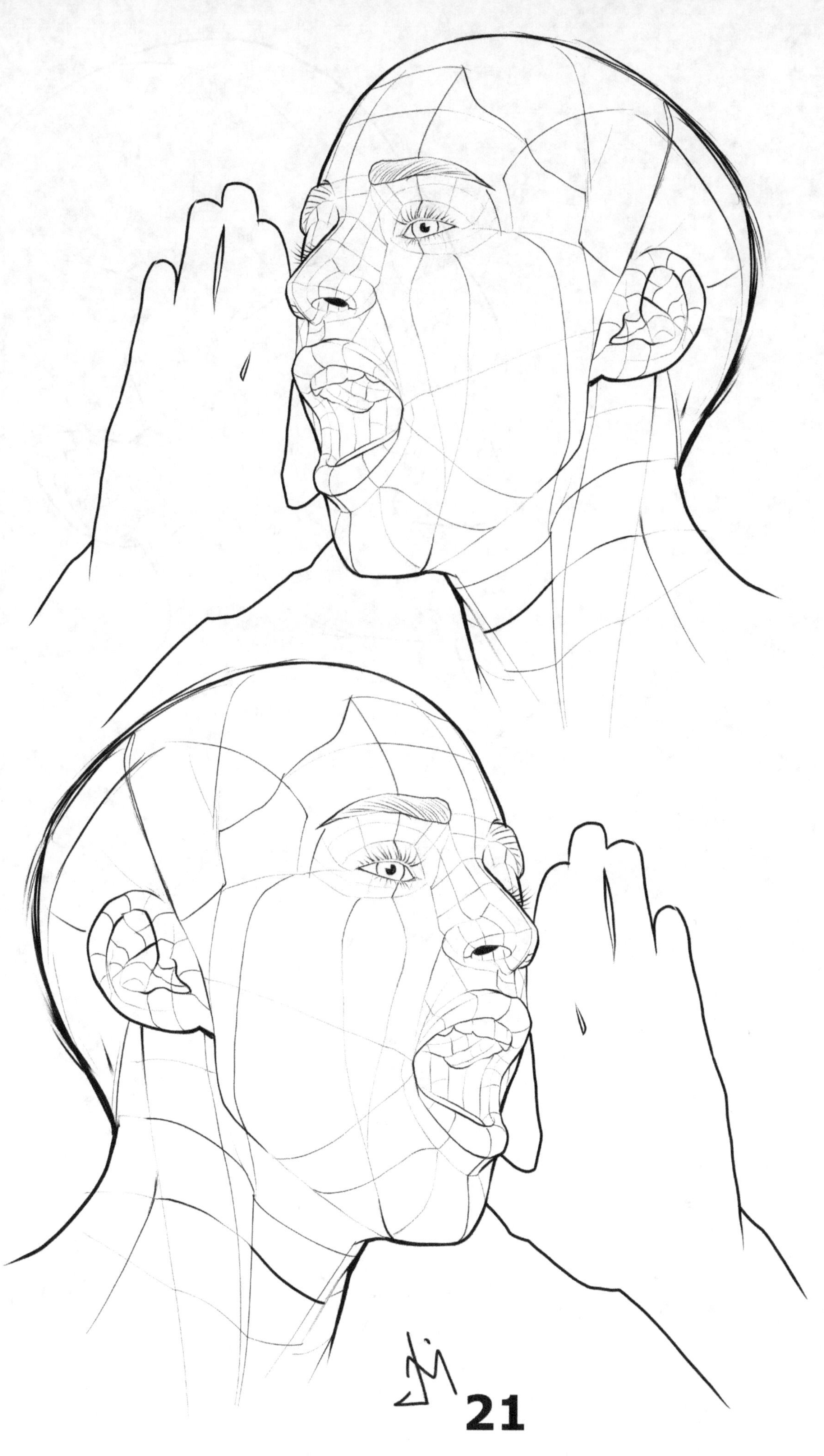

21

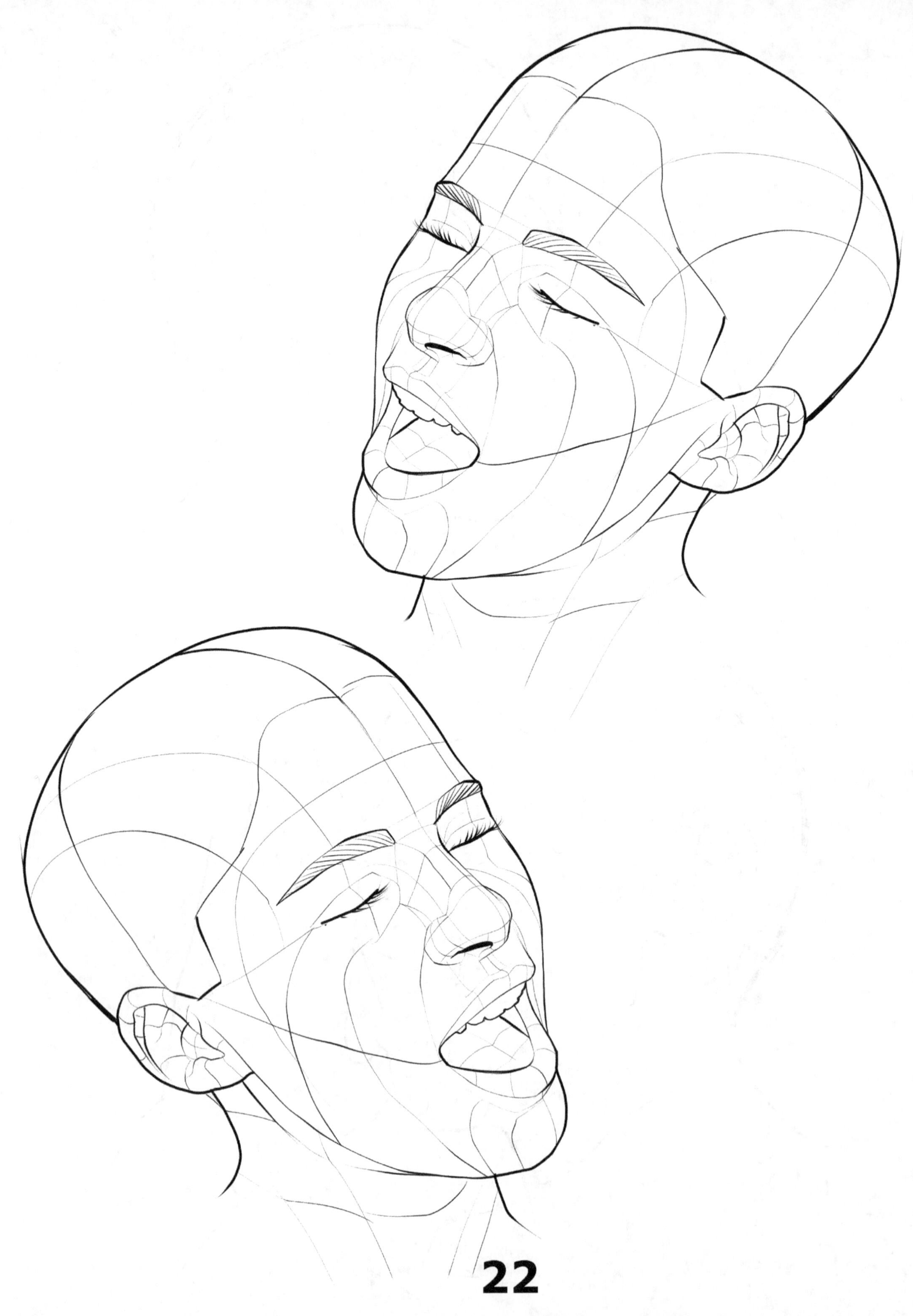

22

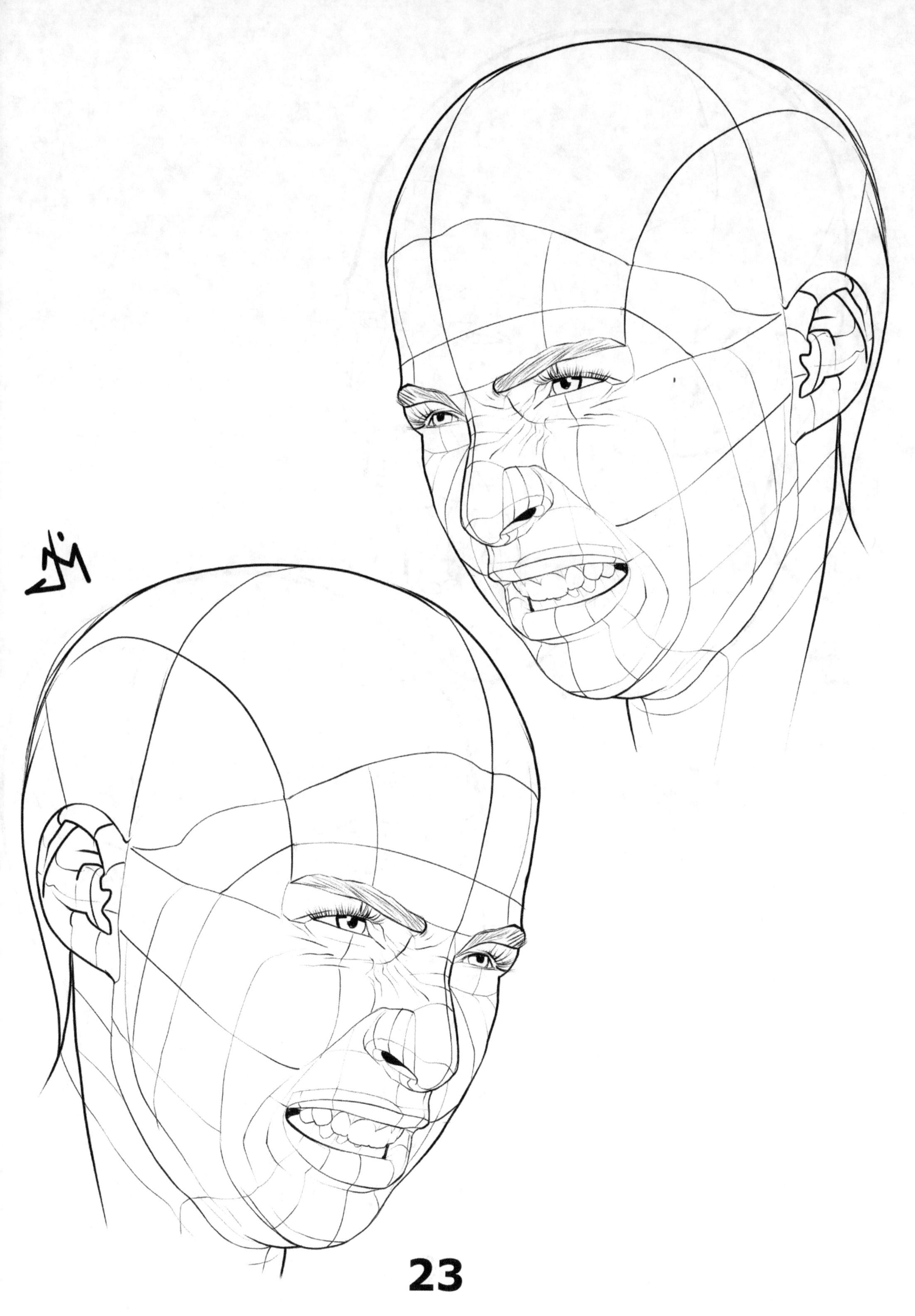

23

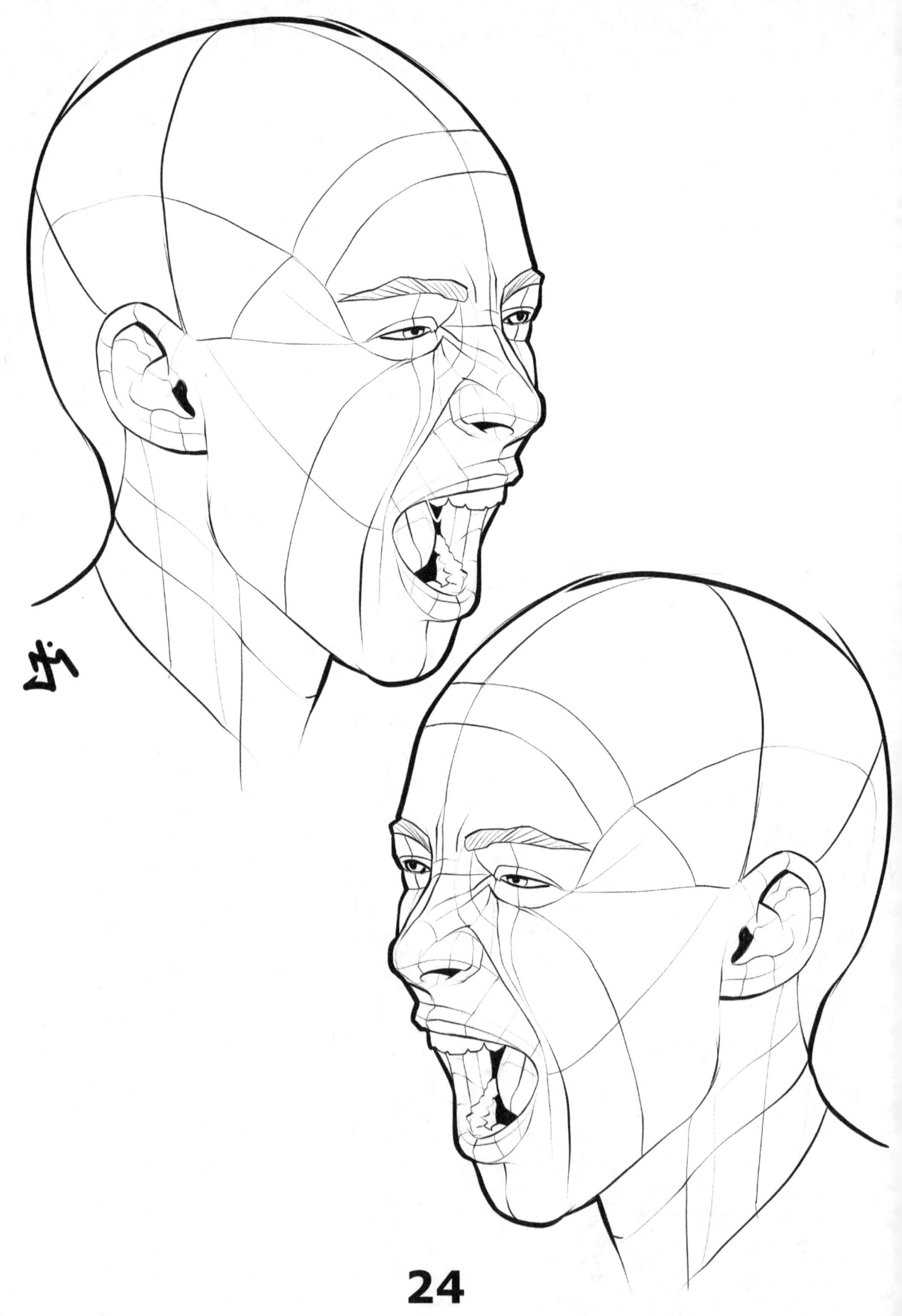

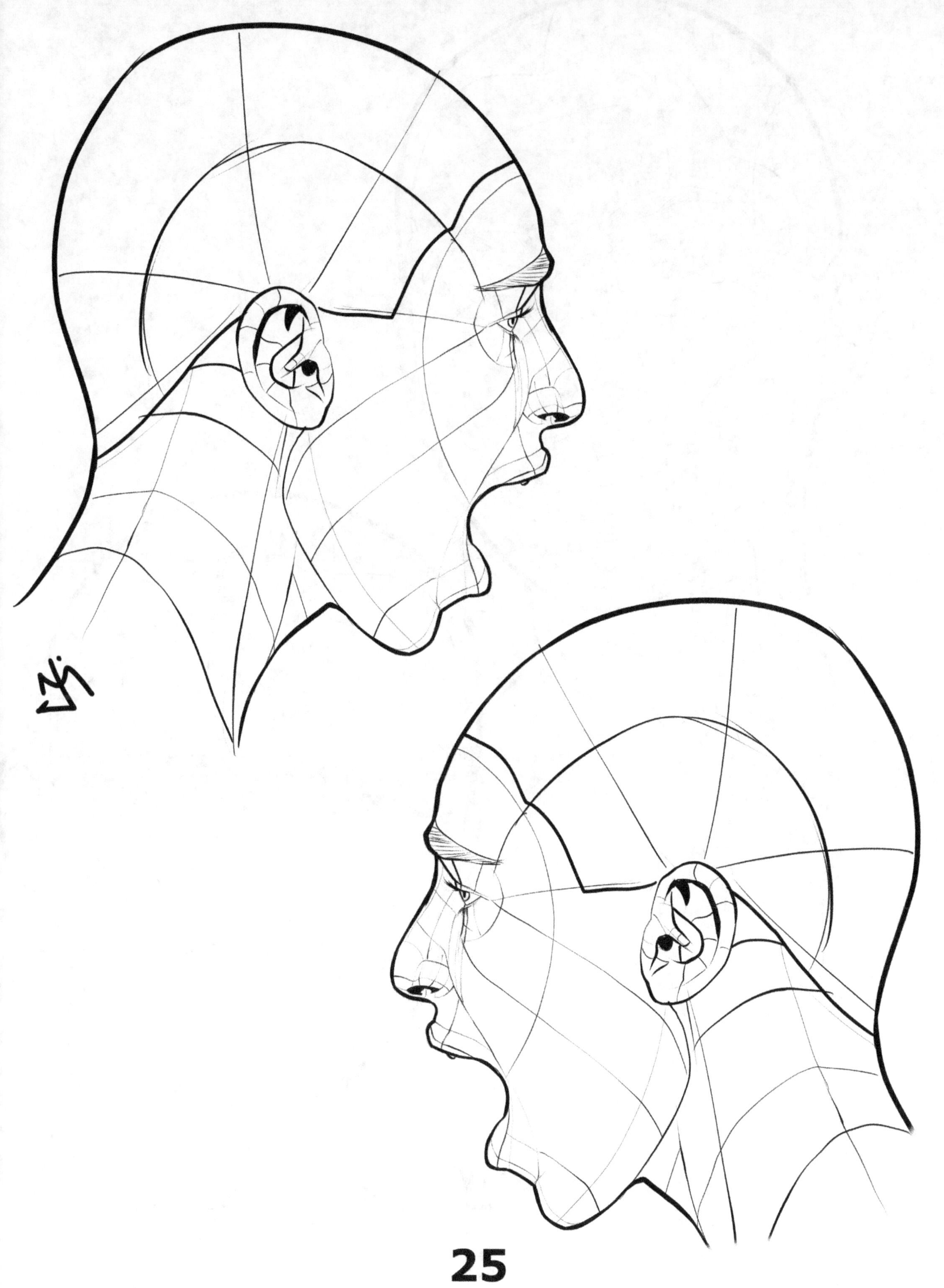

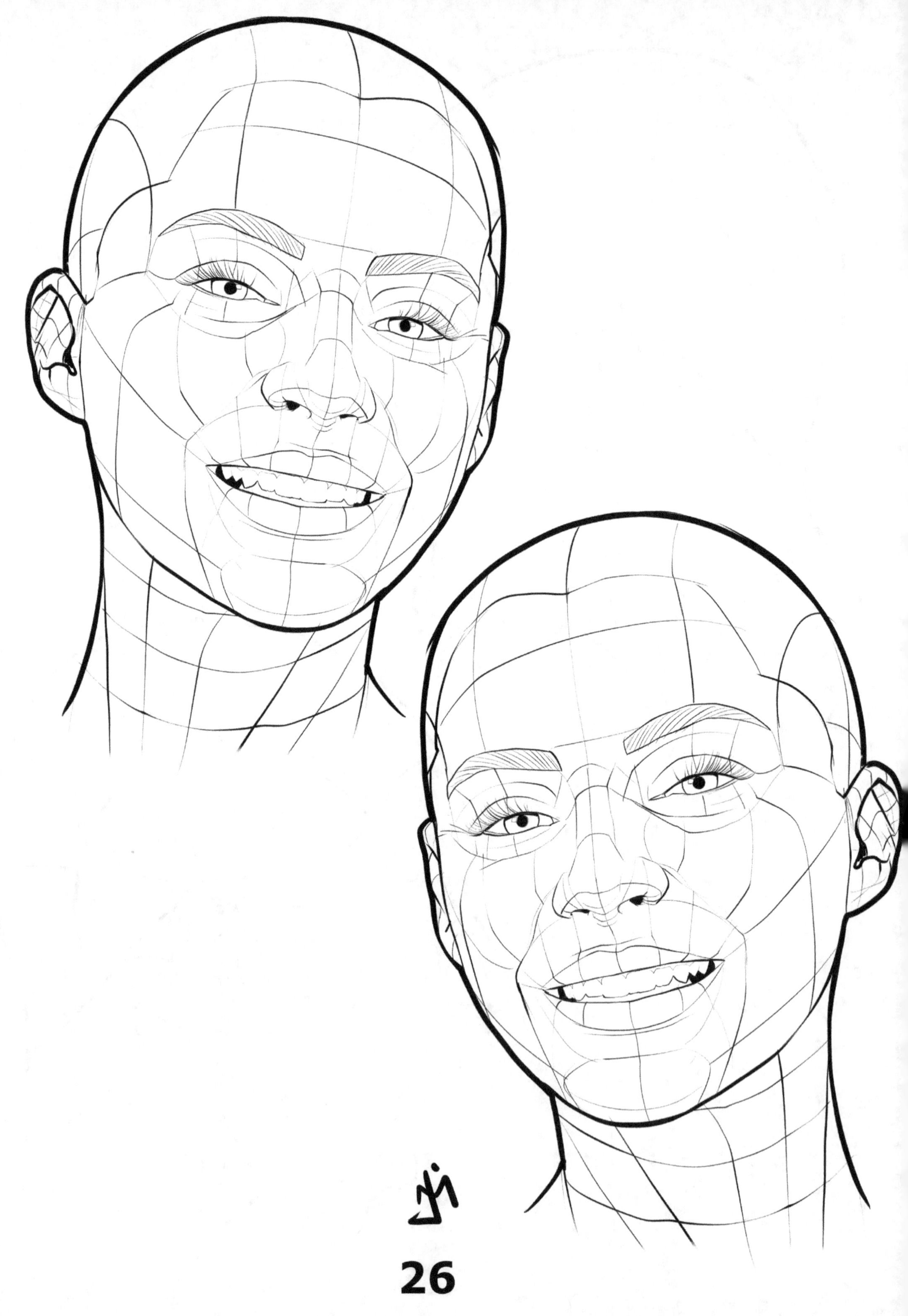

26

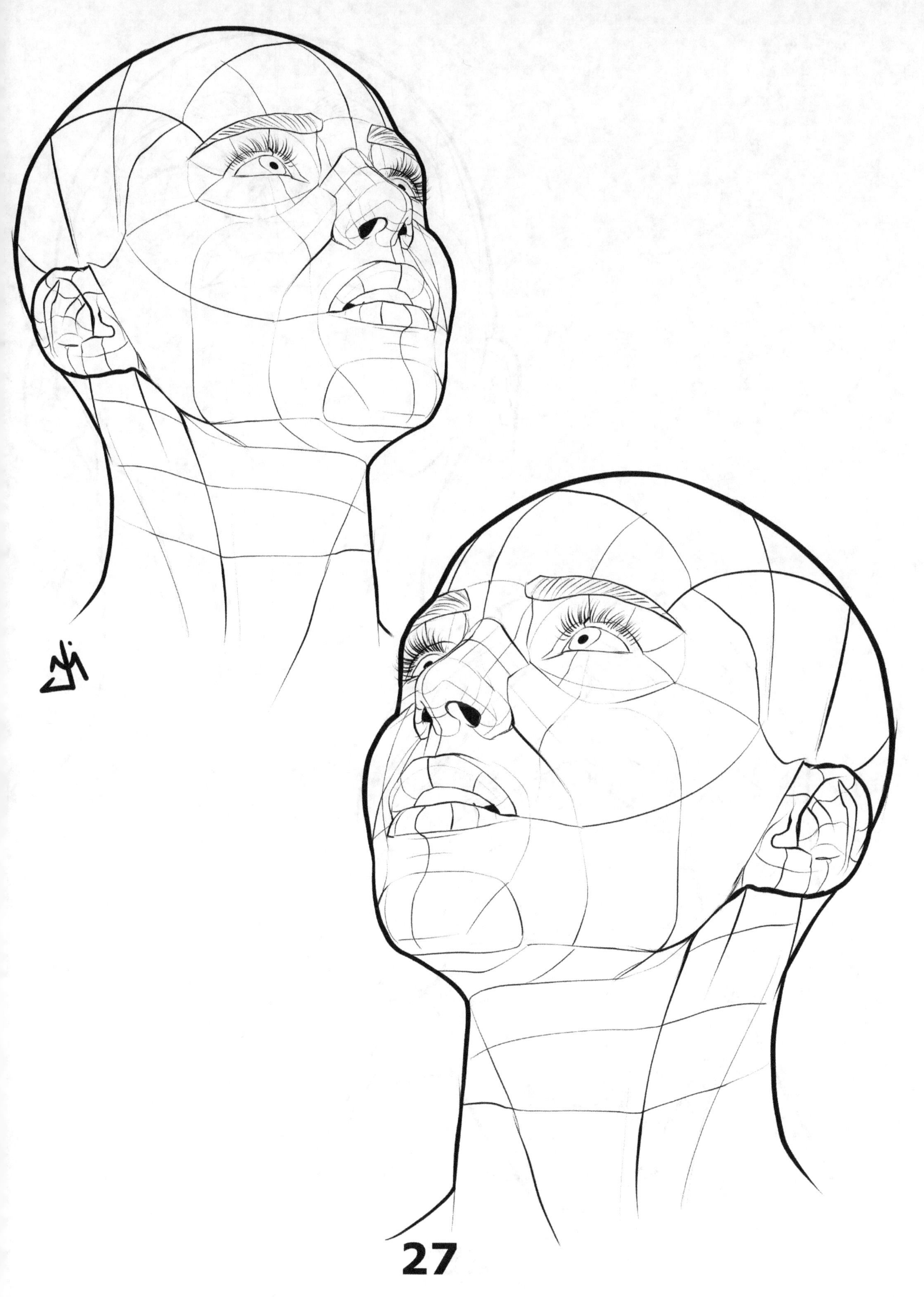

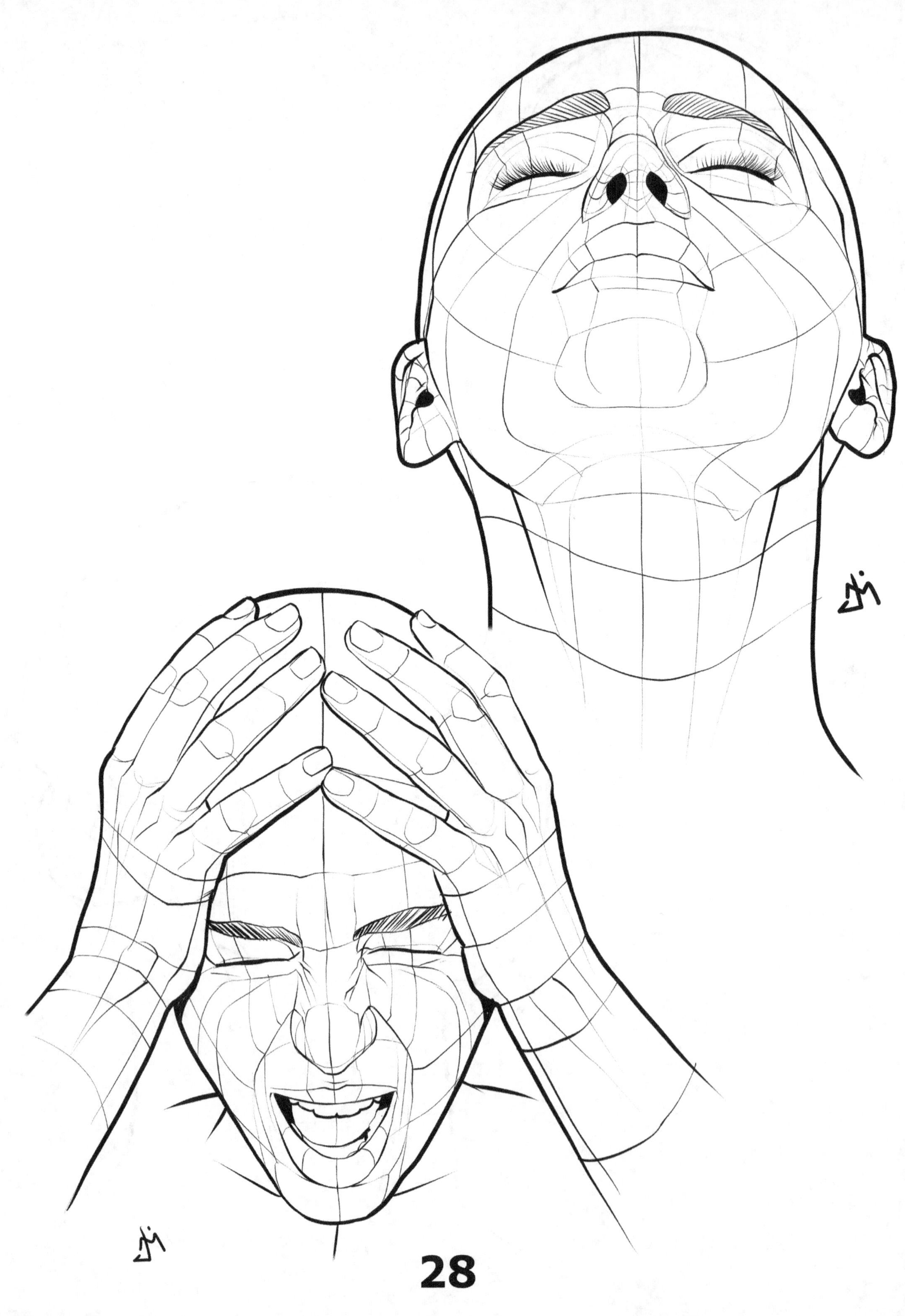

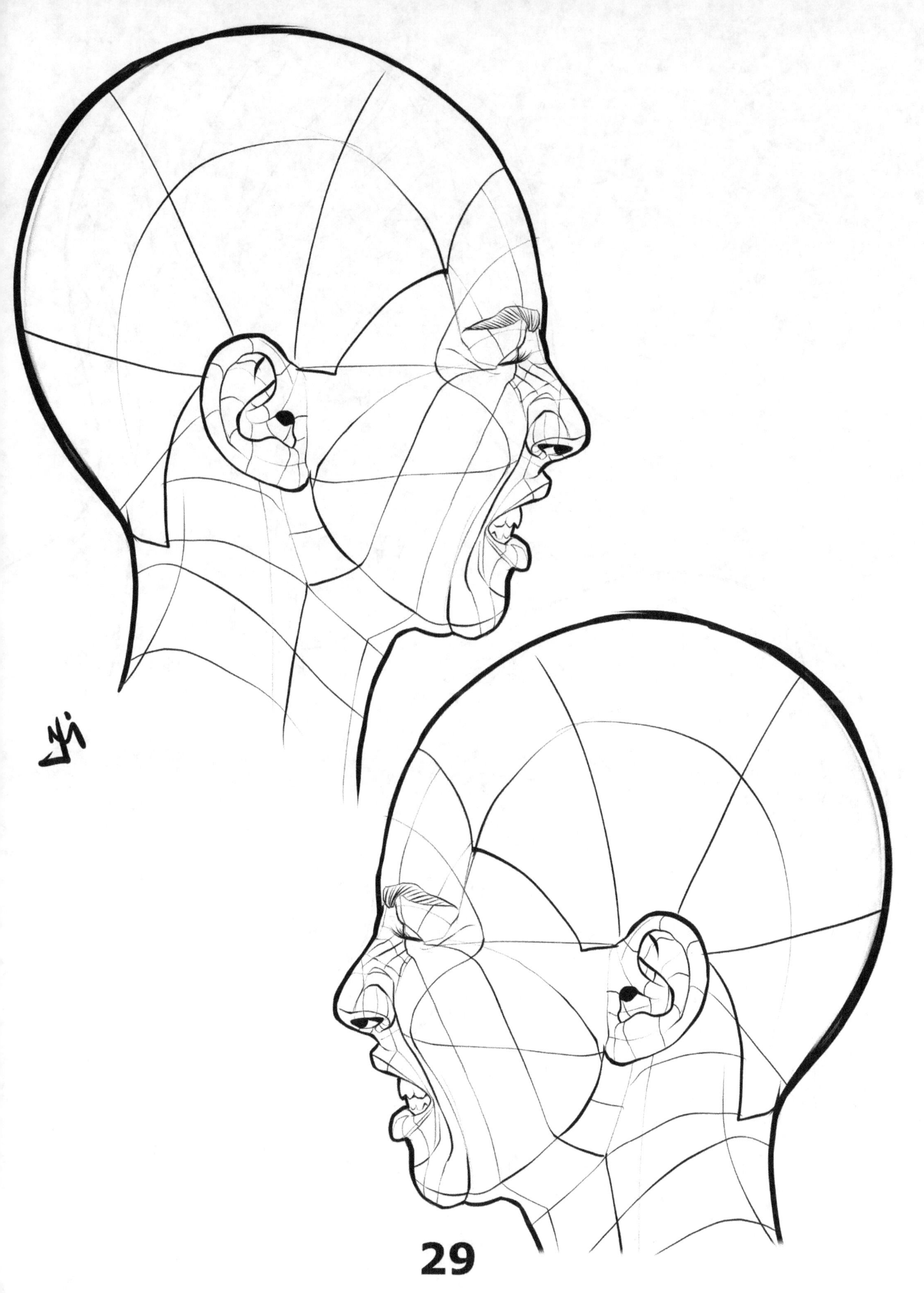

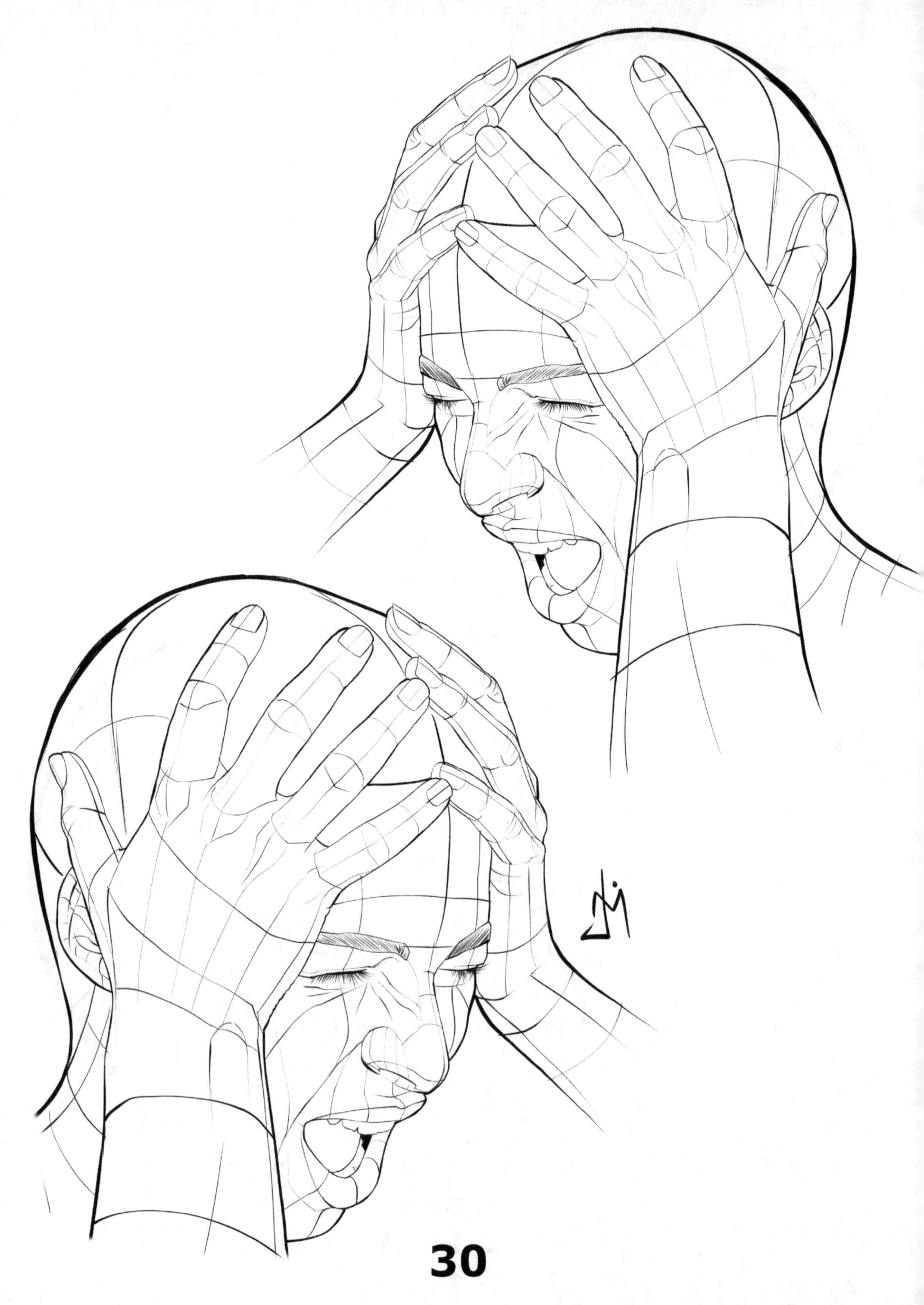

30

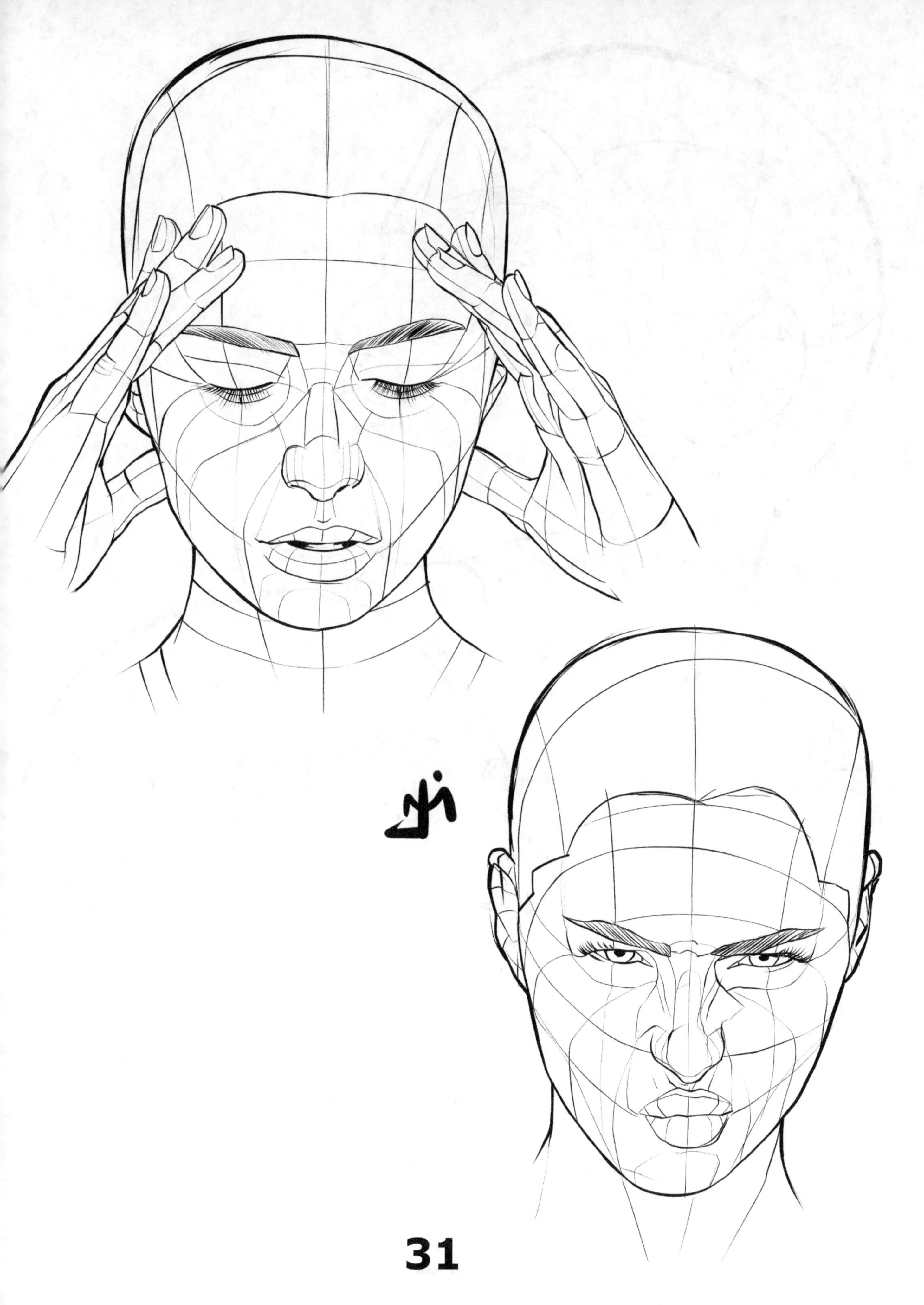

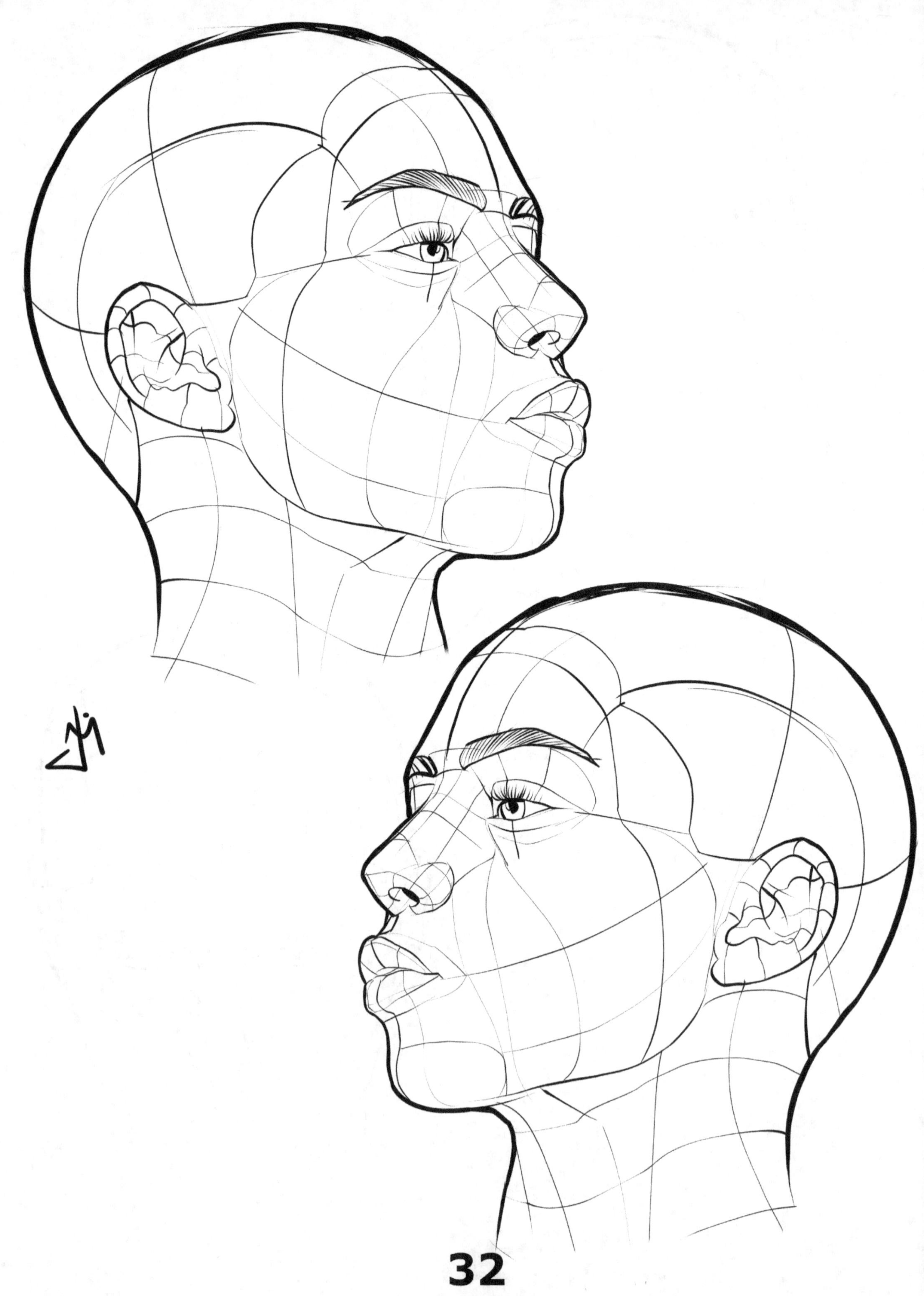

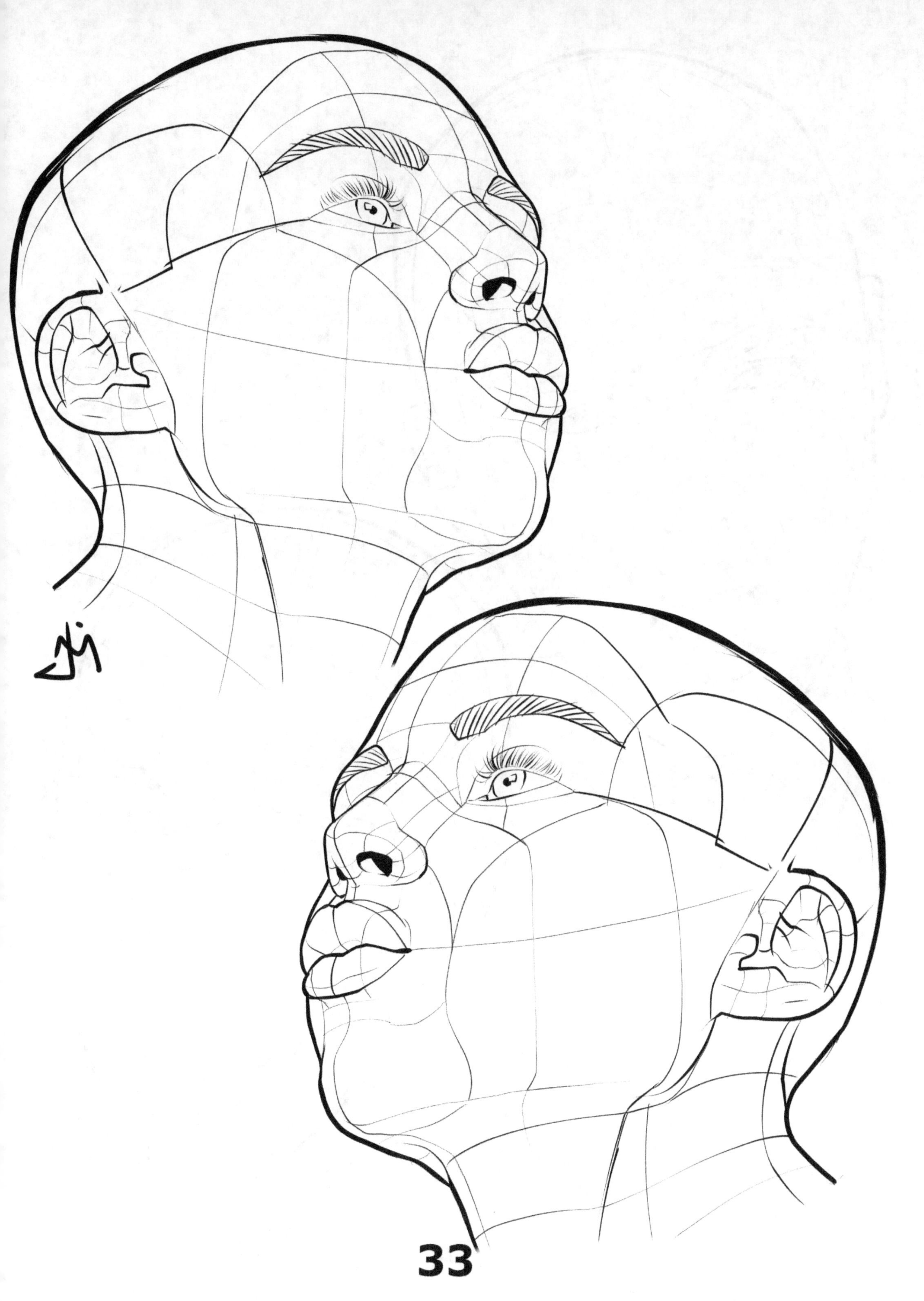

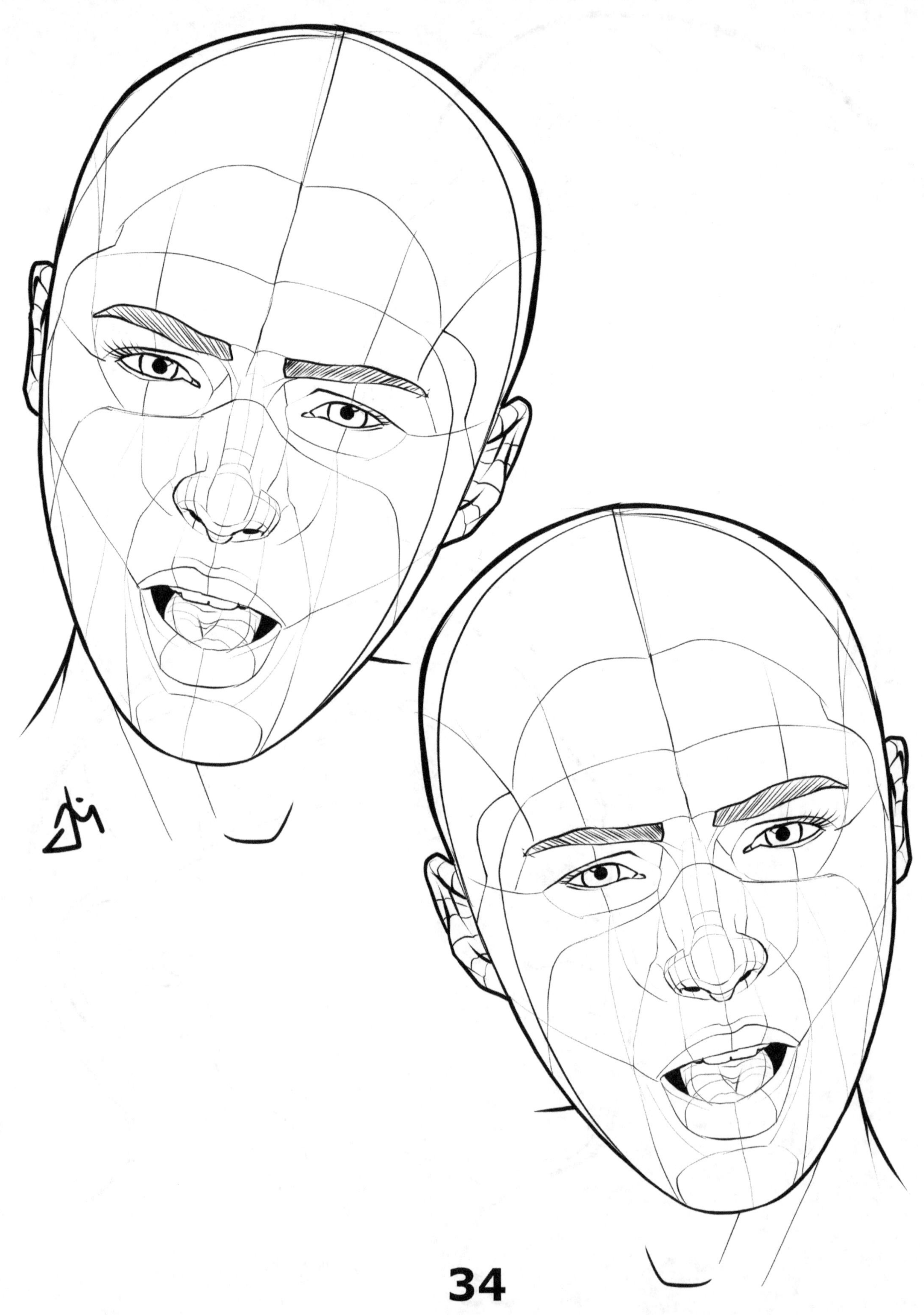

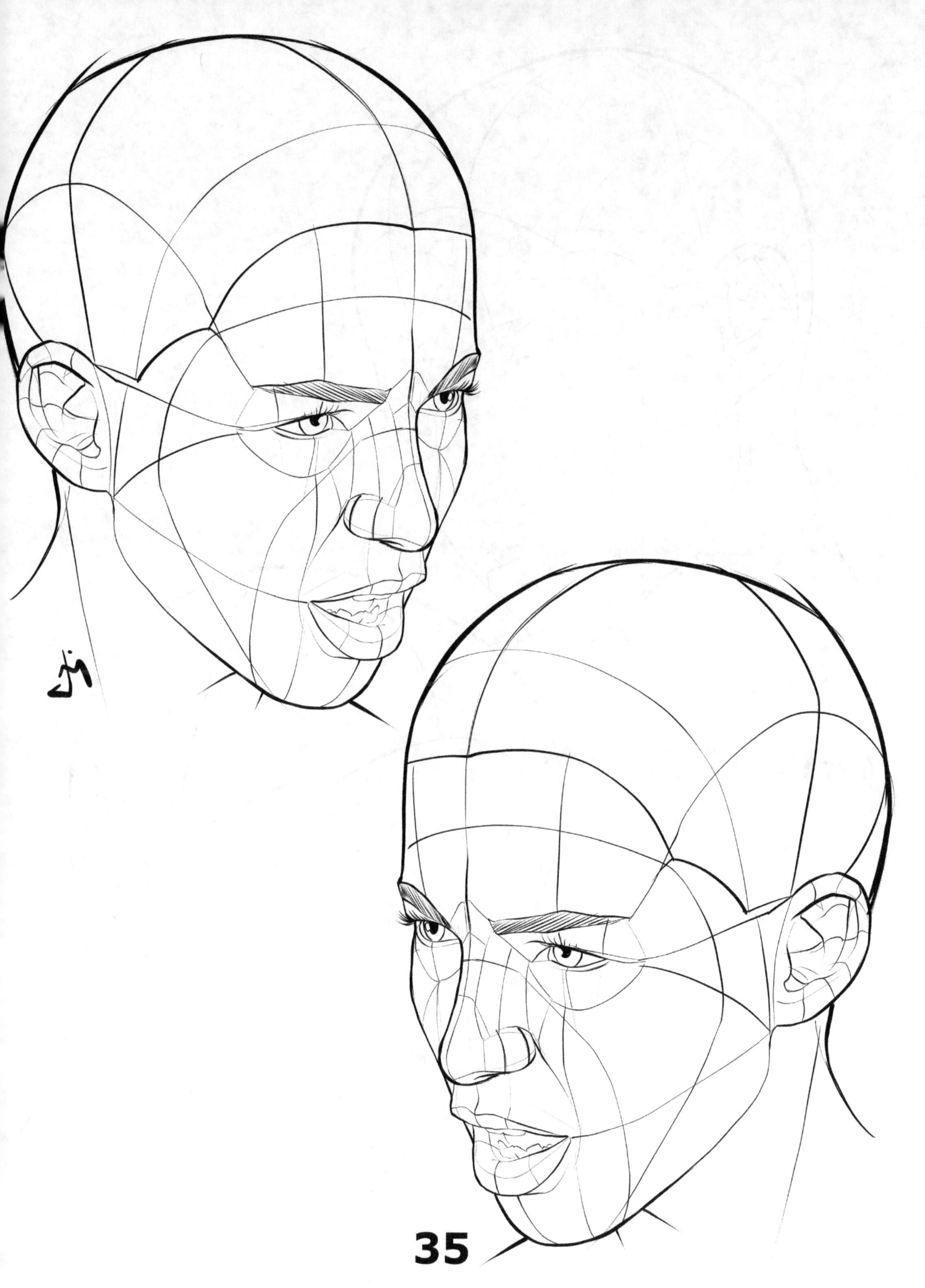

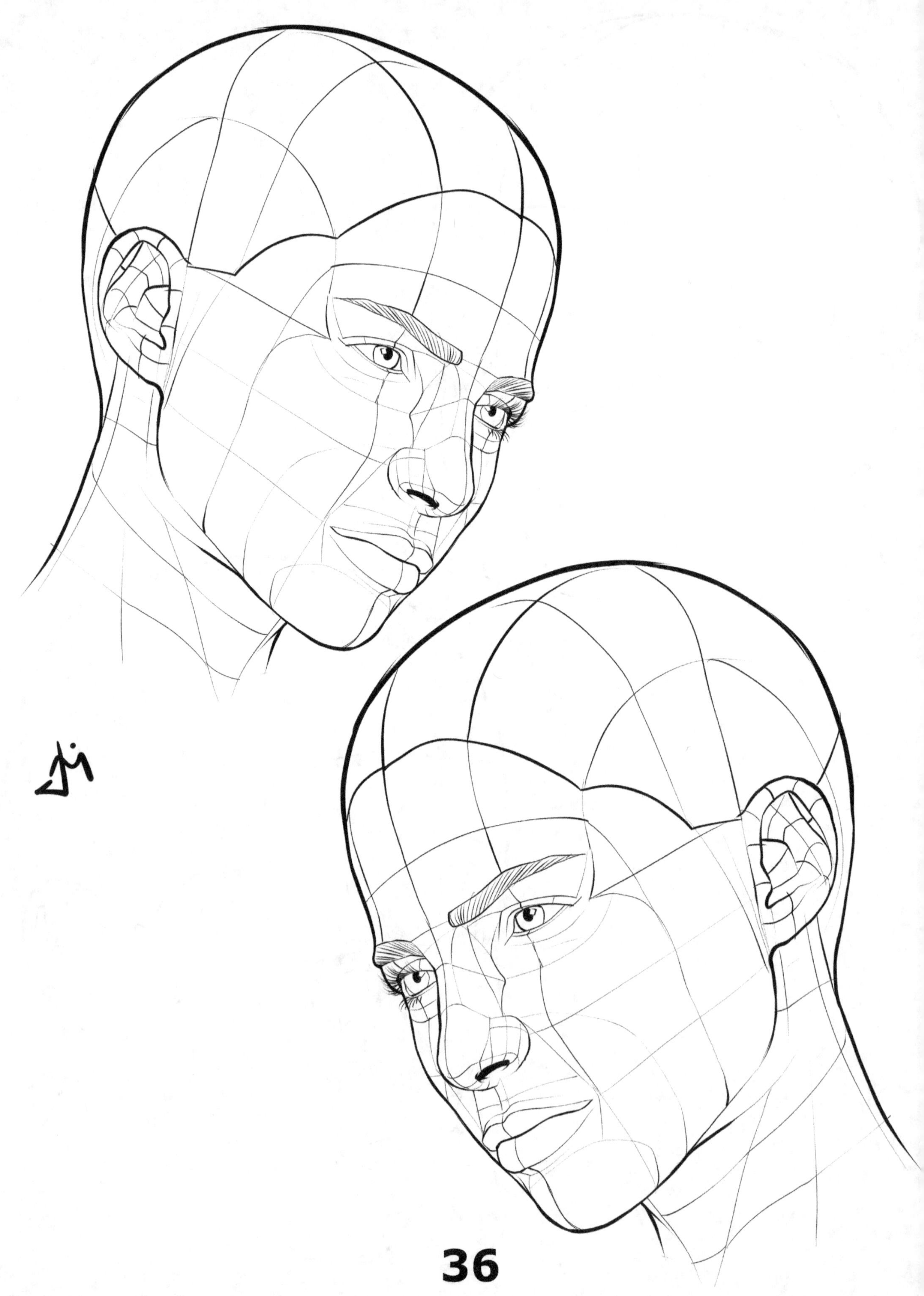

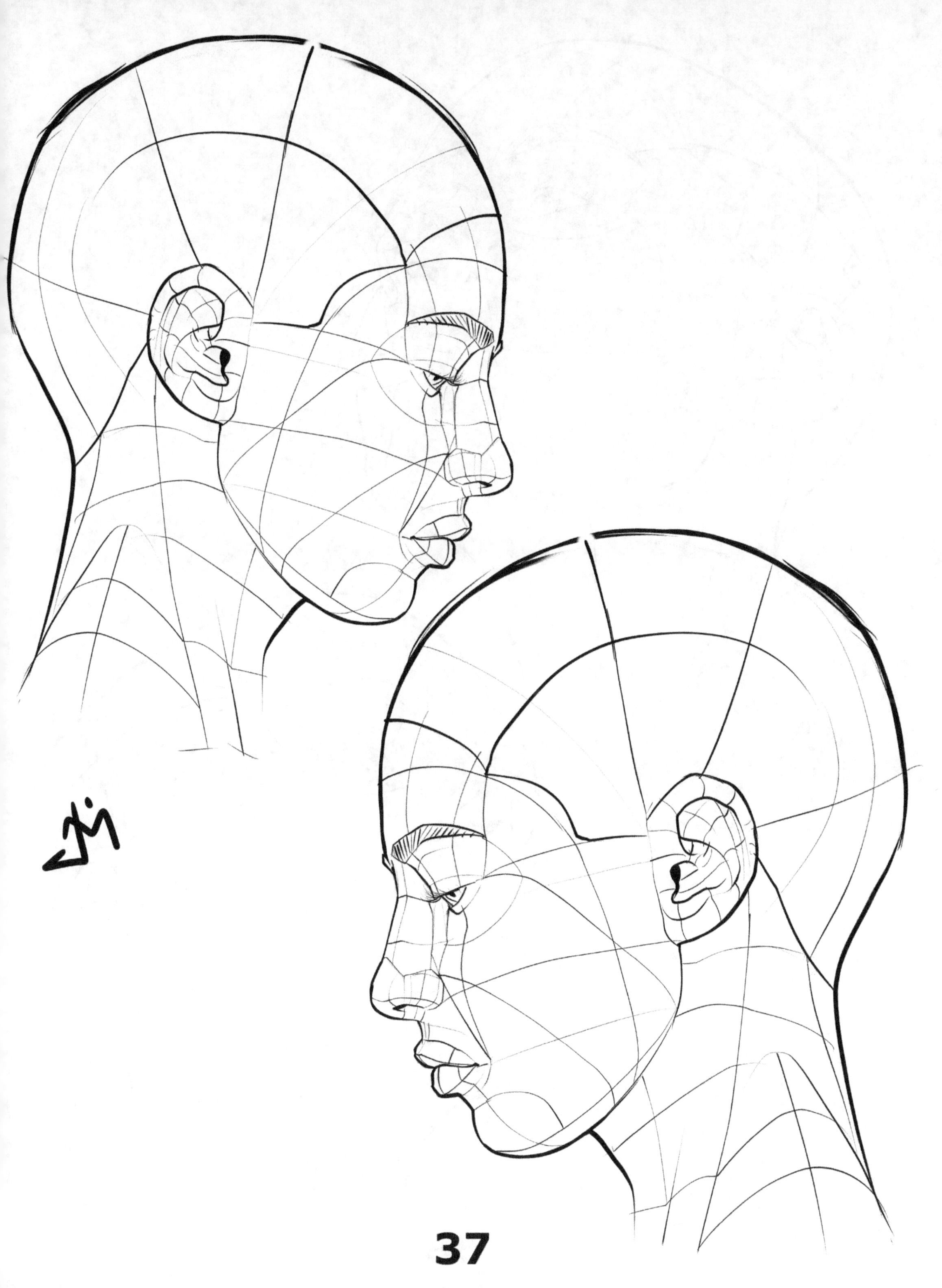

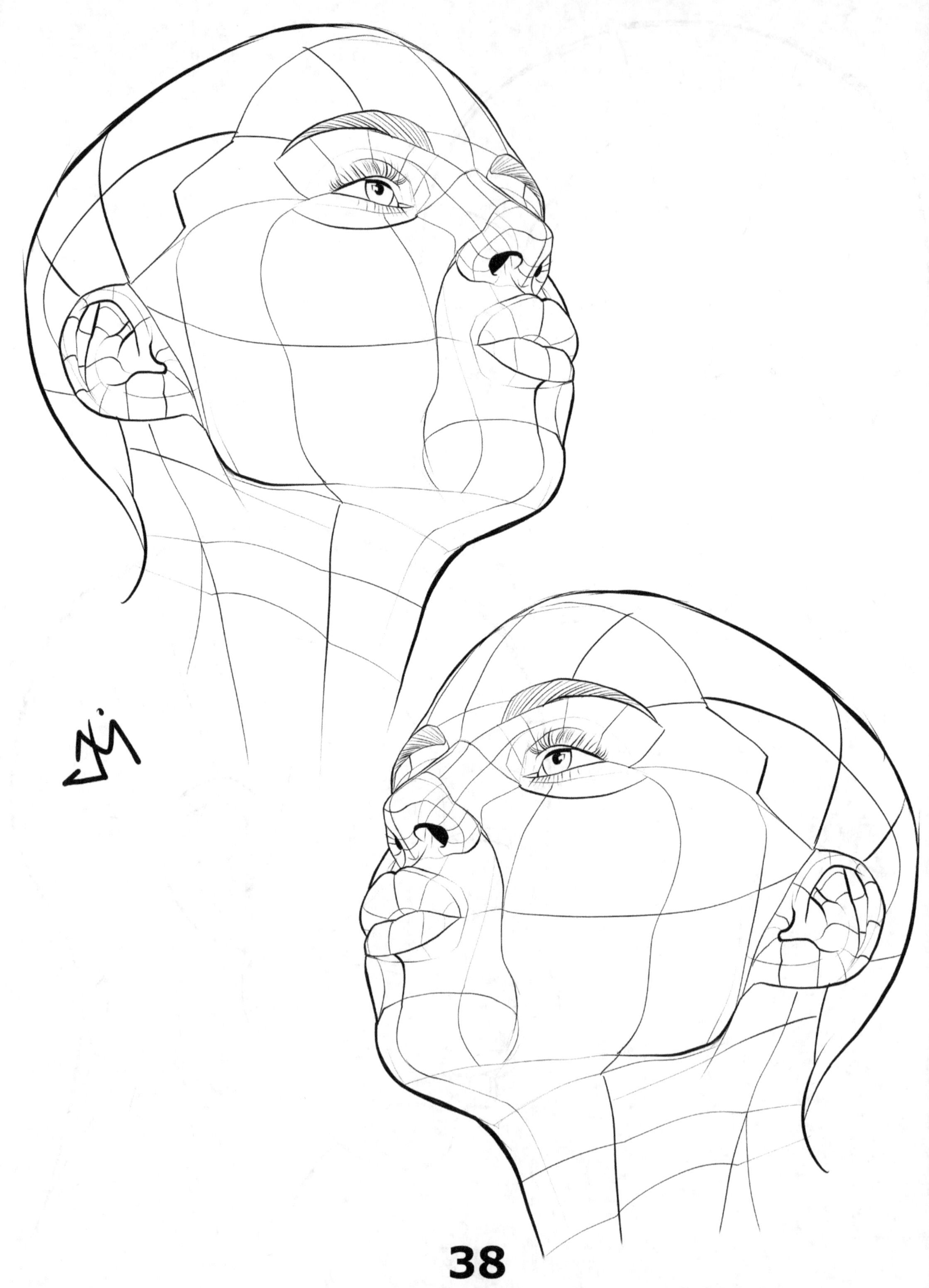

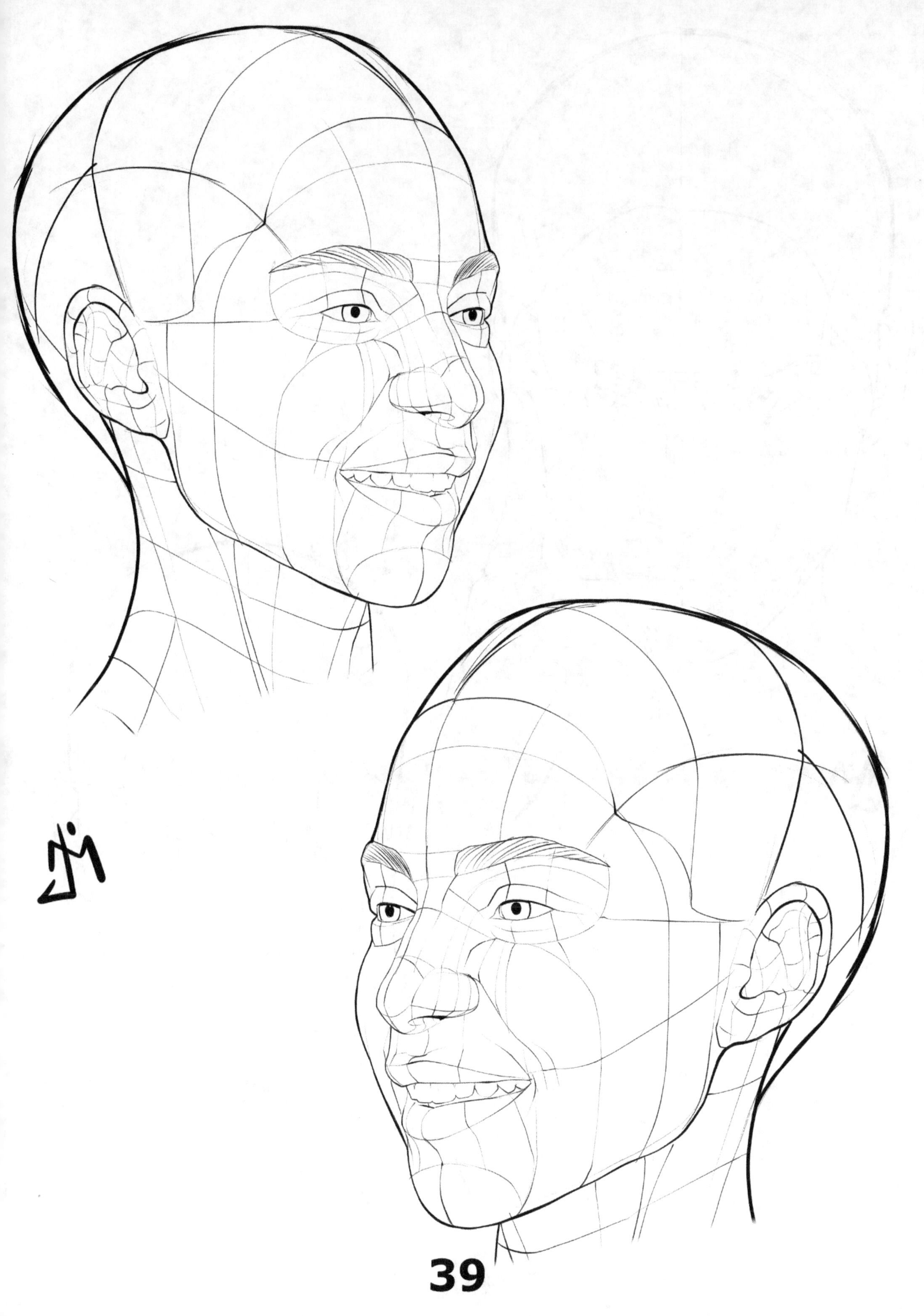

39

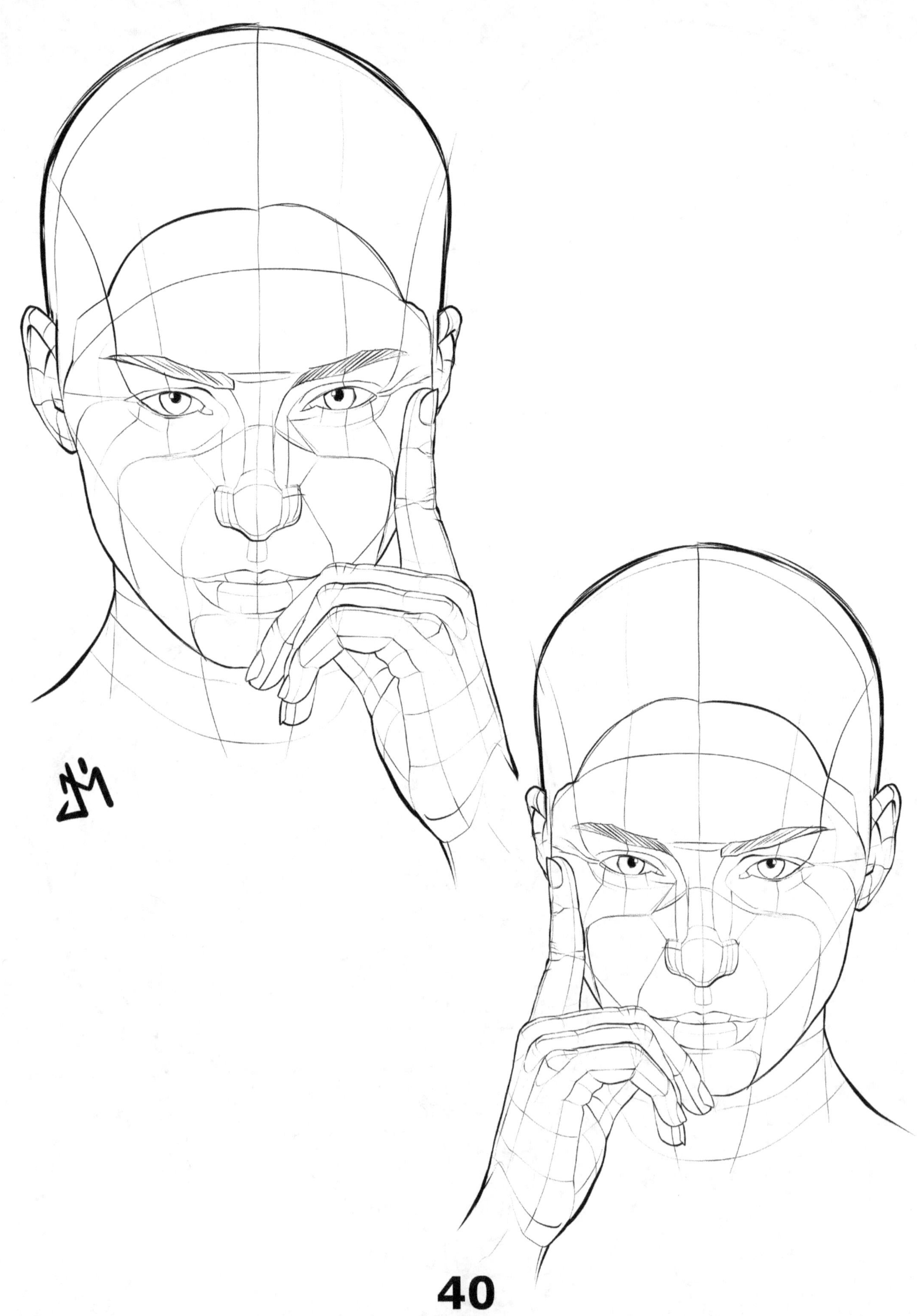

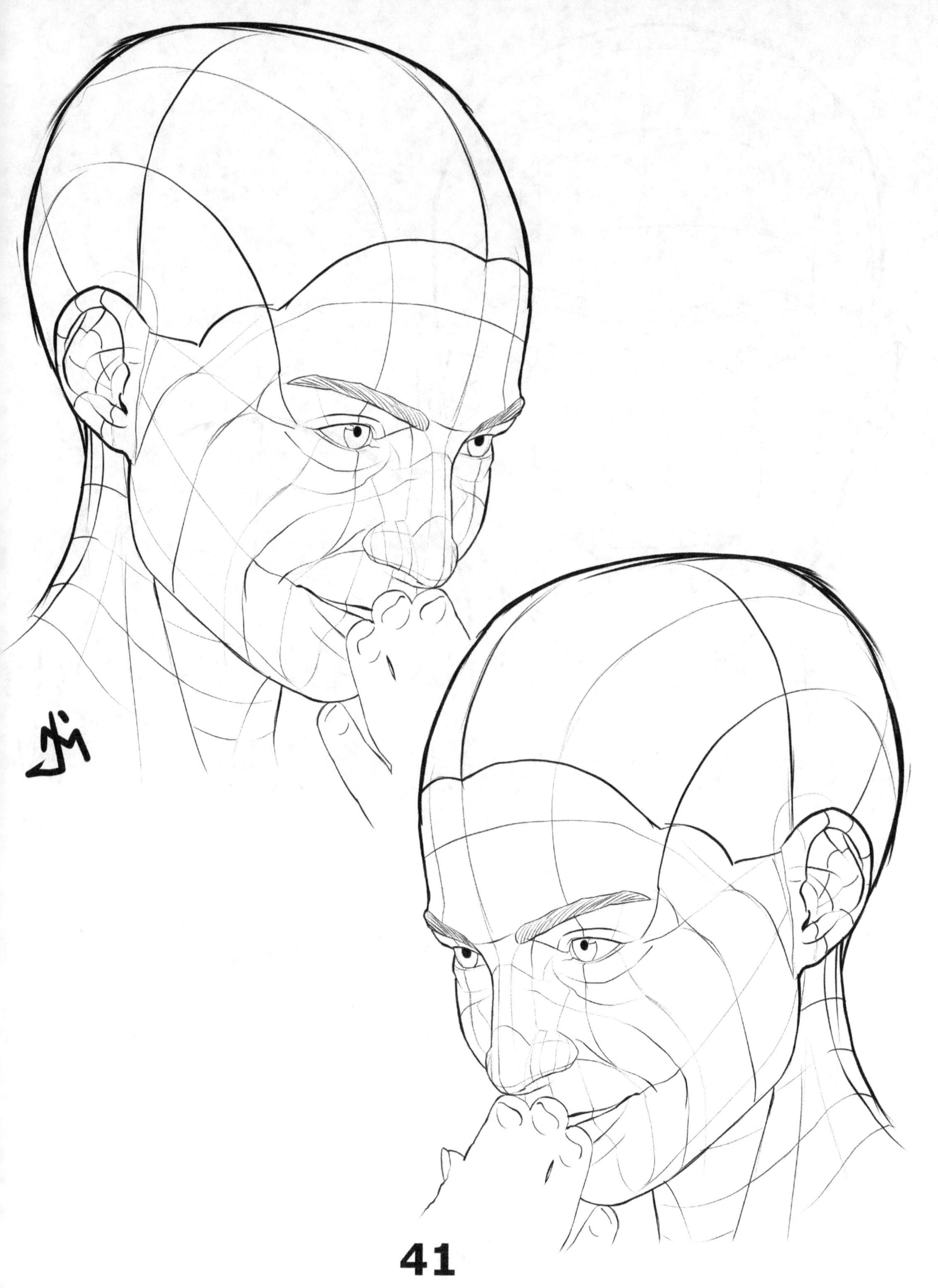

41

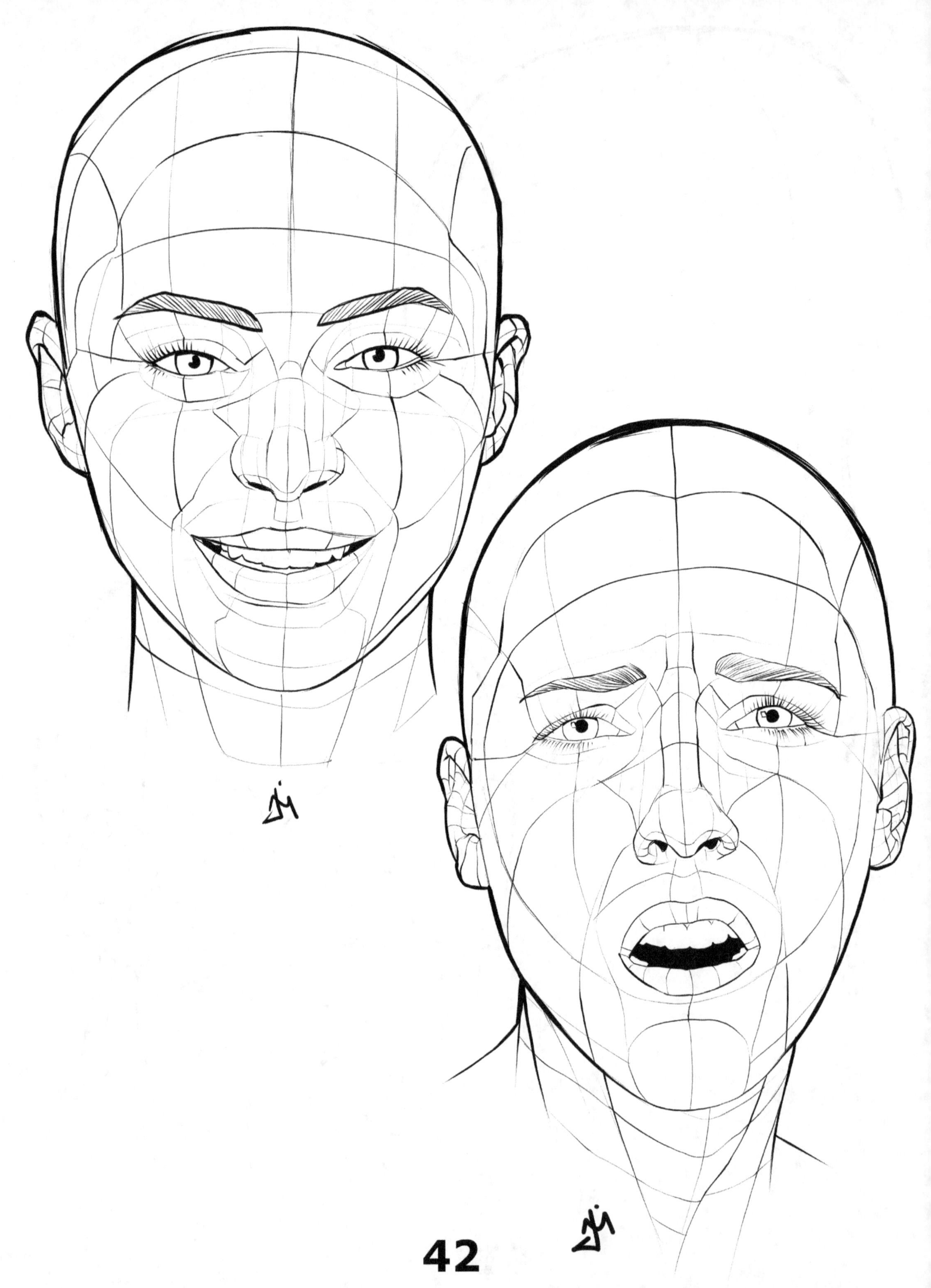

42

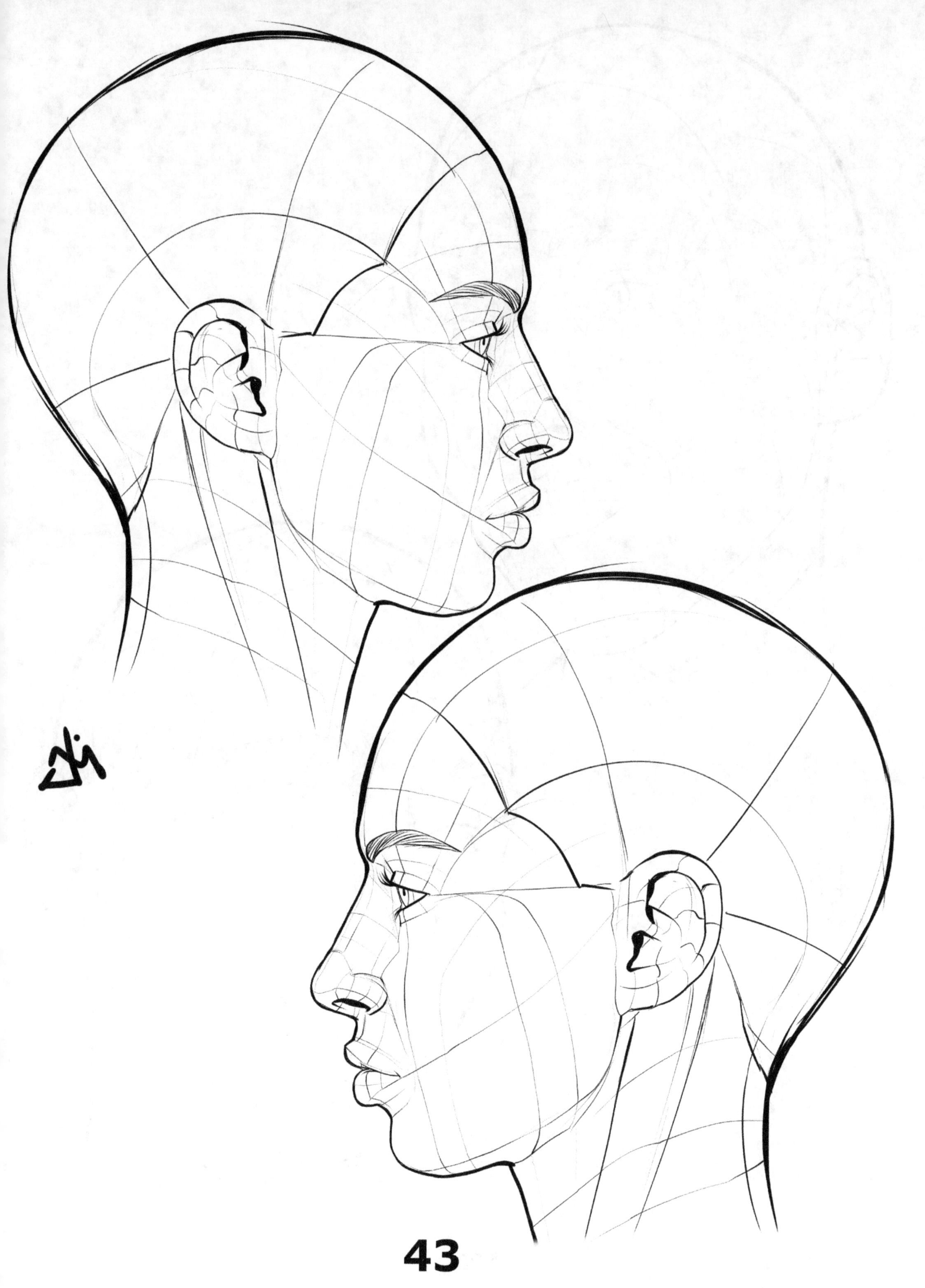

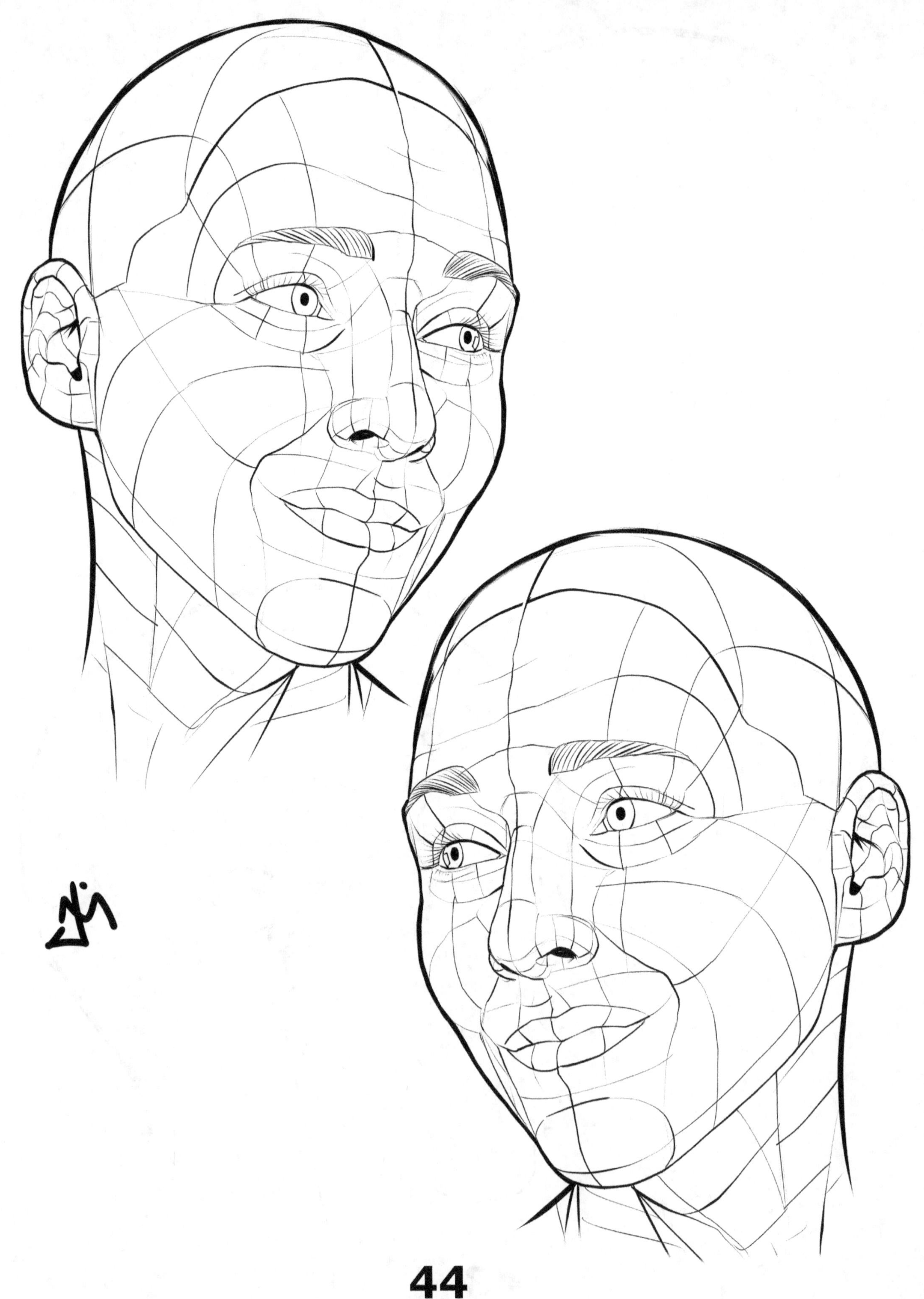

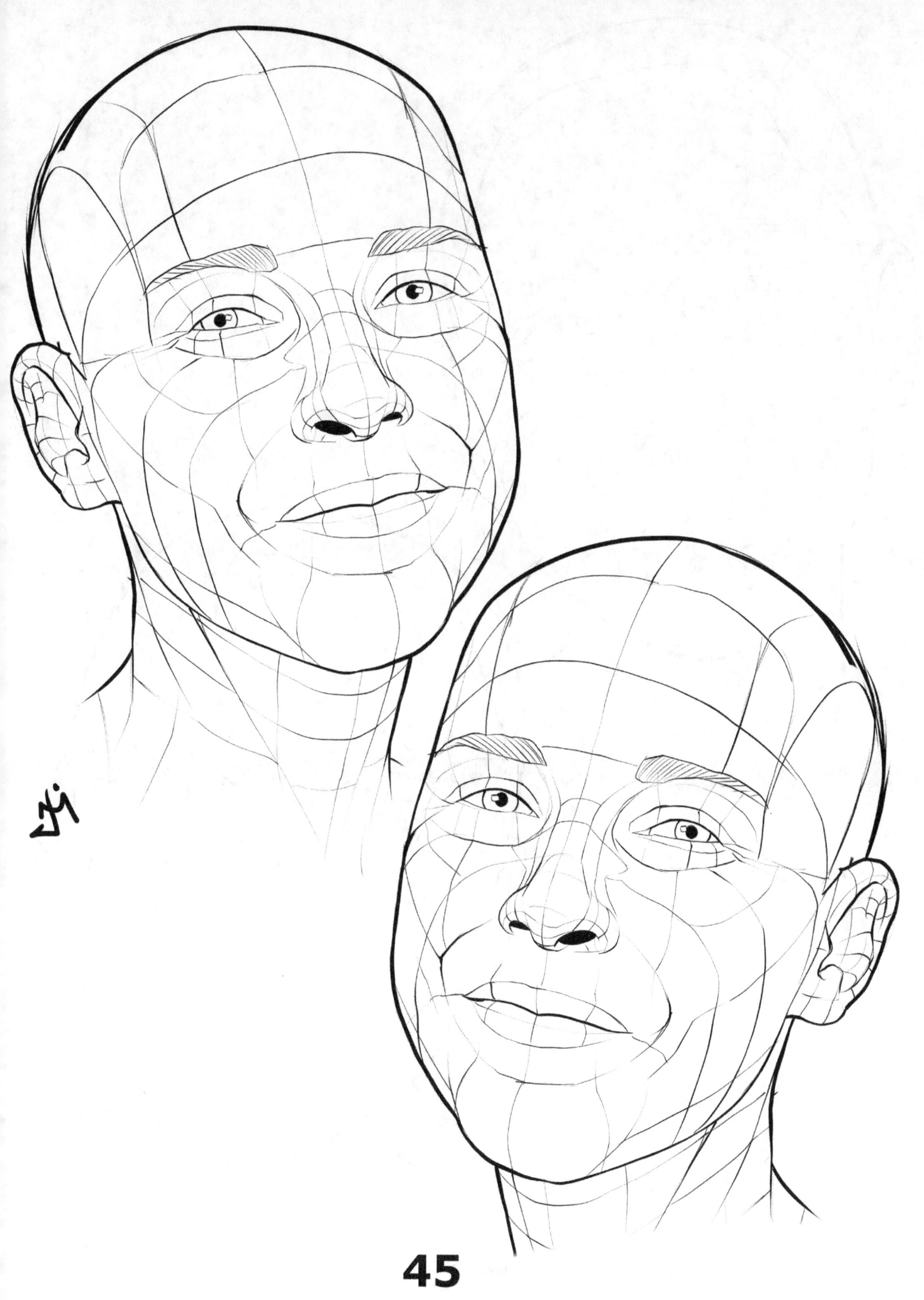

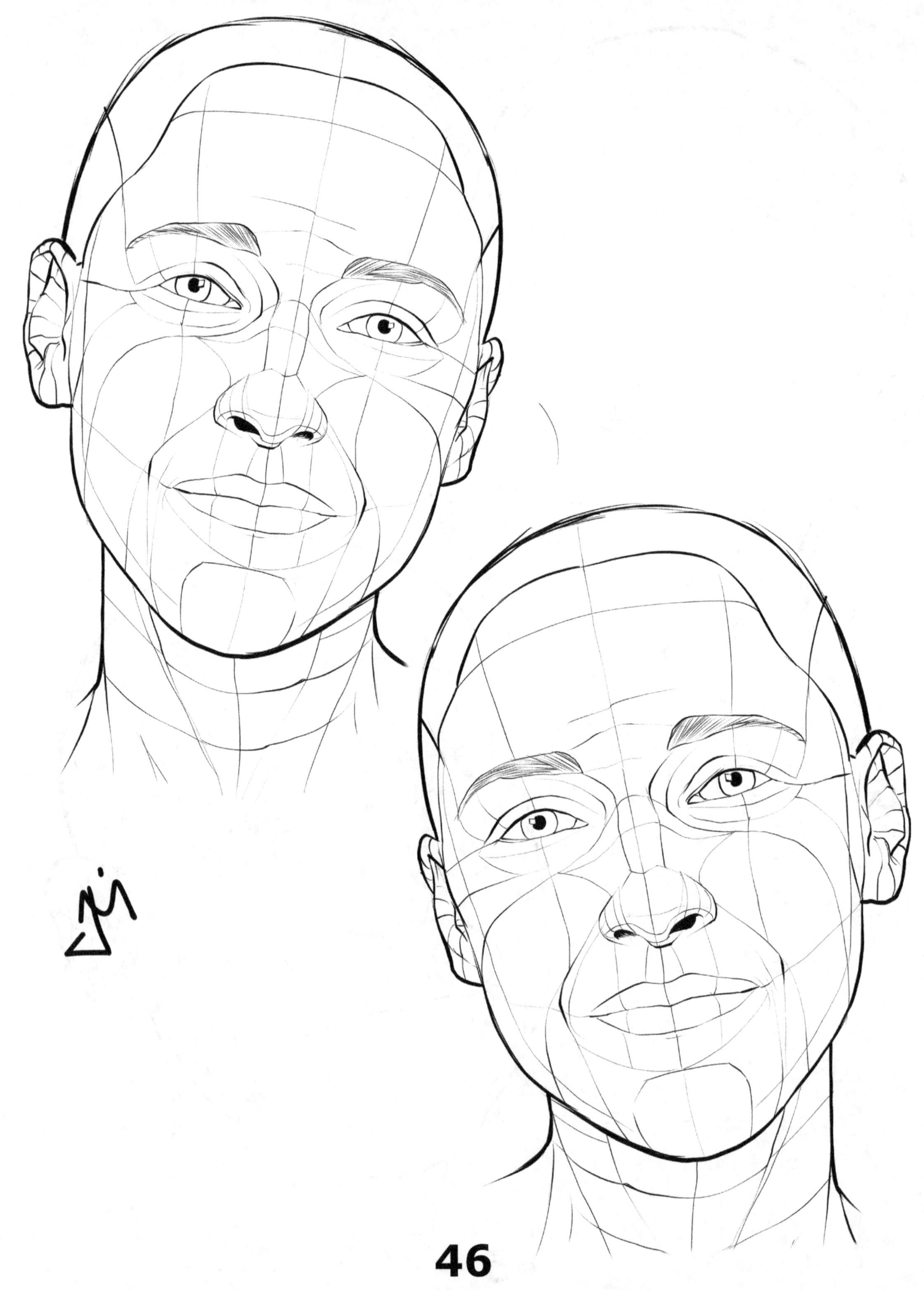

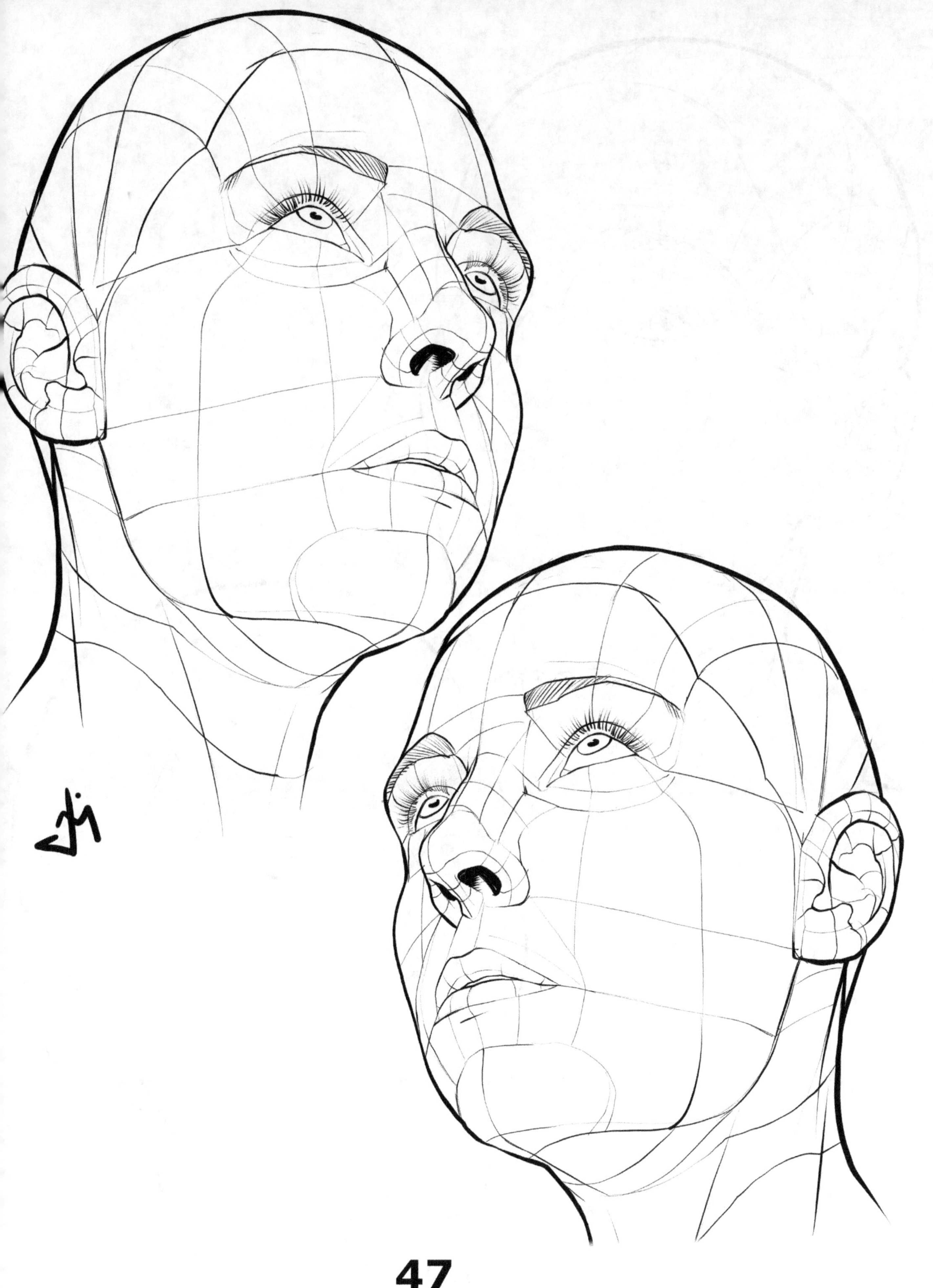

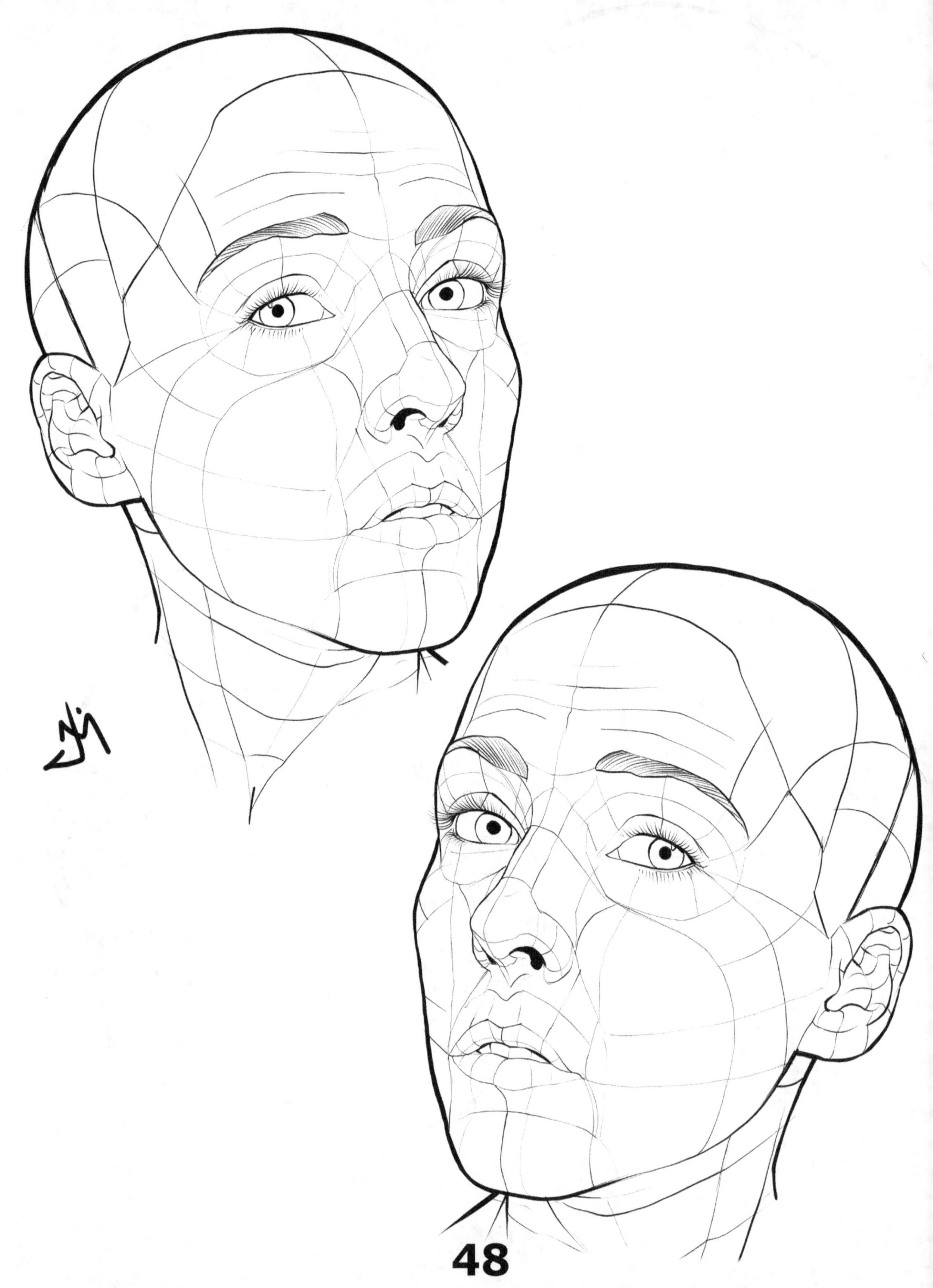

48

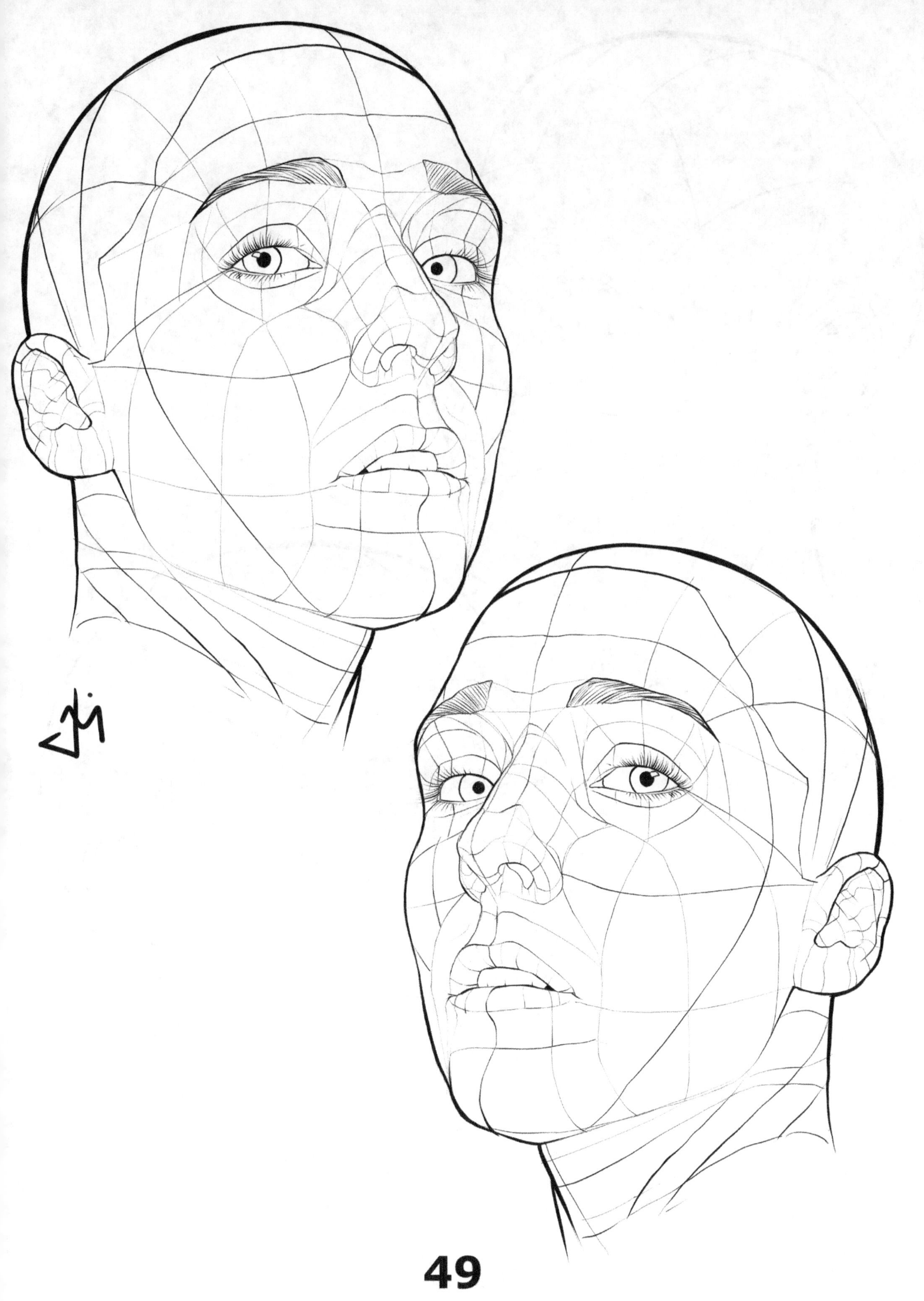

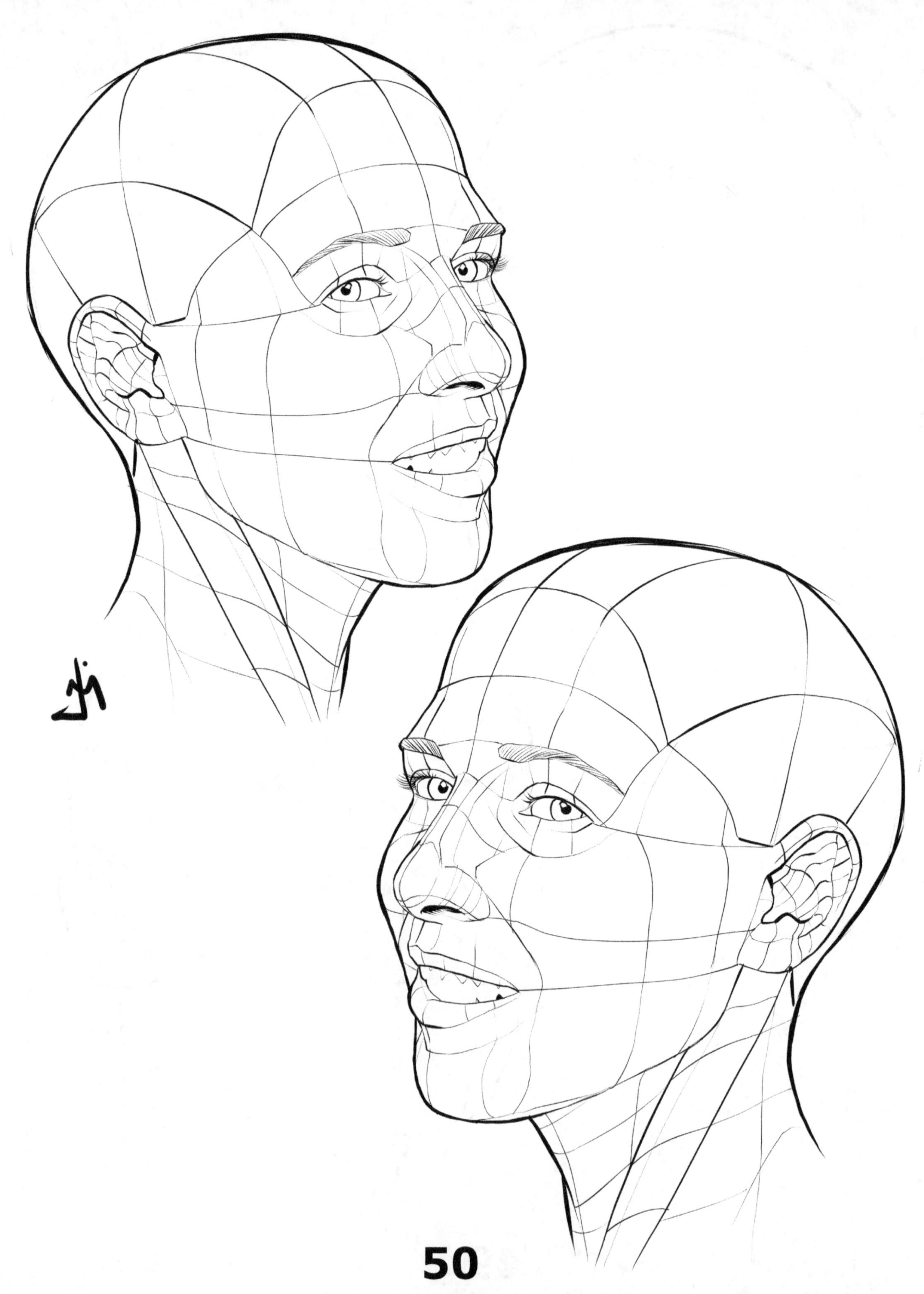

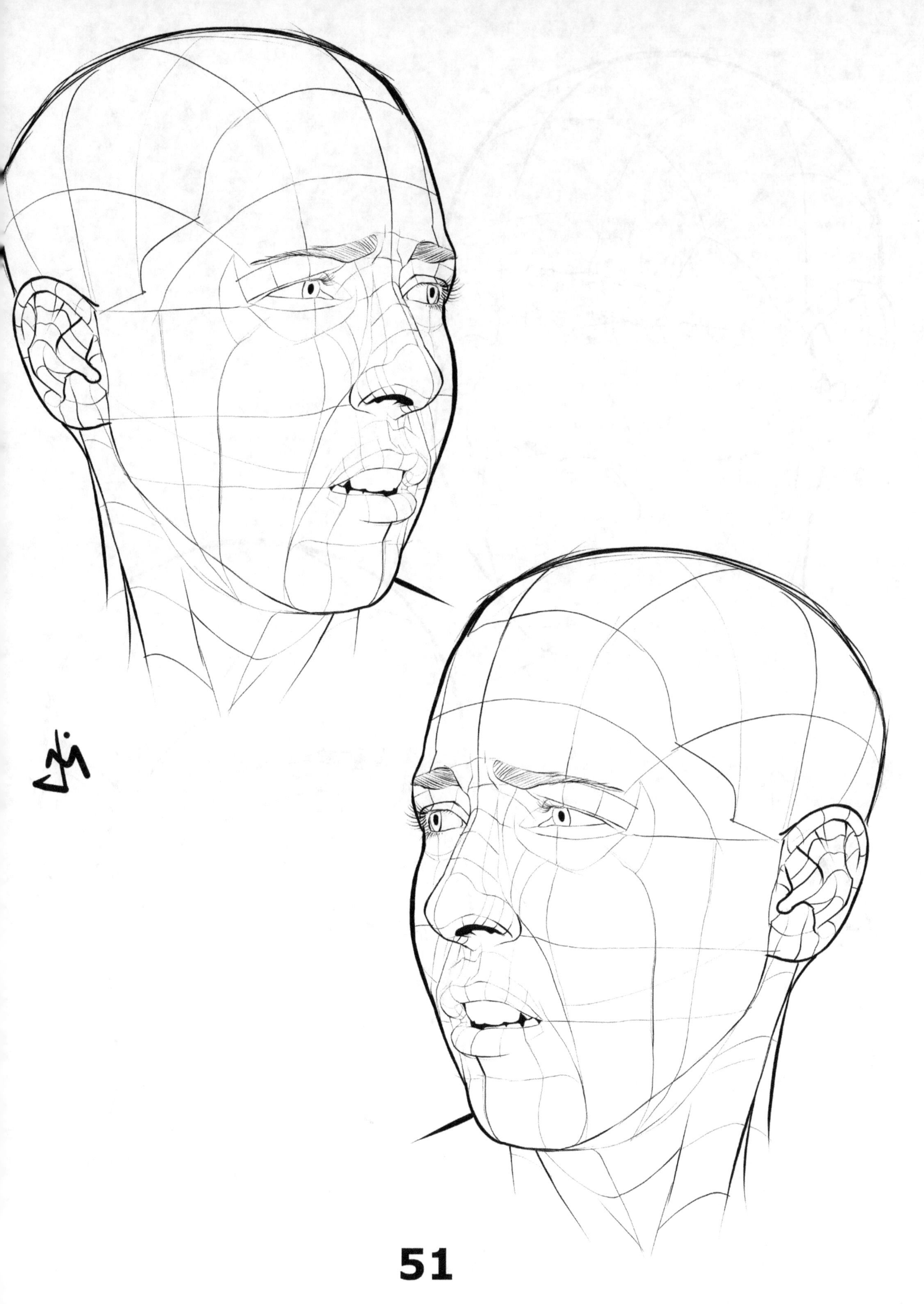

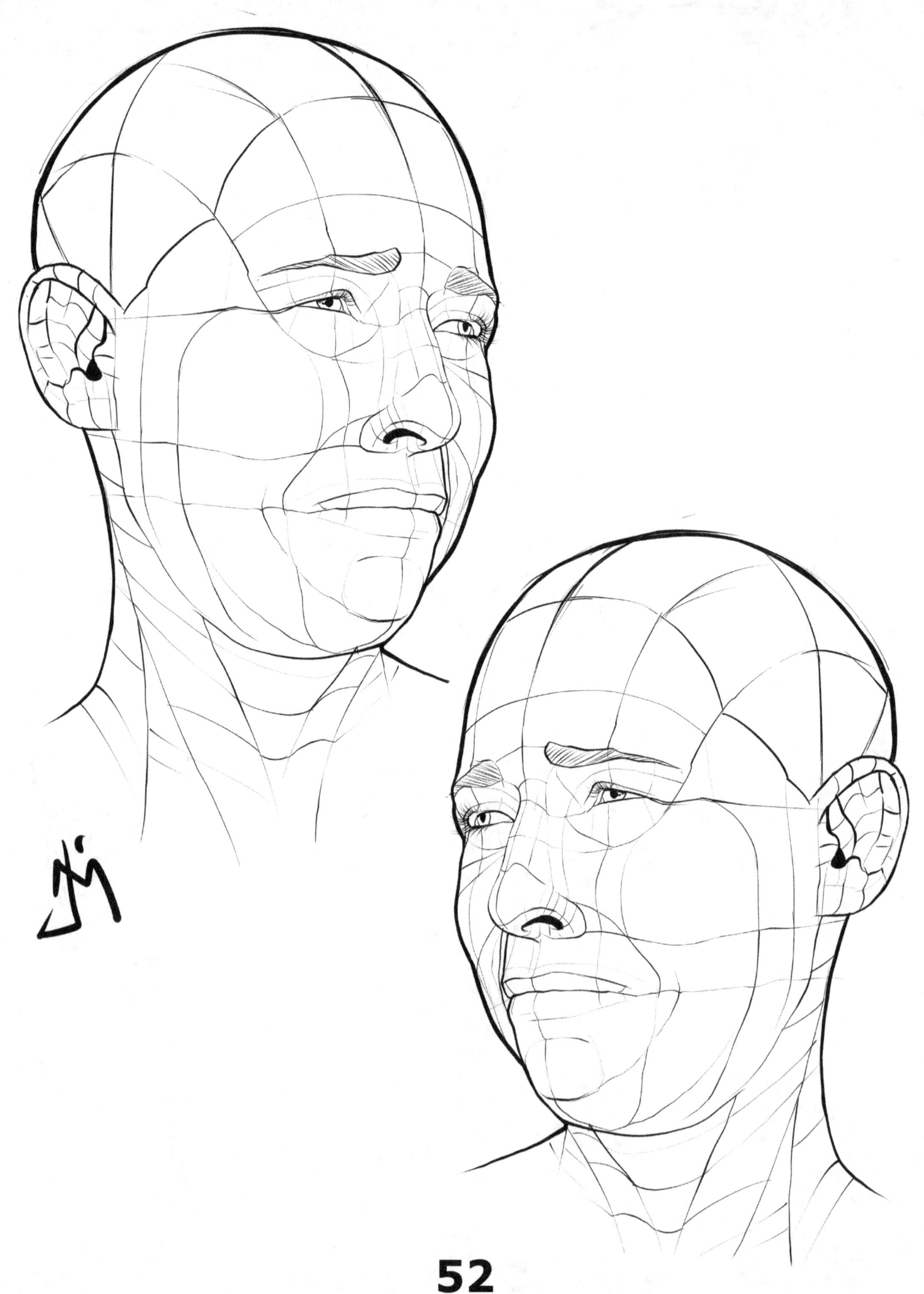

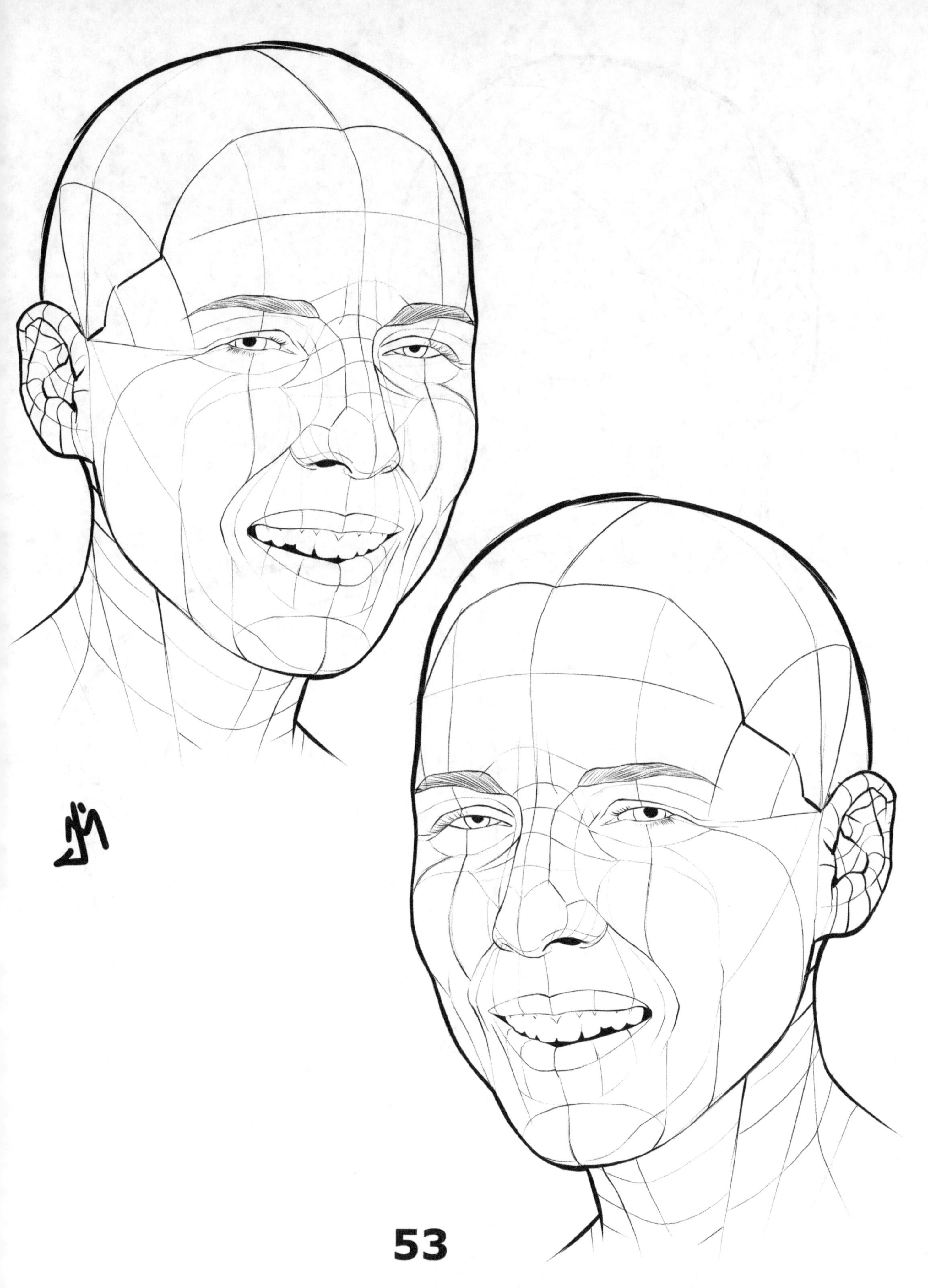

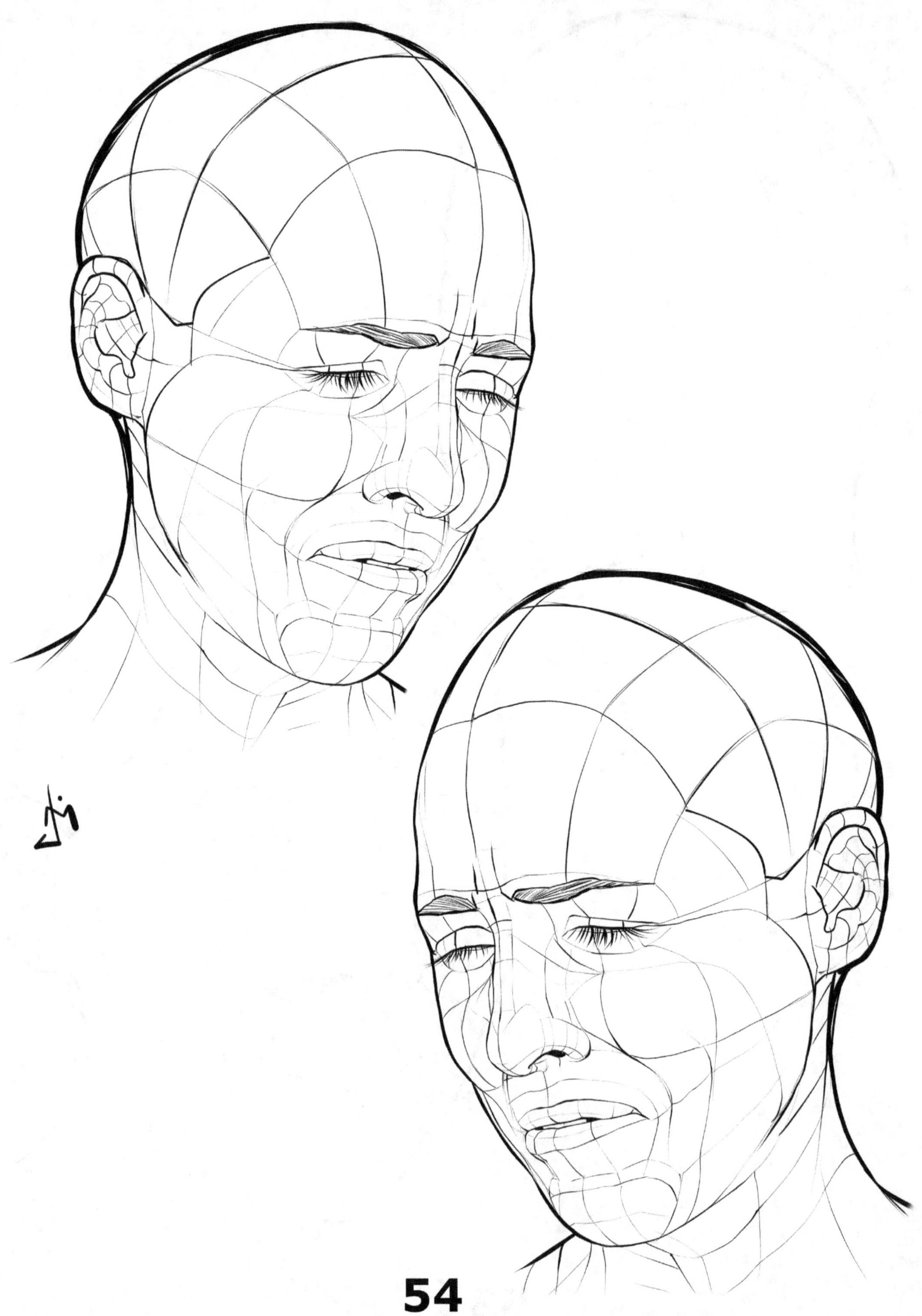

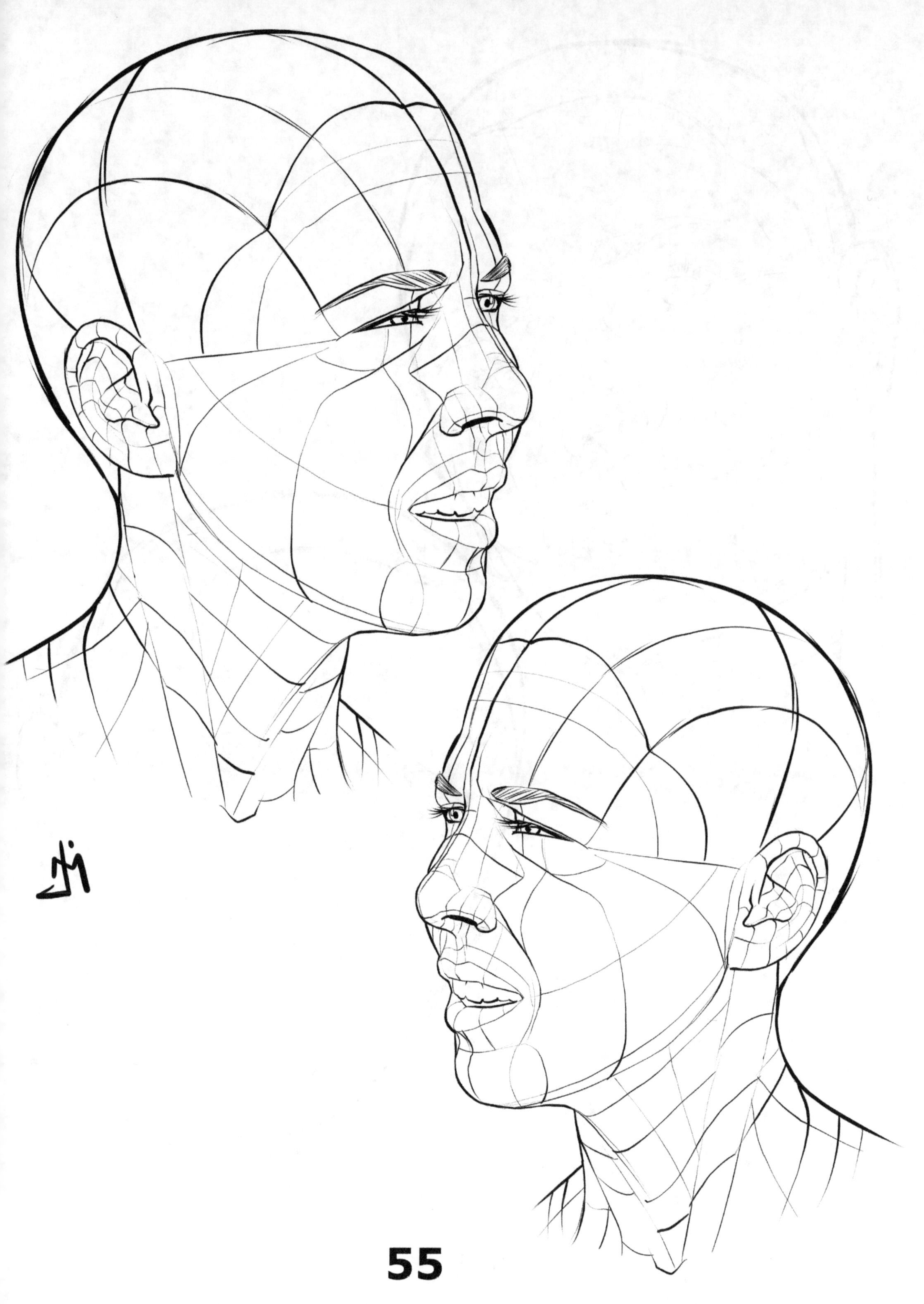

55

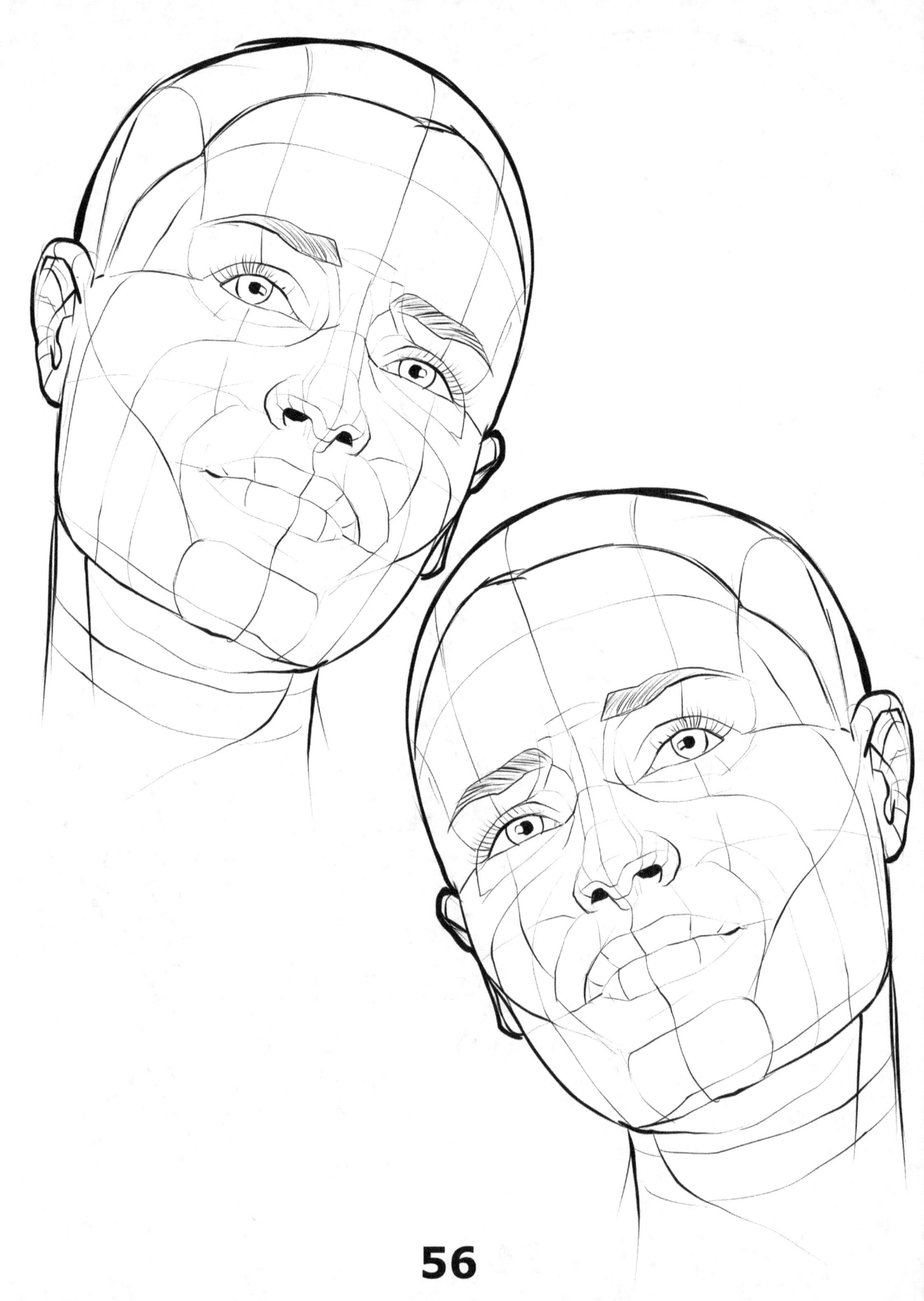

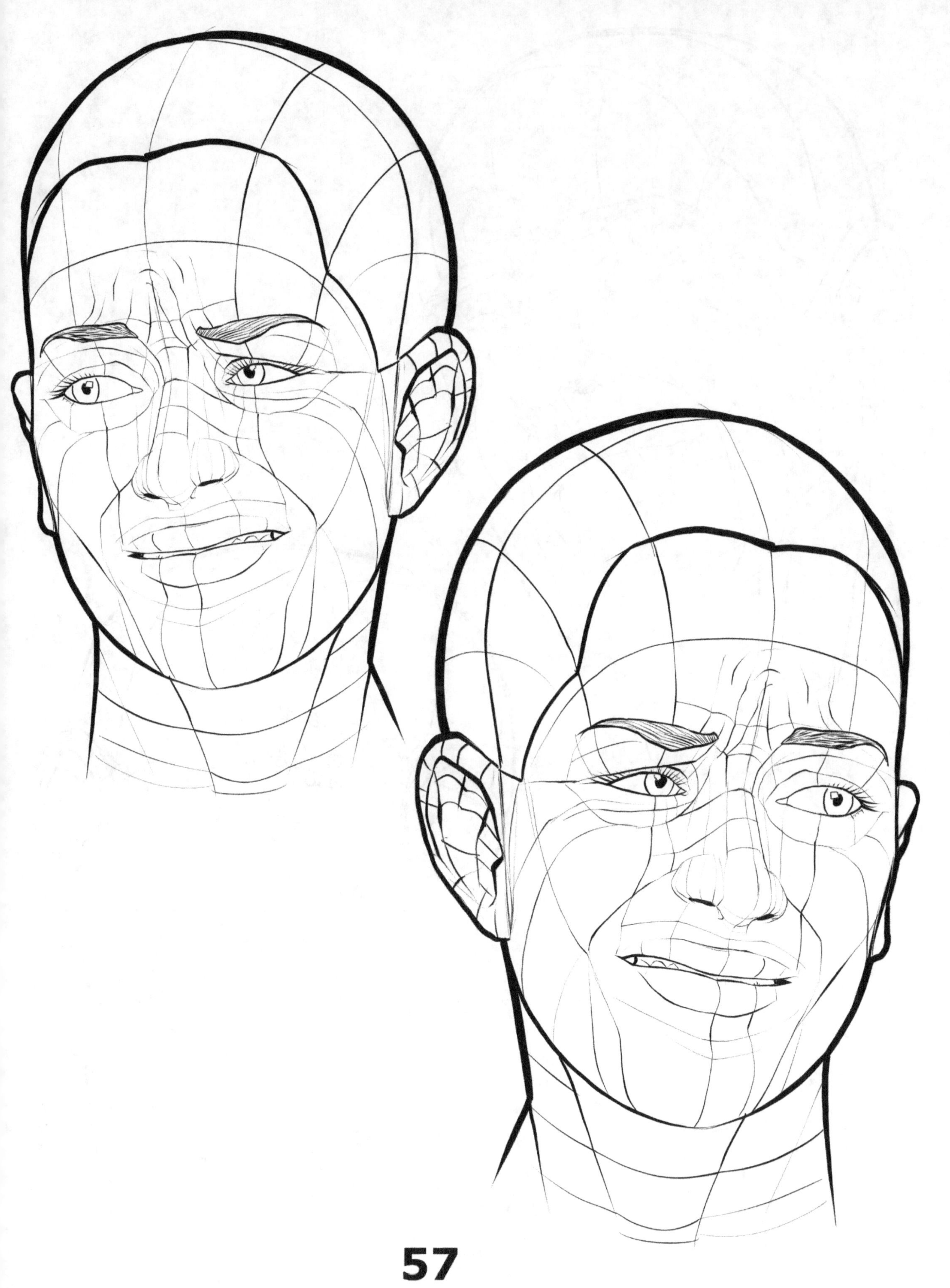

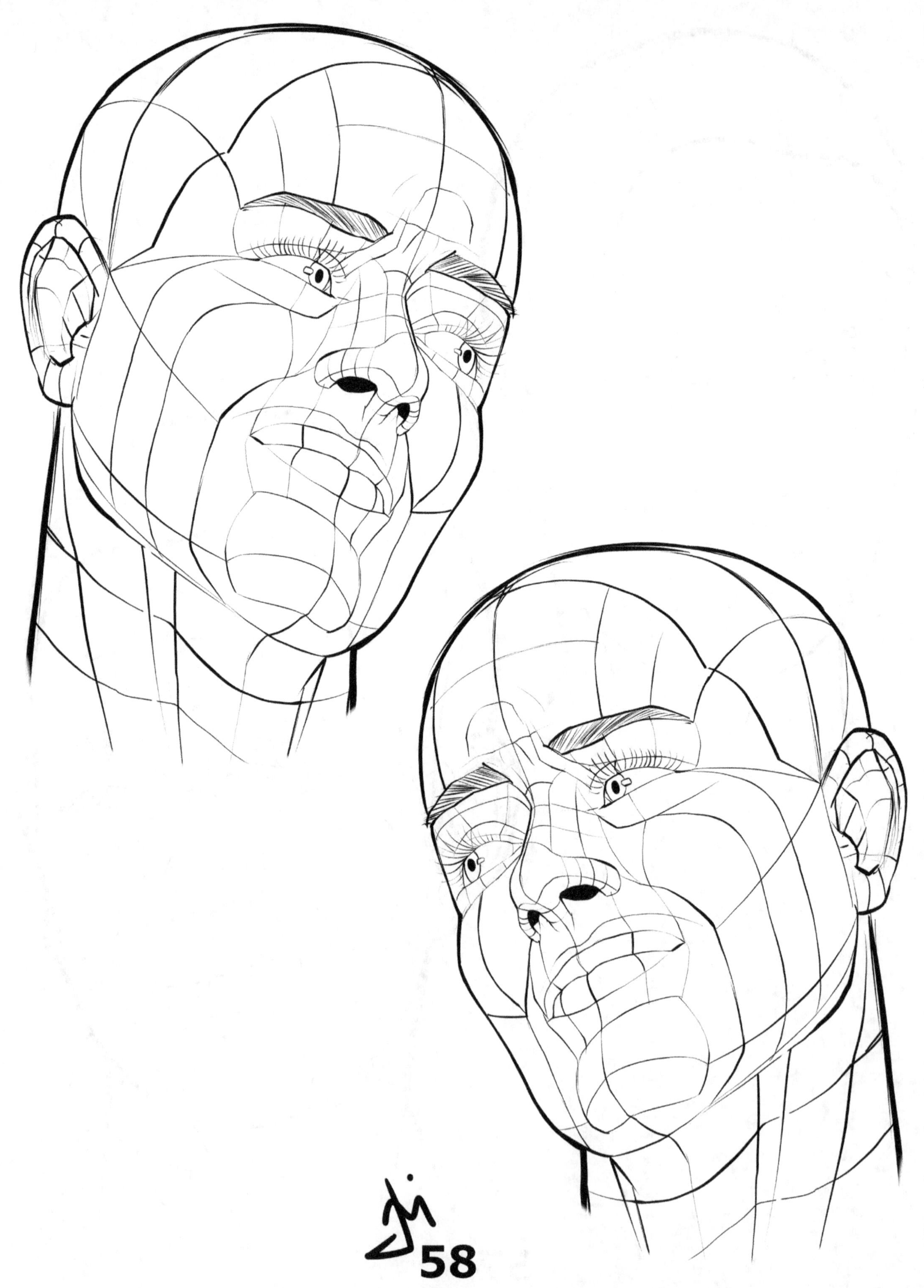

58

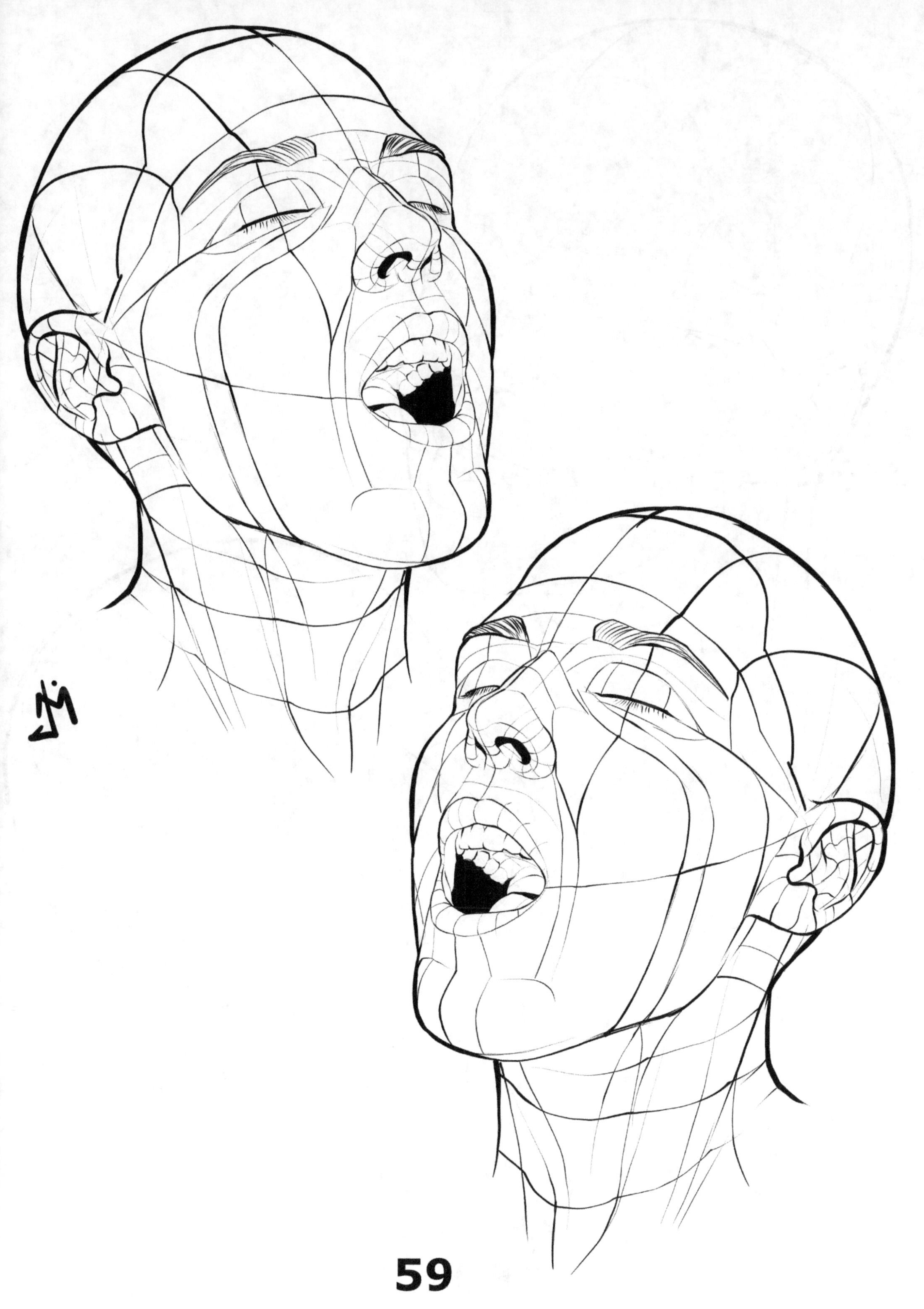

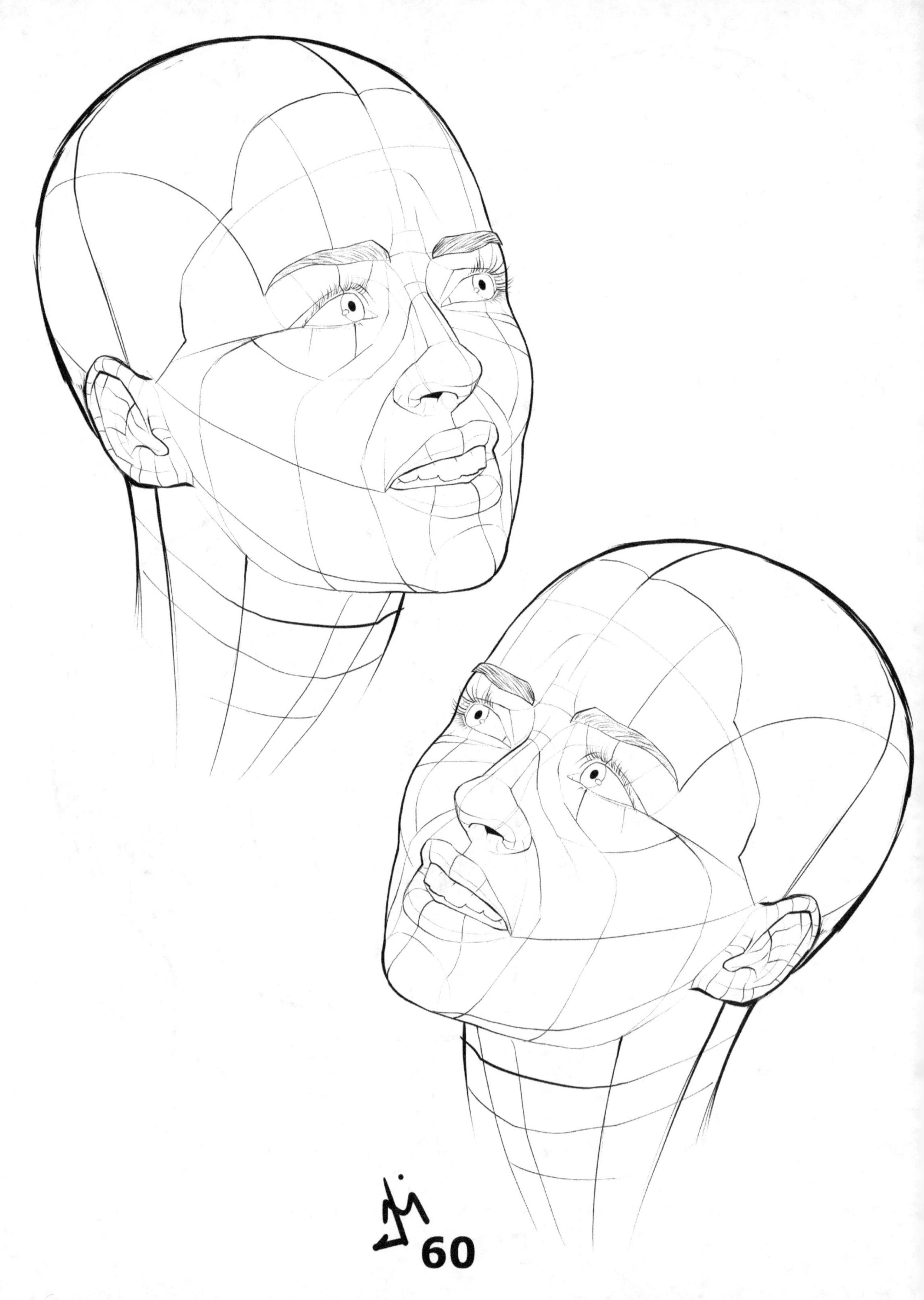
60

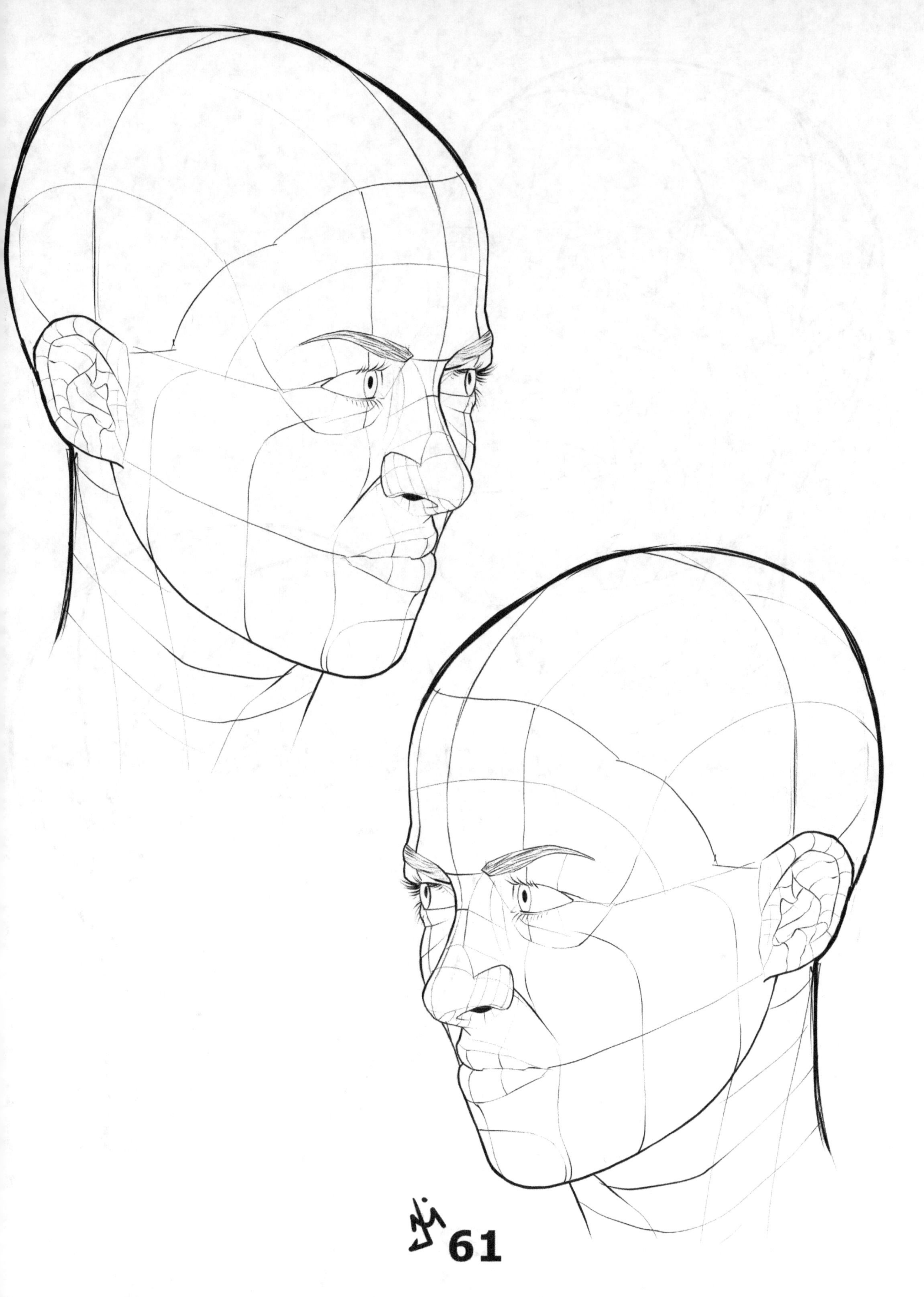

61

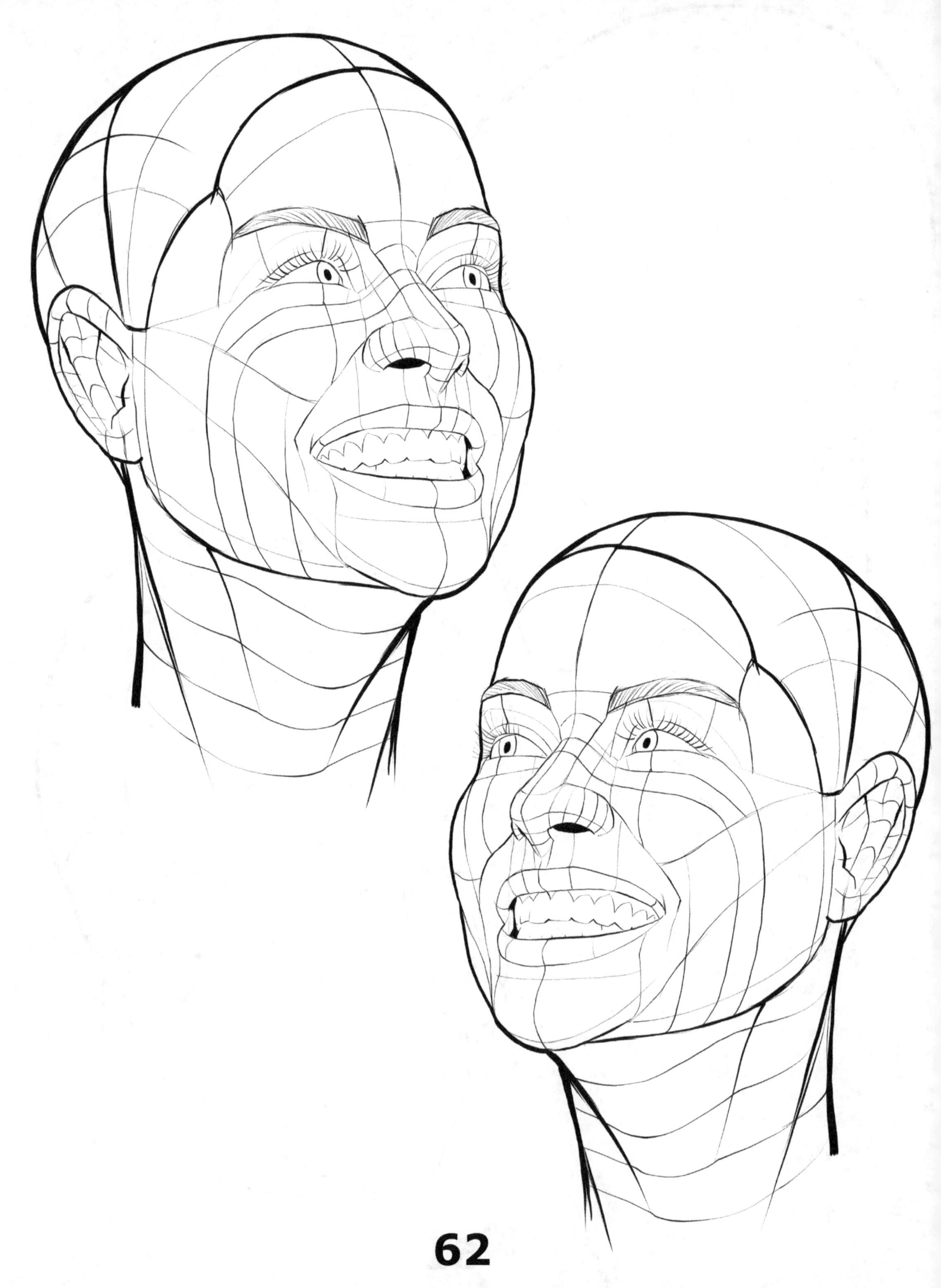

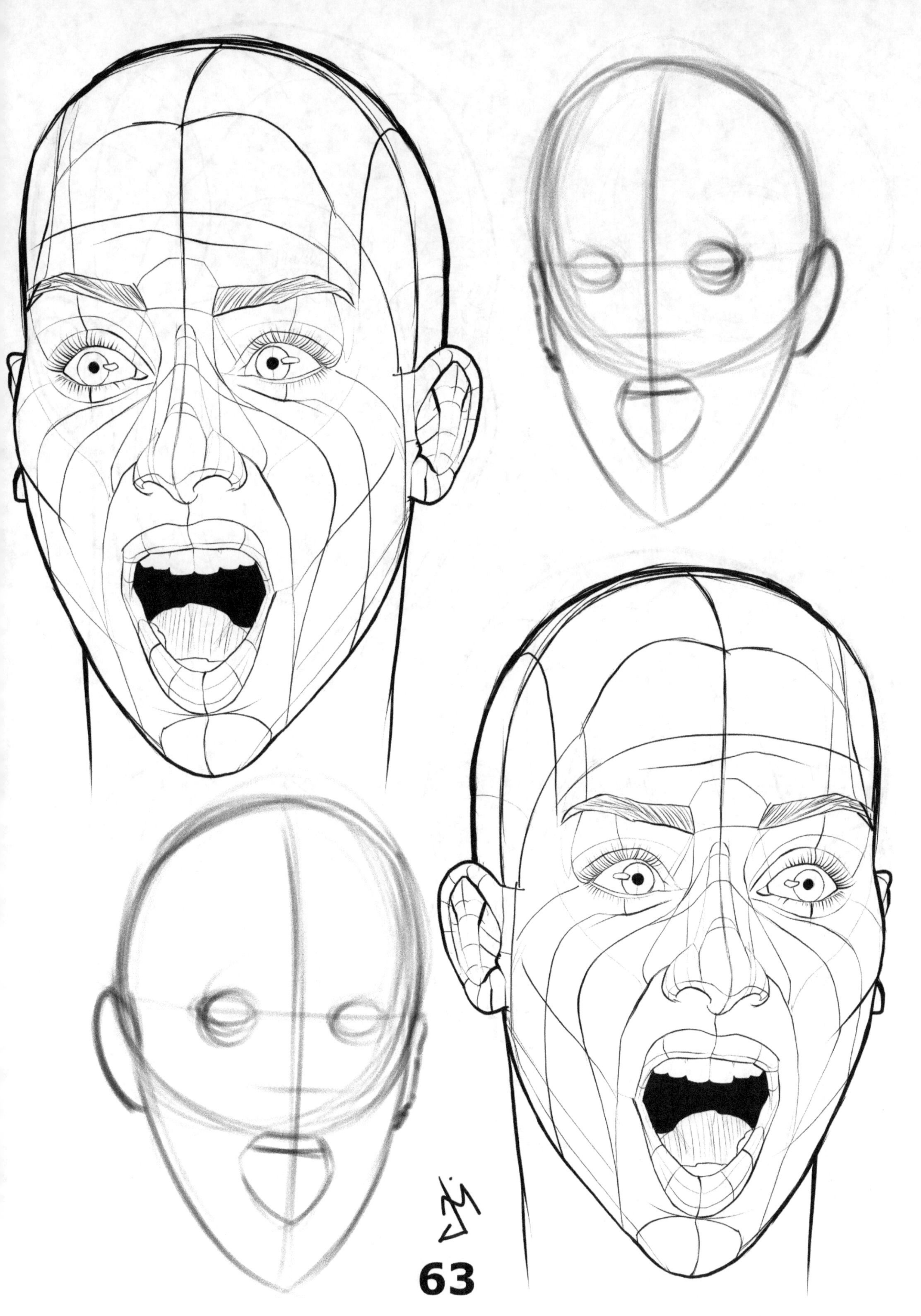

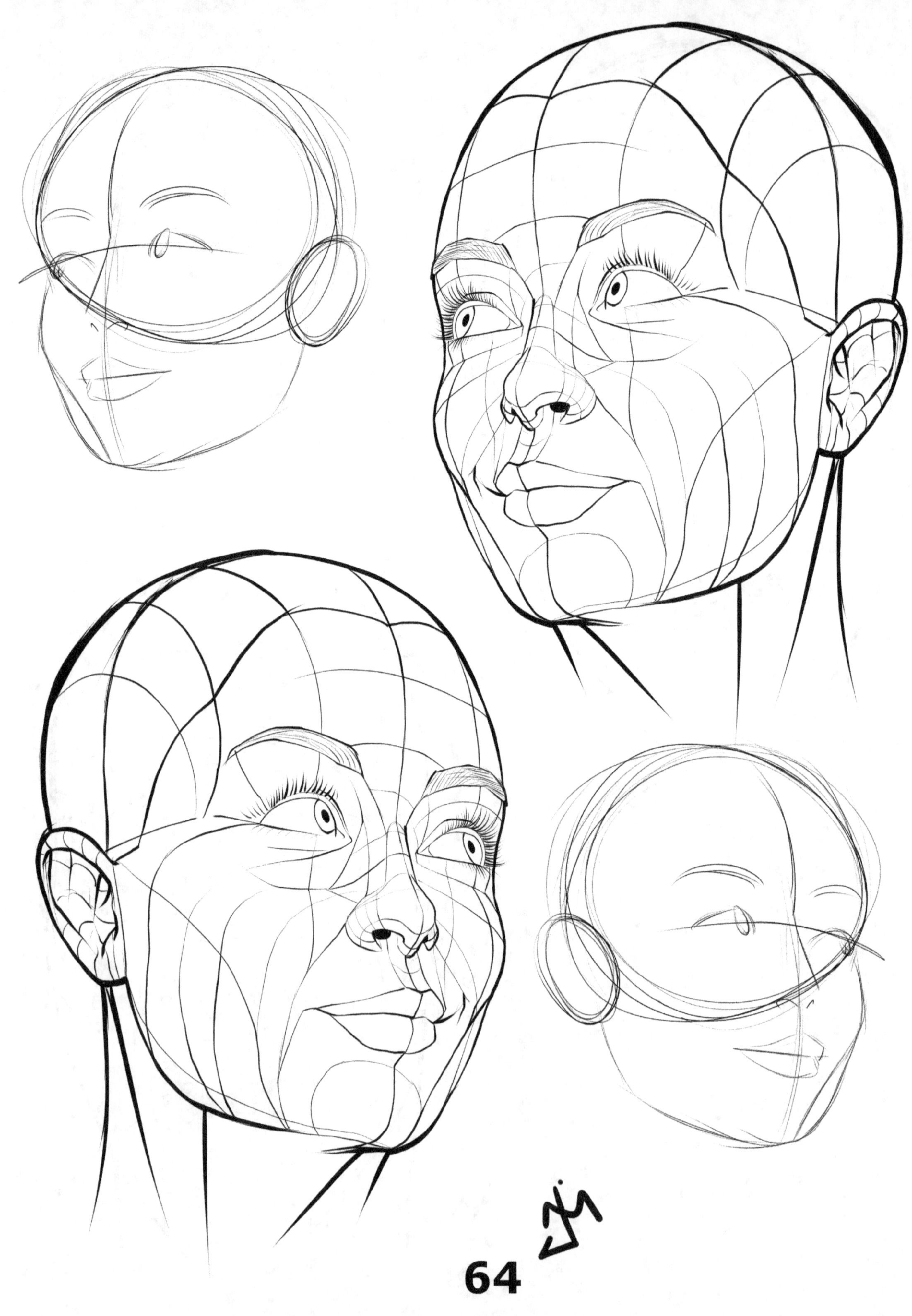

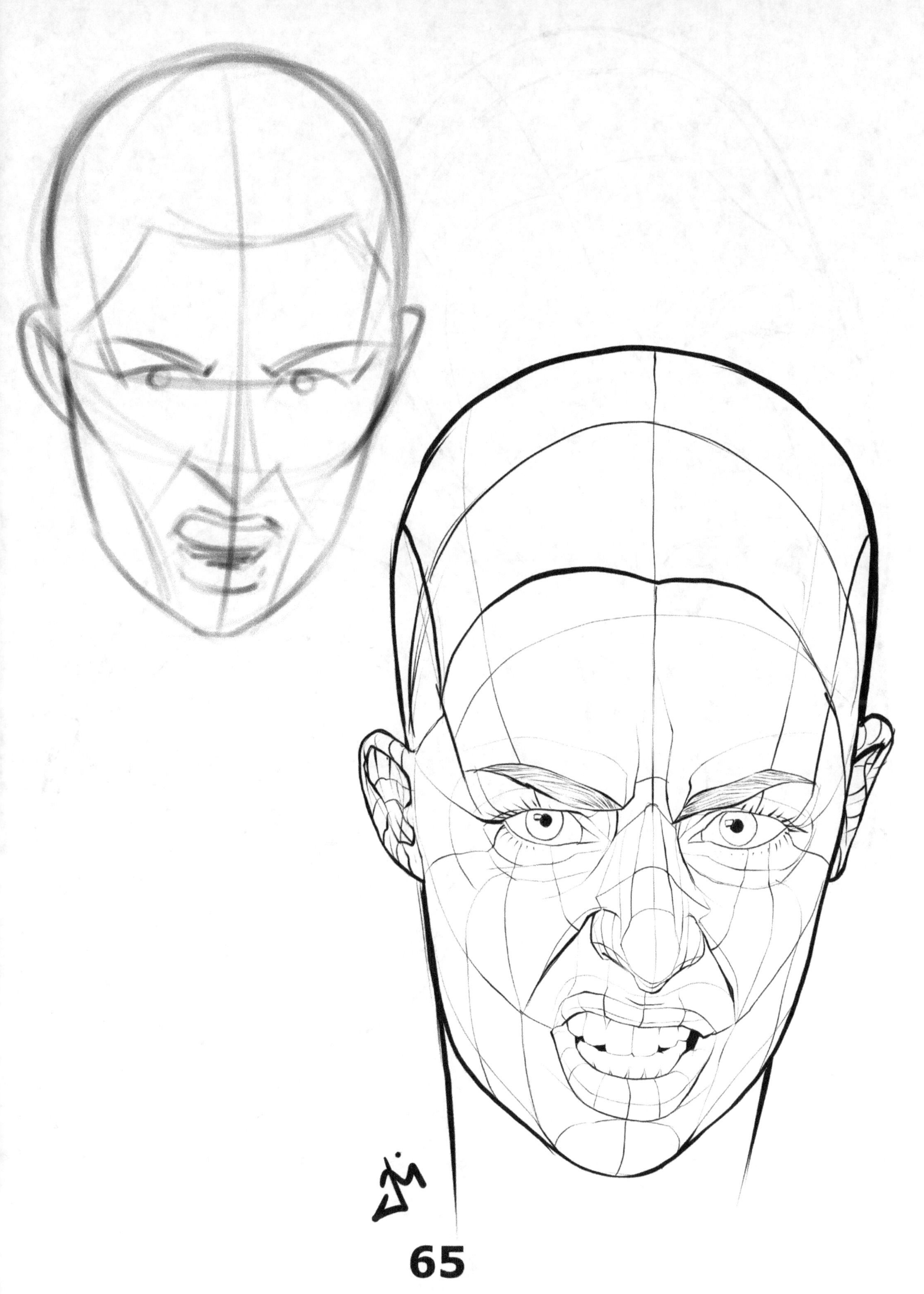

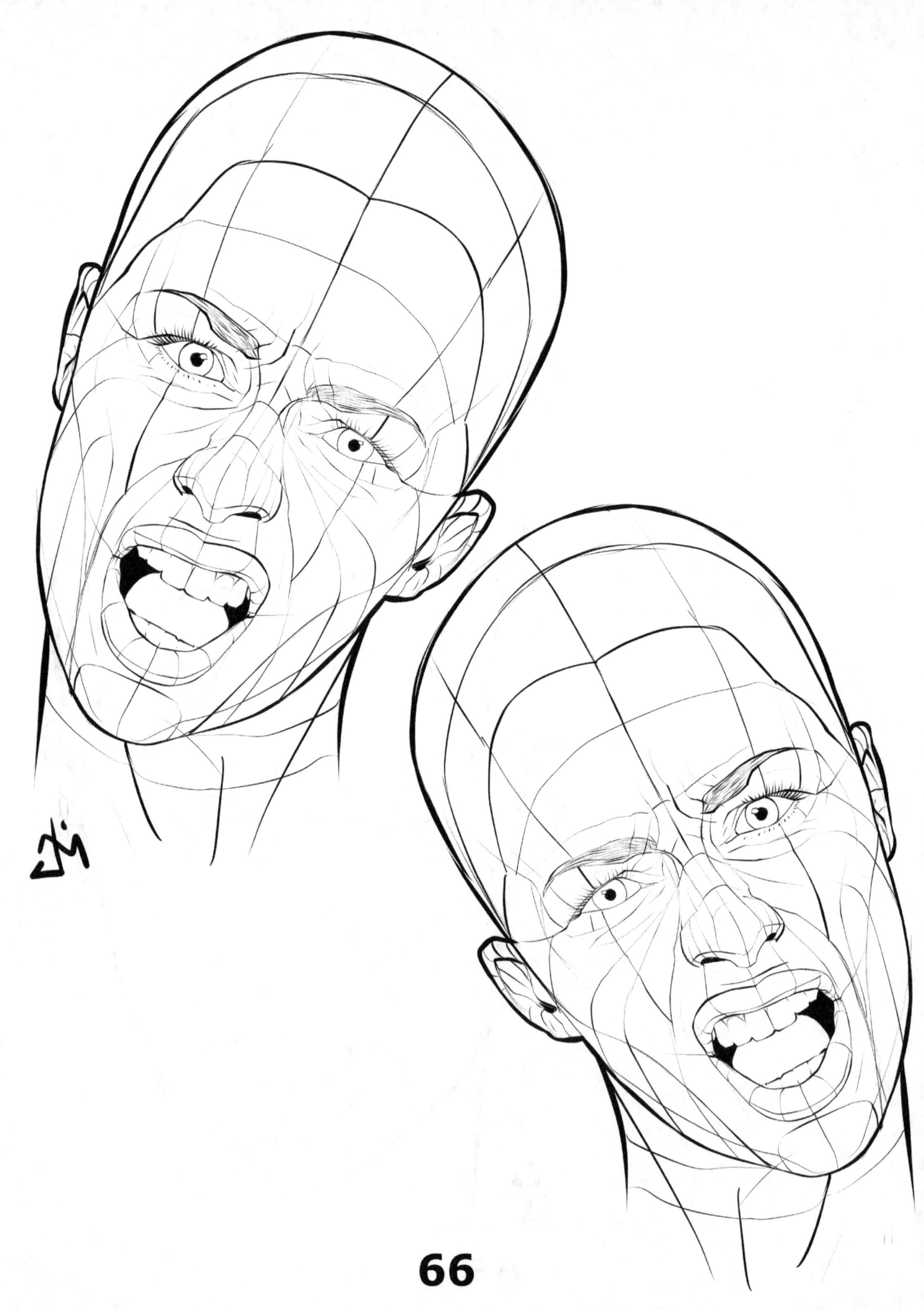

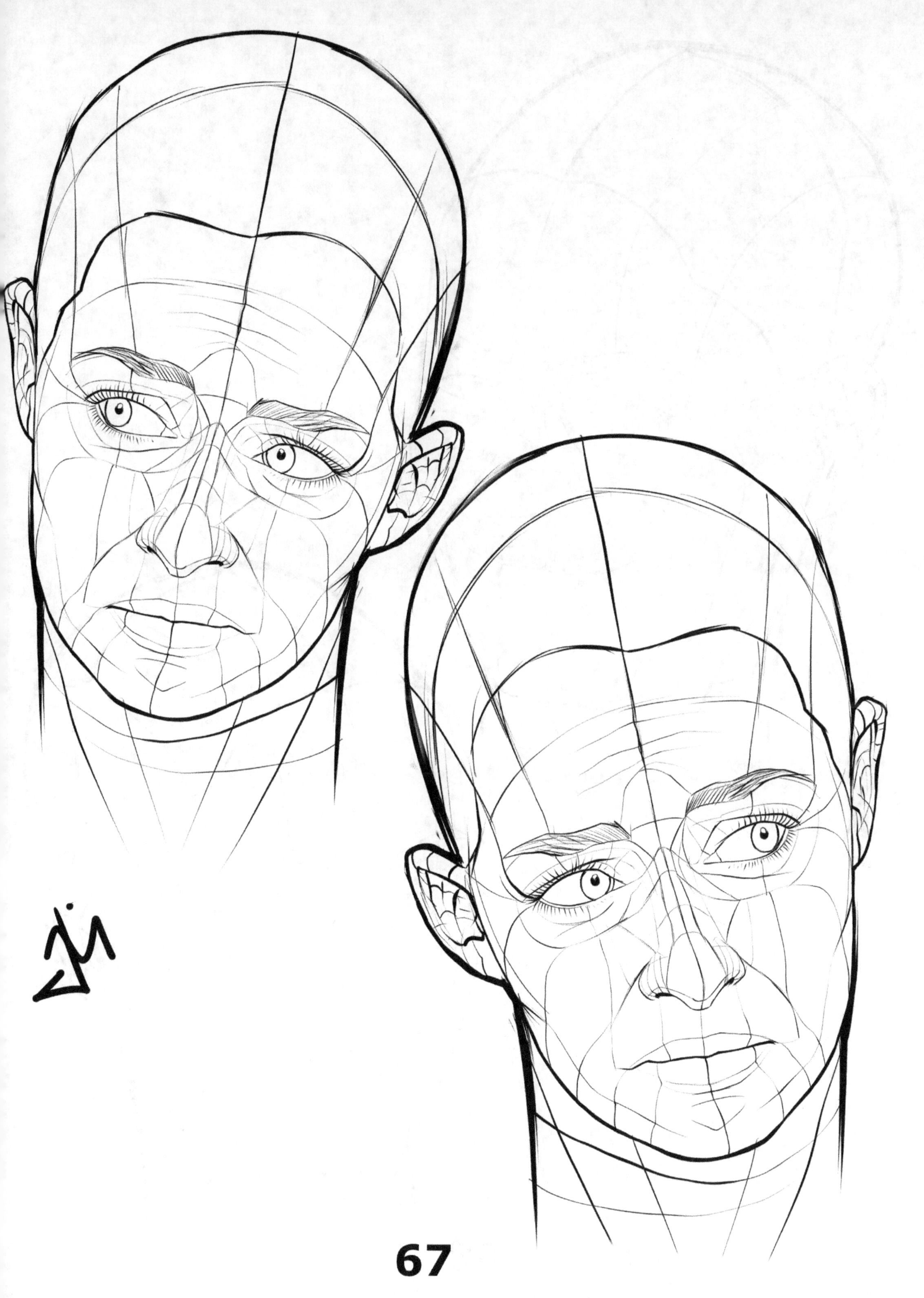

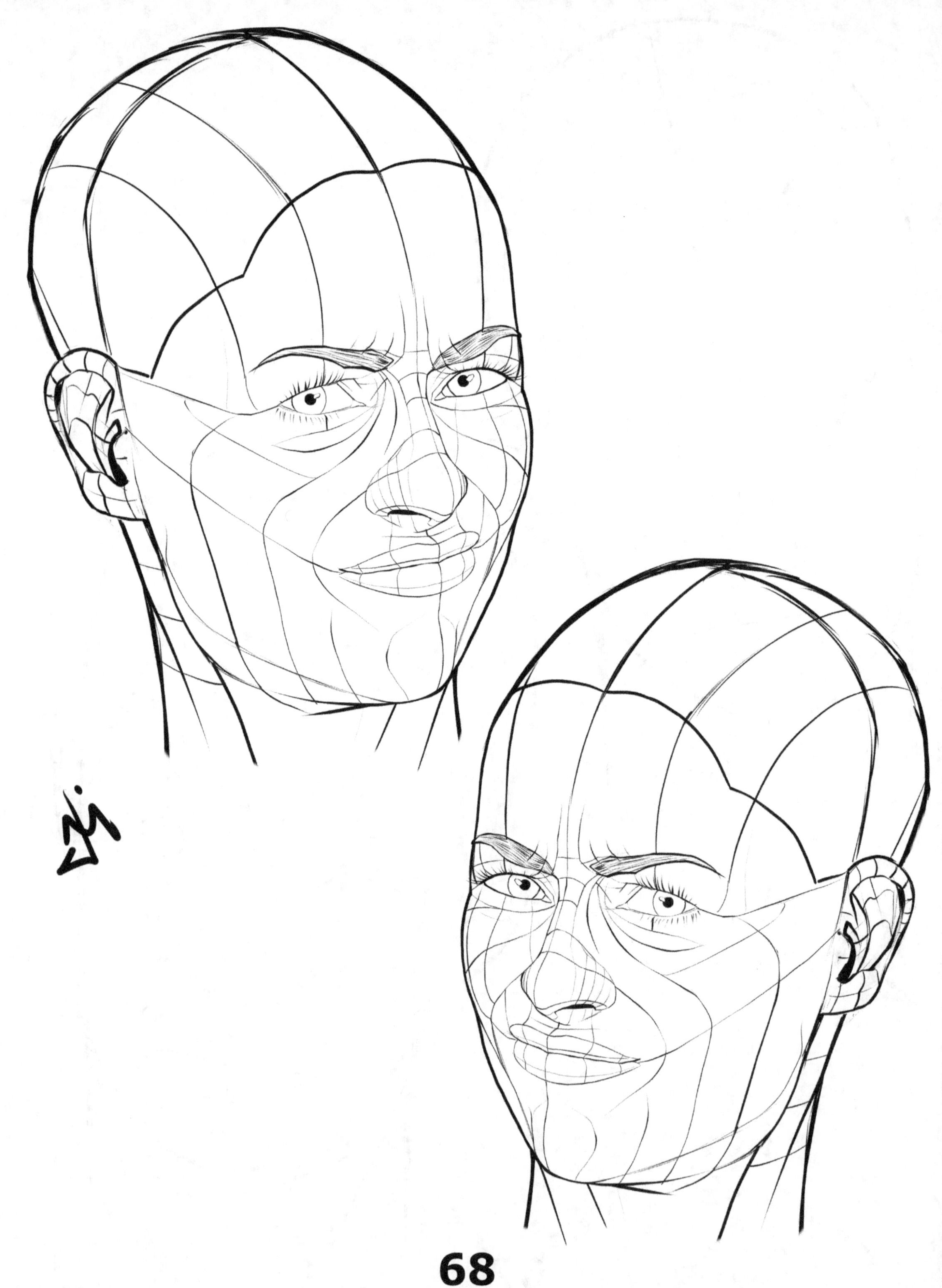

68

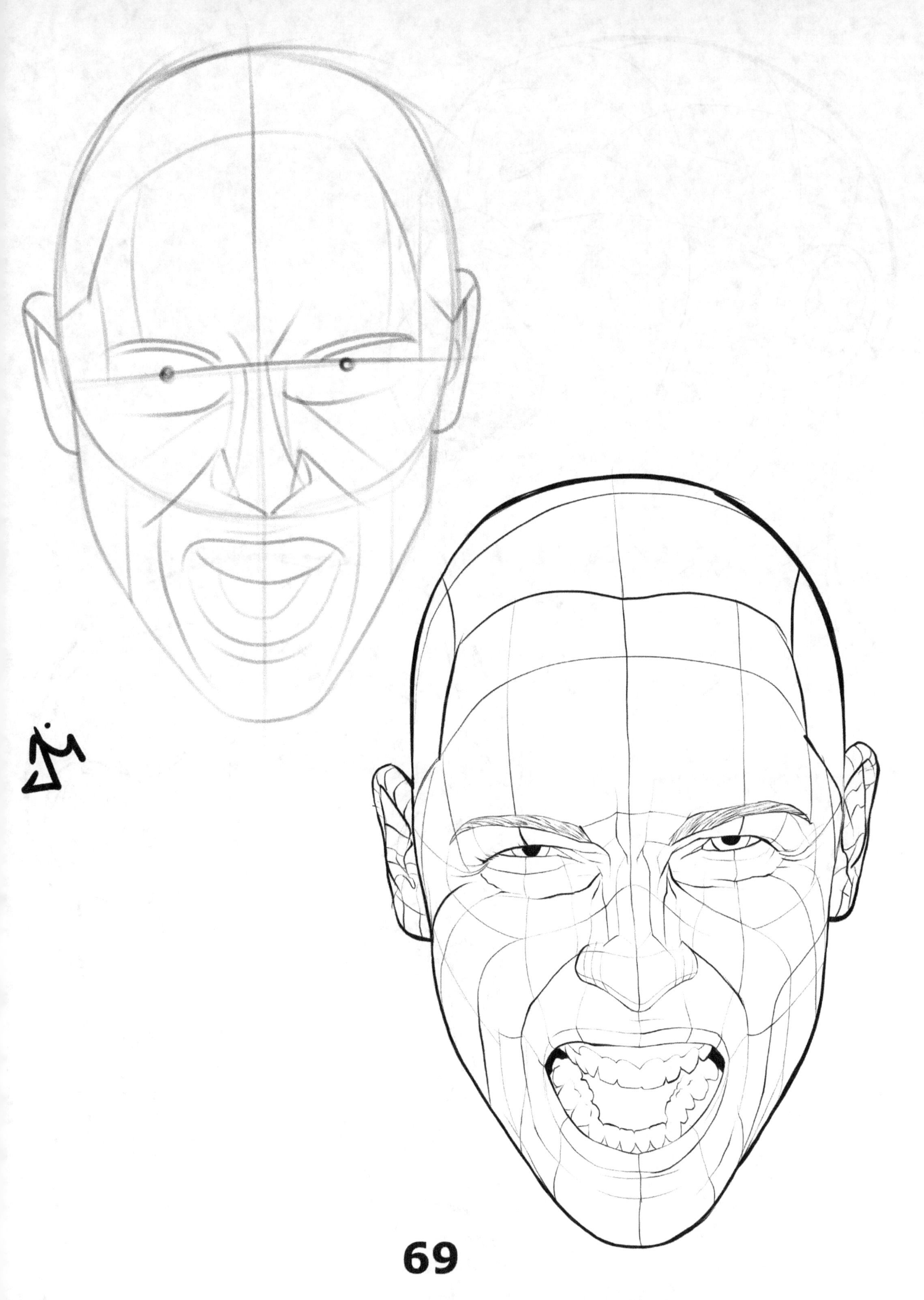

69

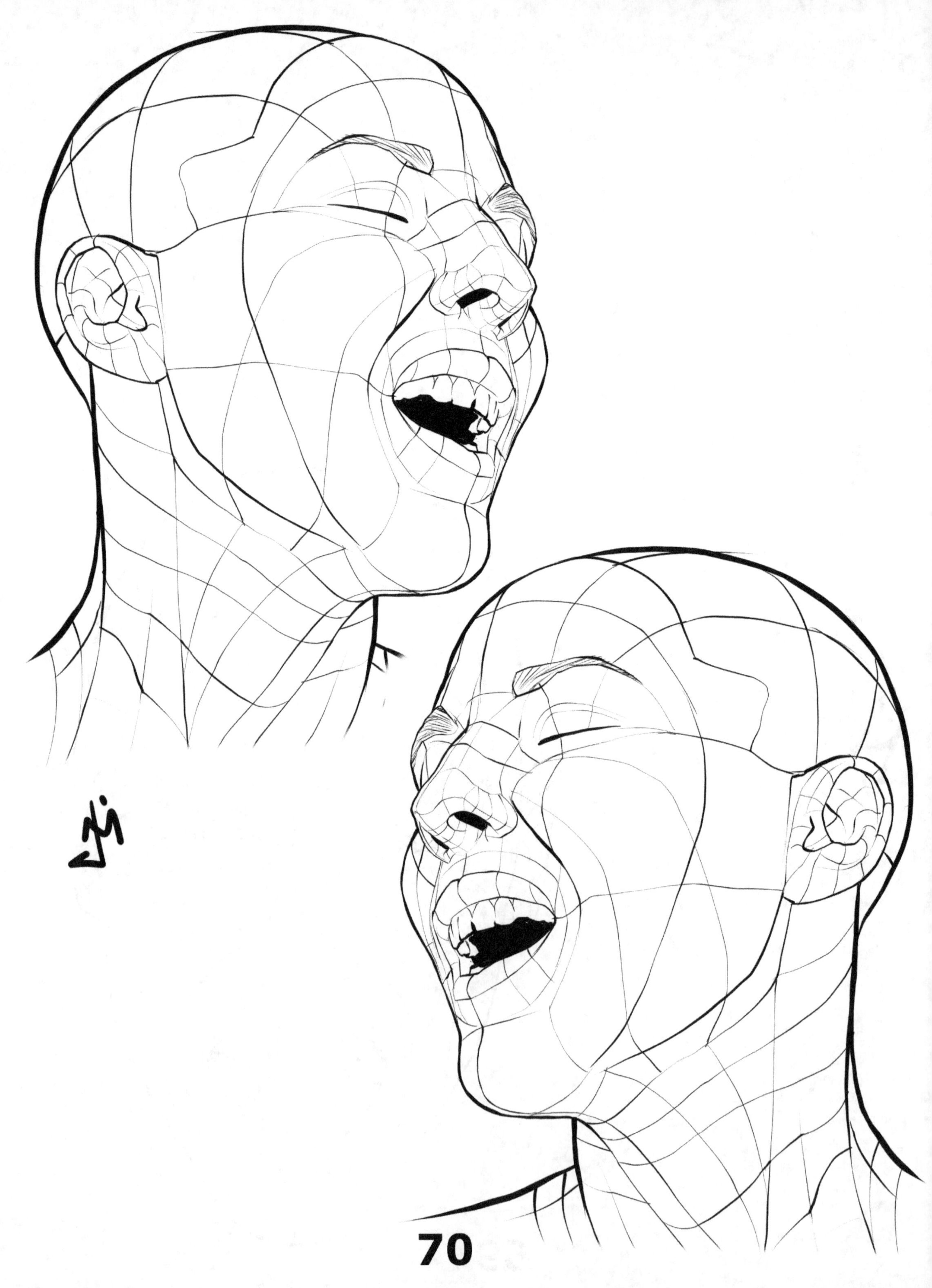

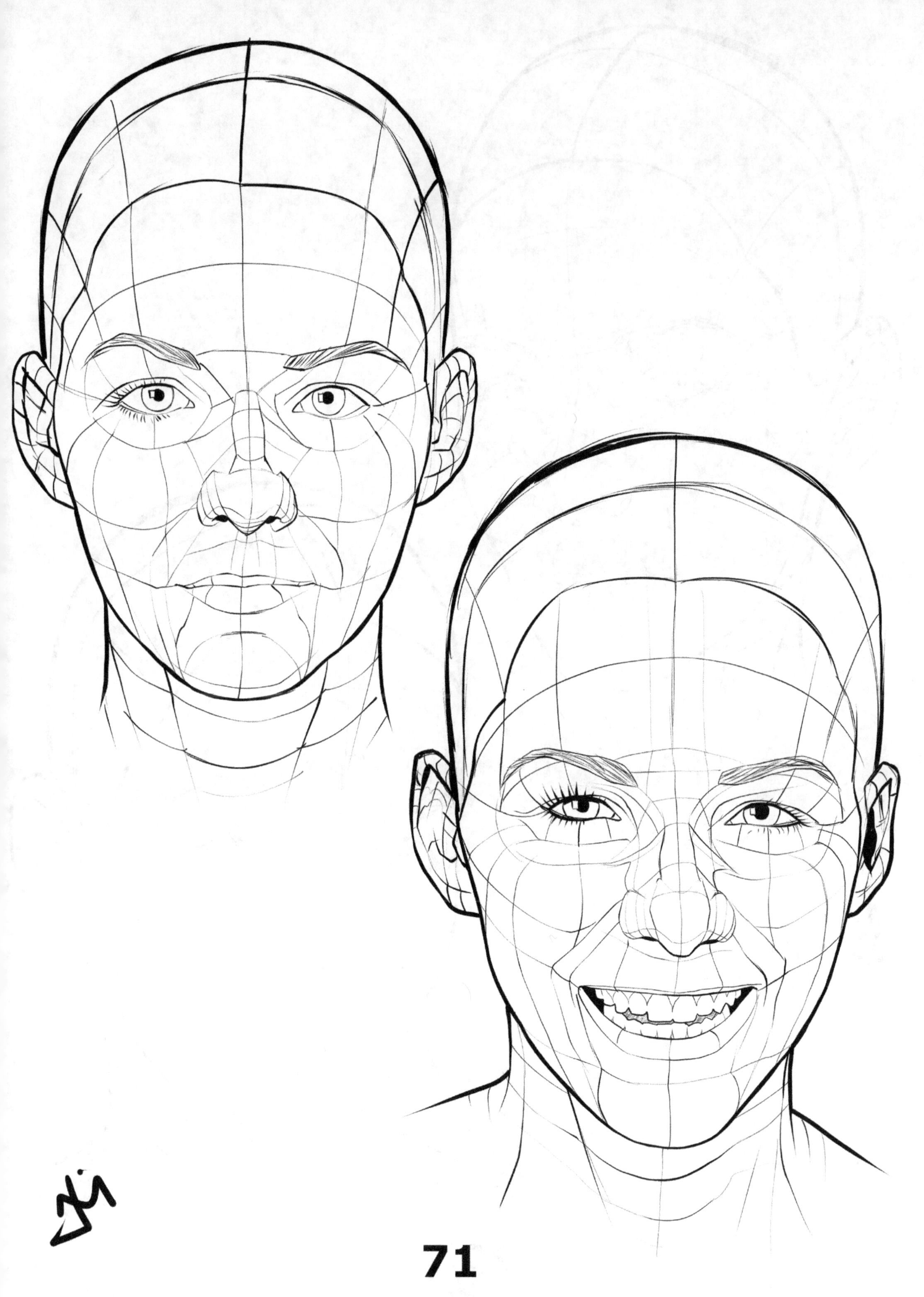

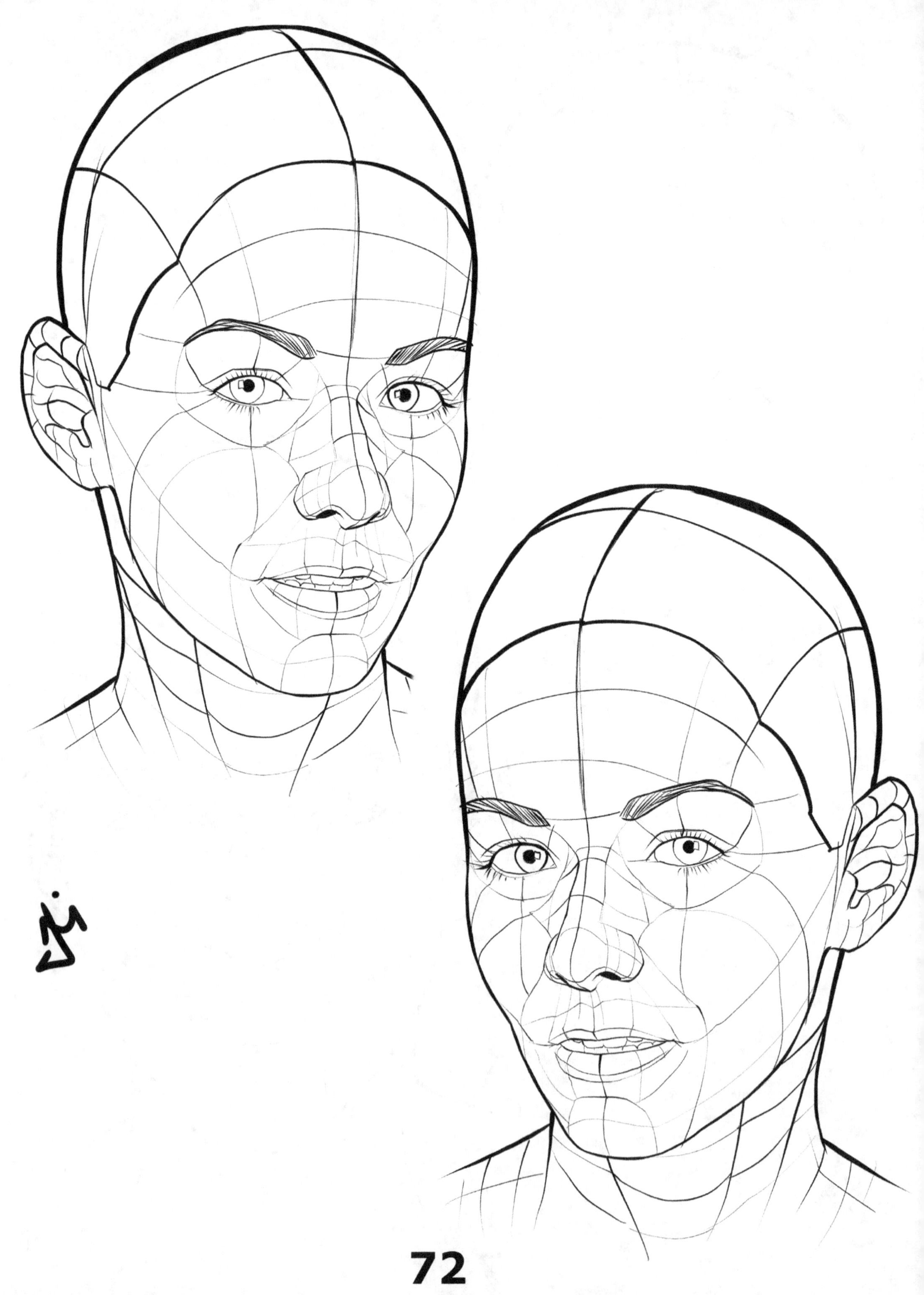

72

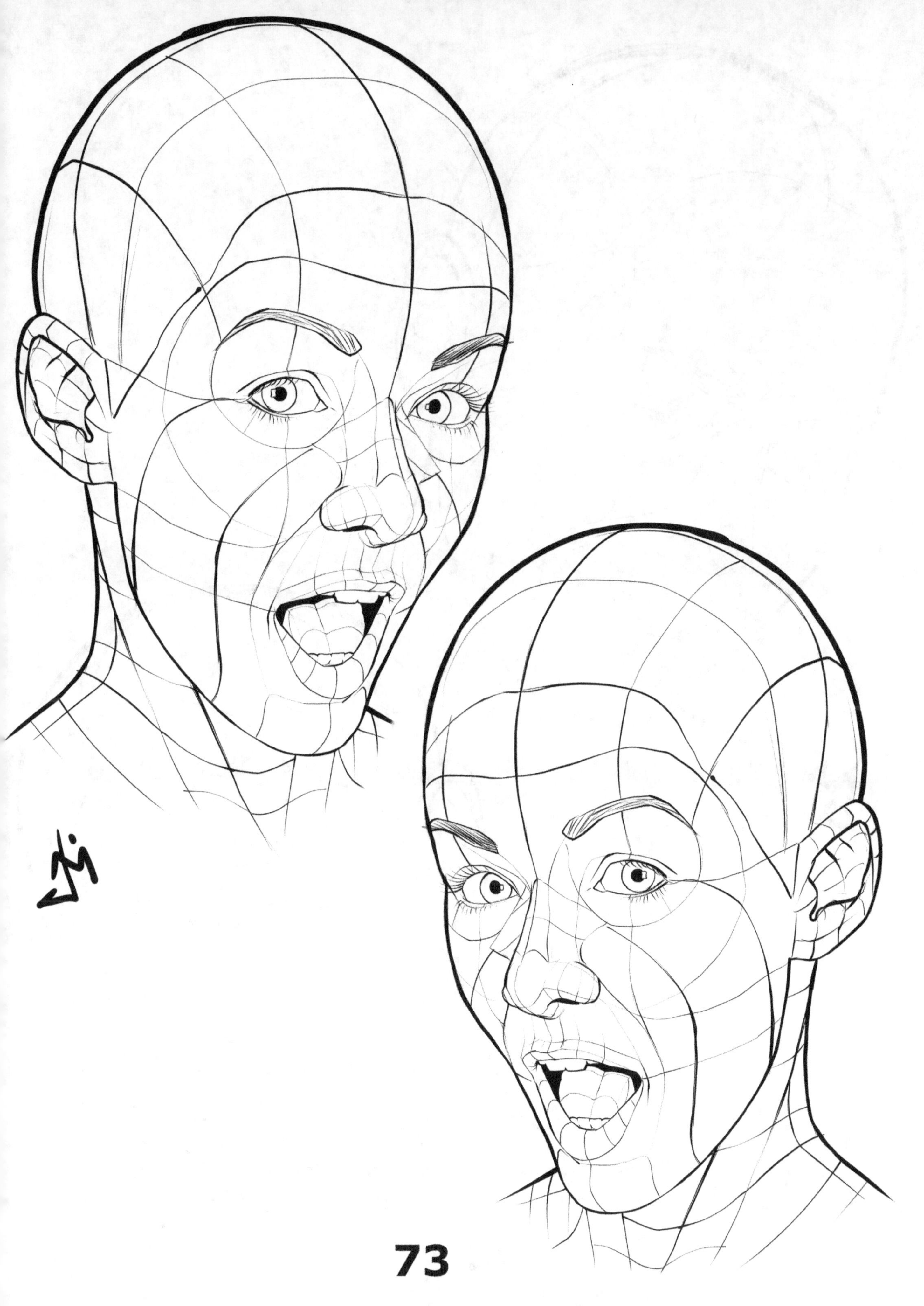

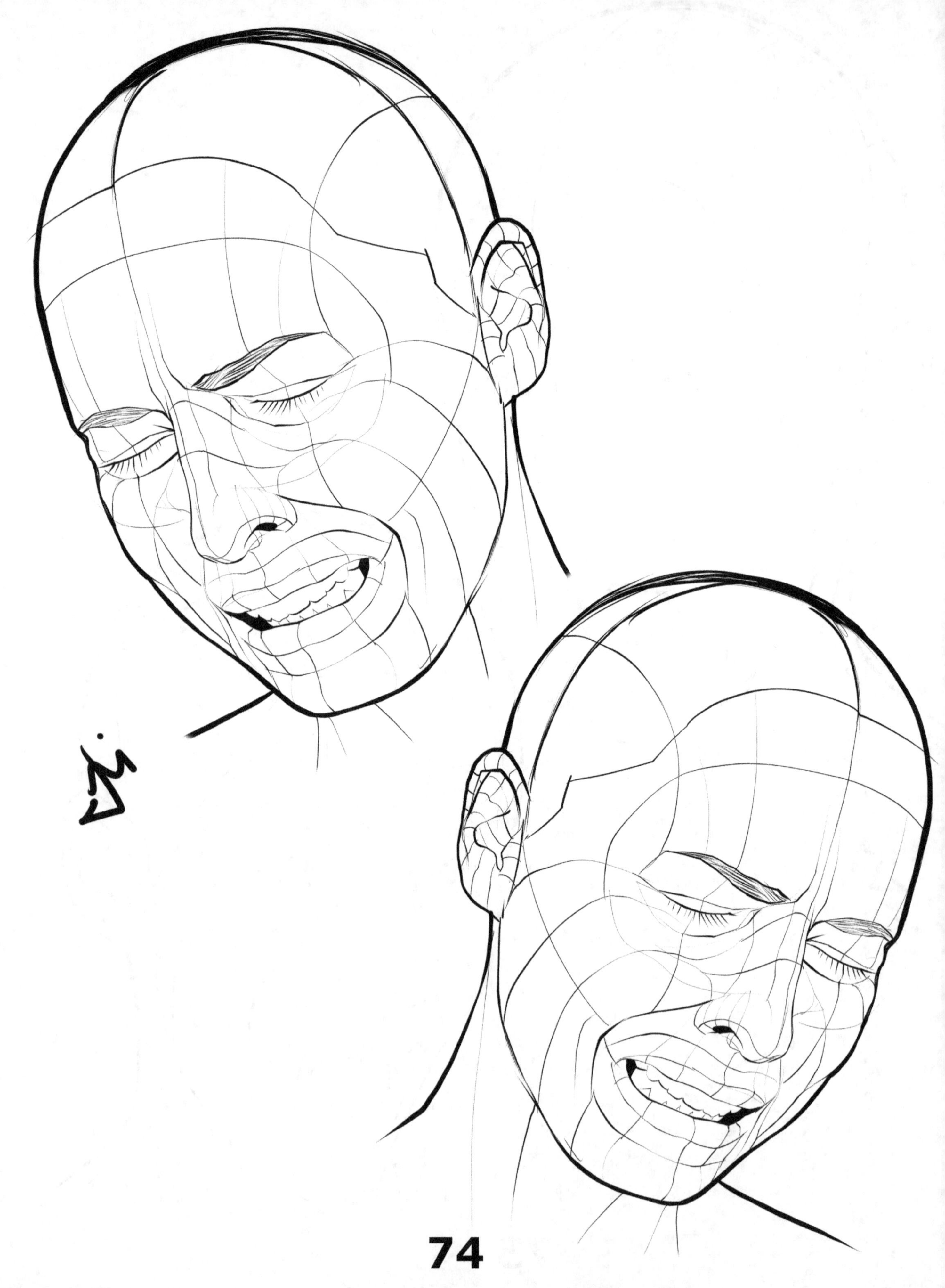

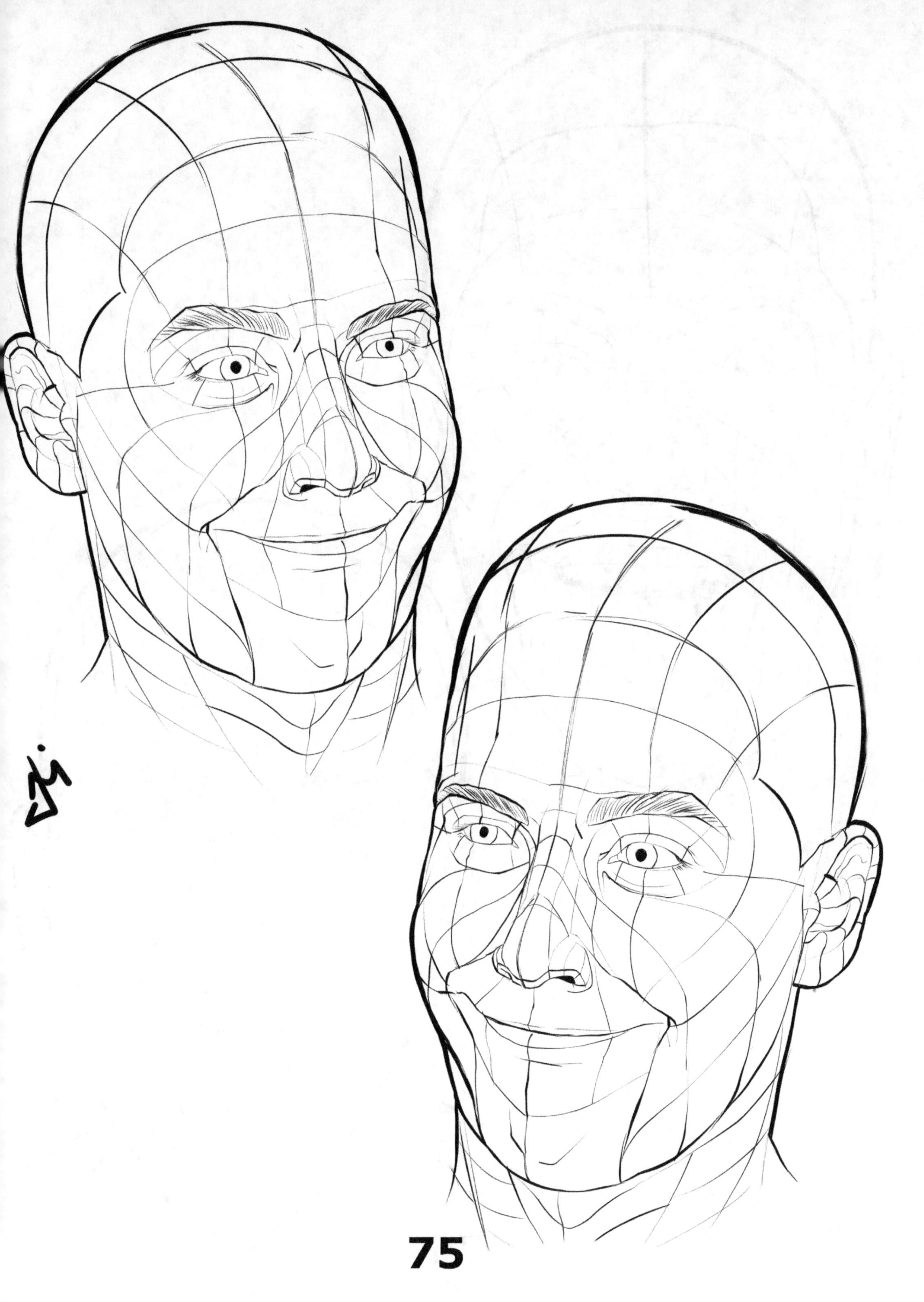

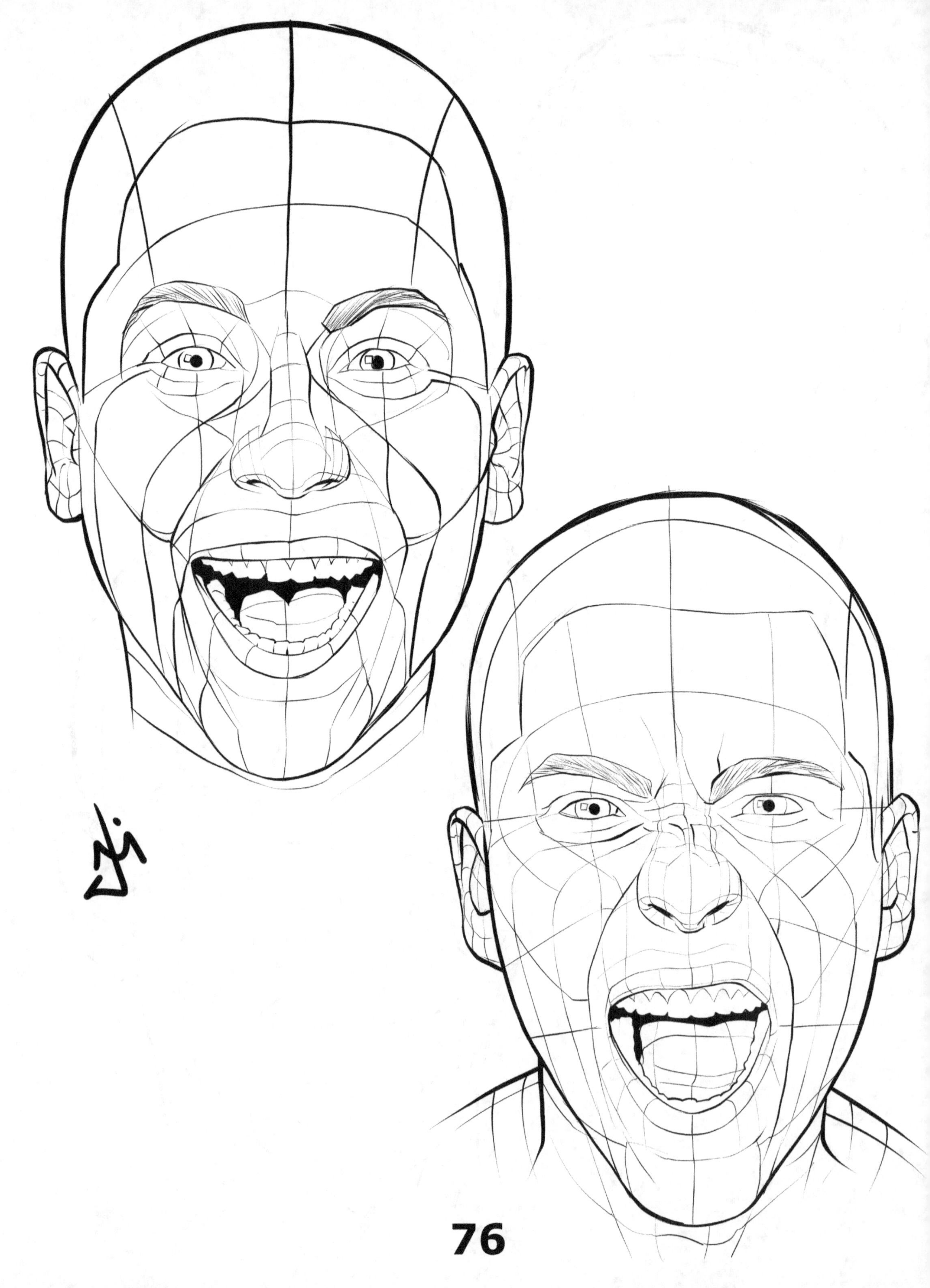

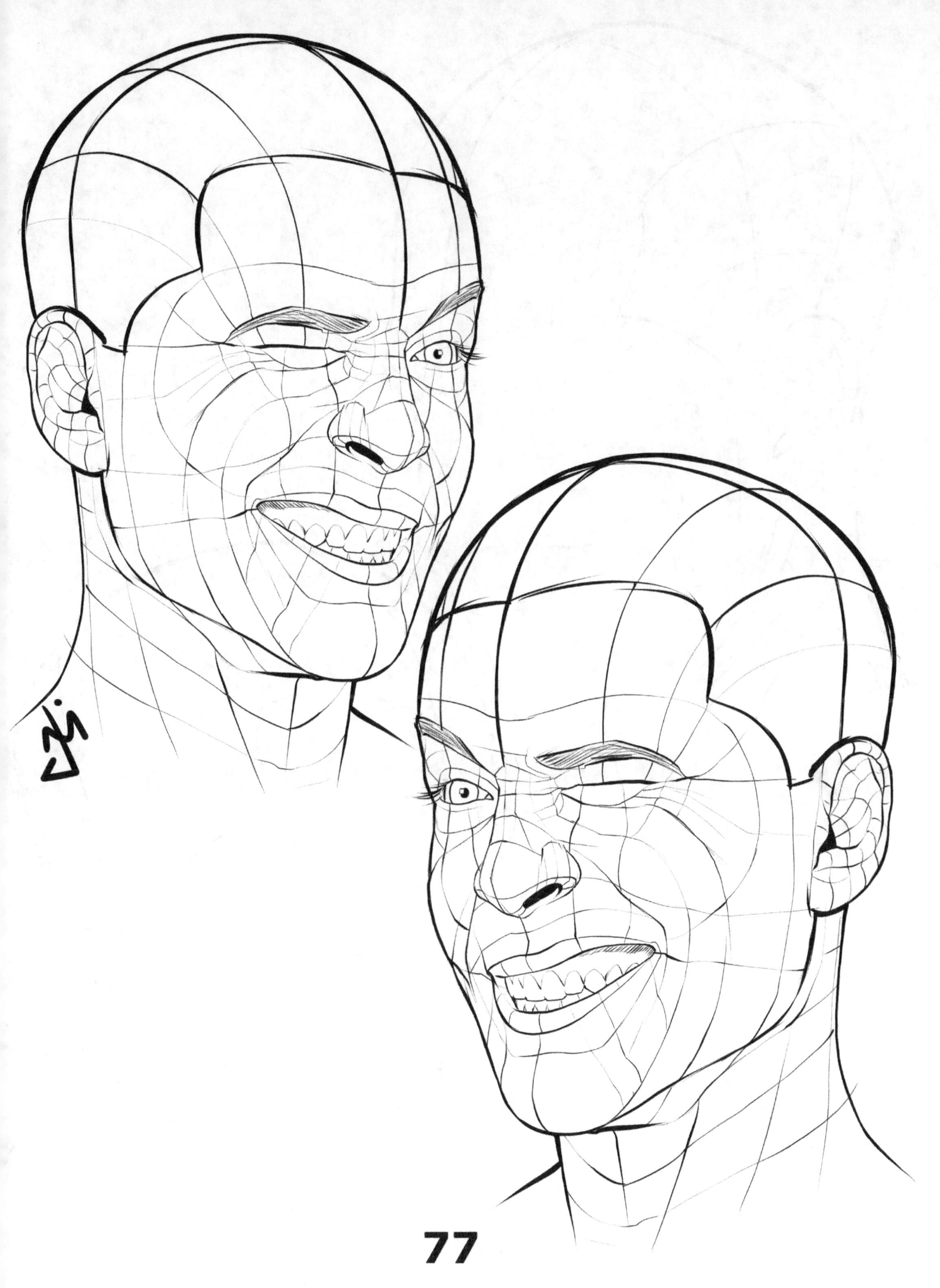

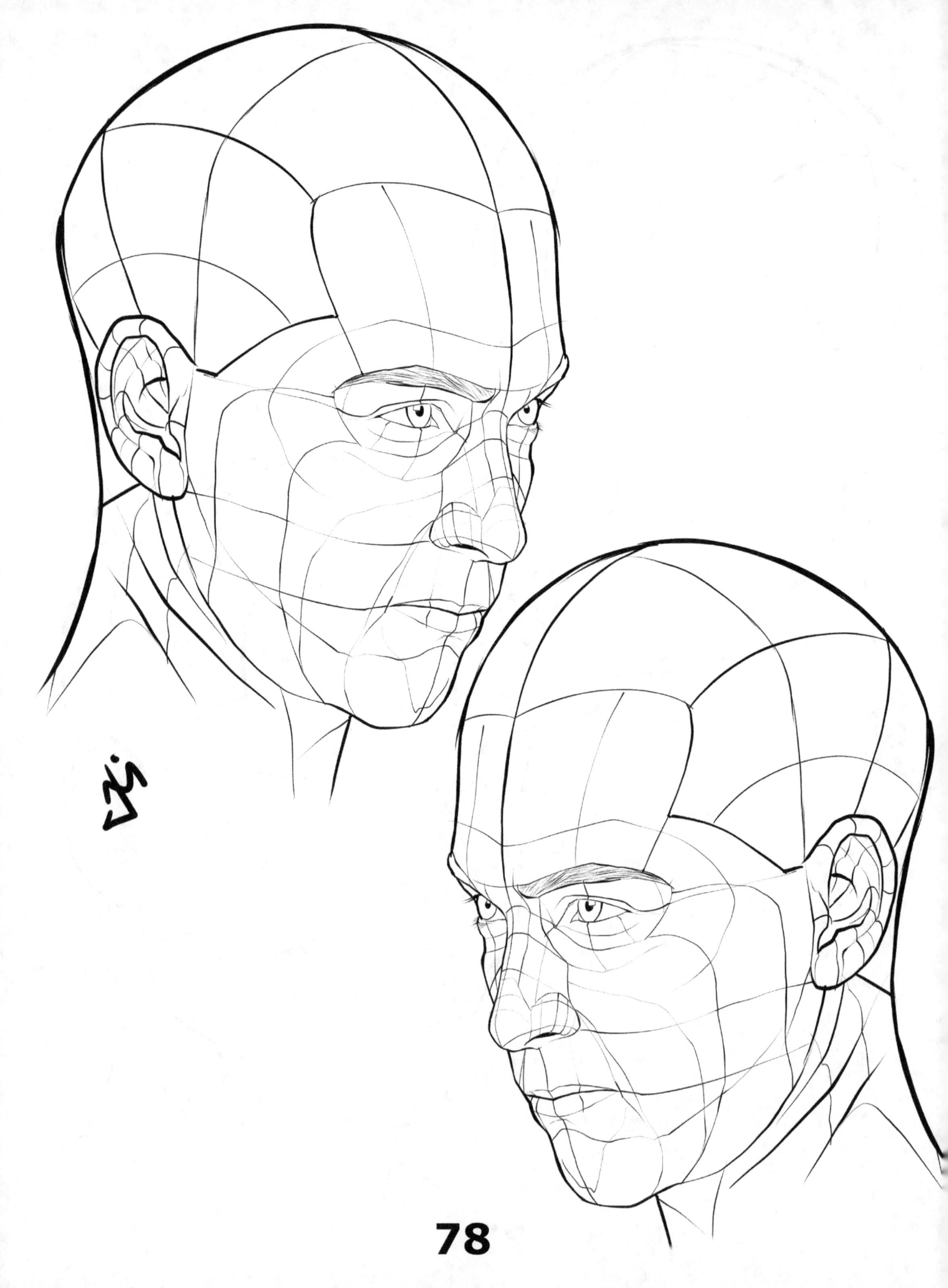

78

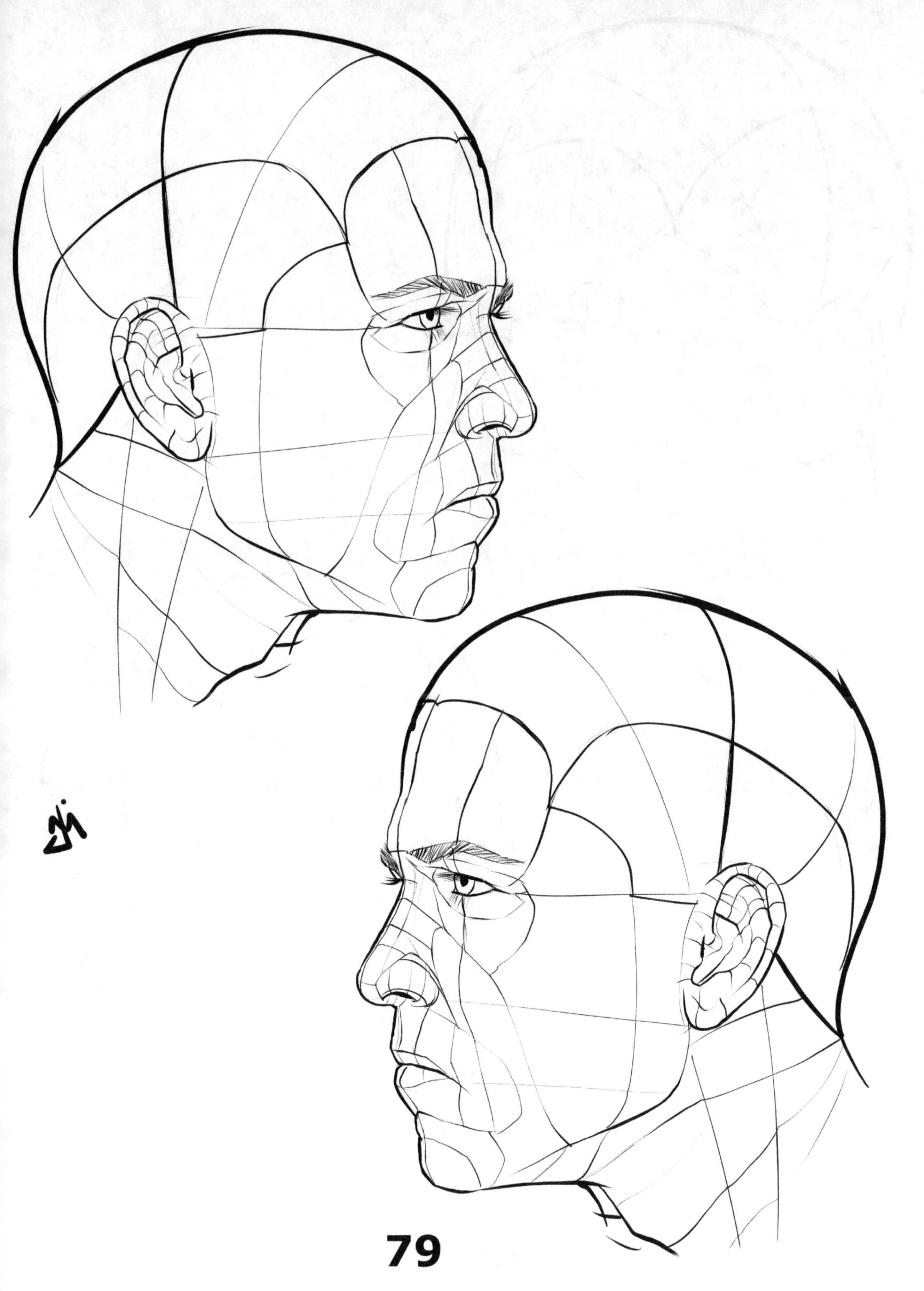

79

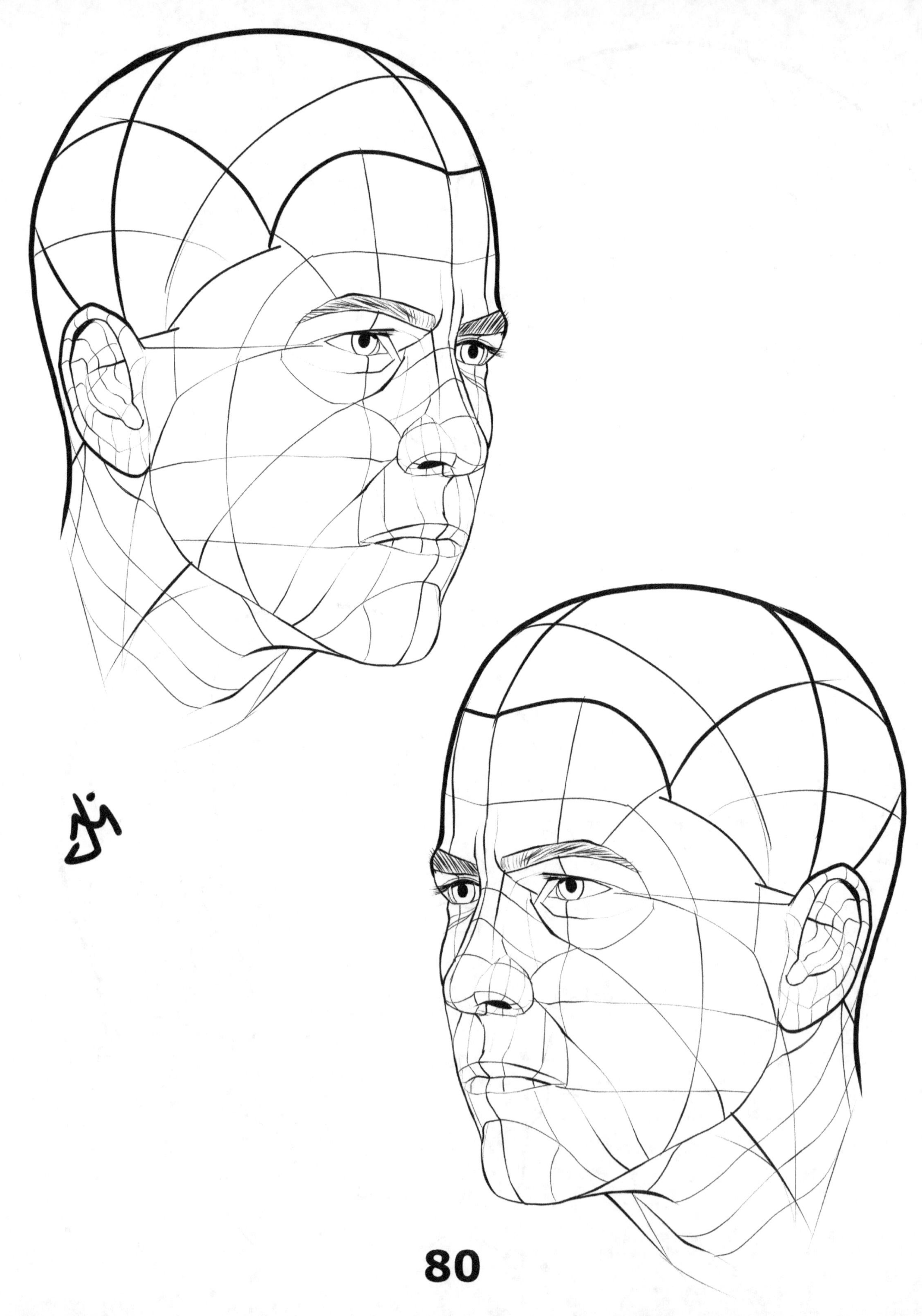

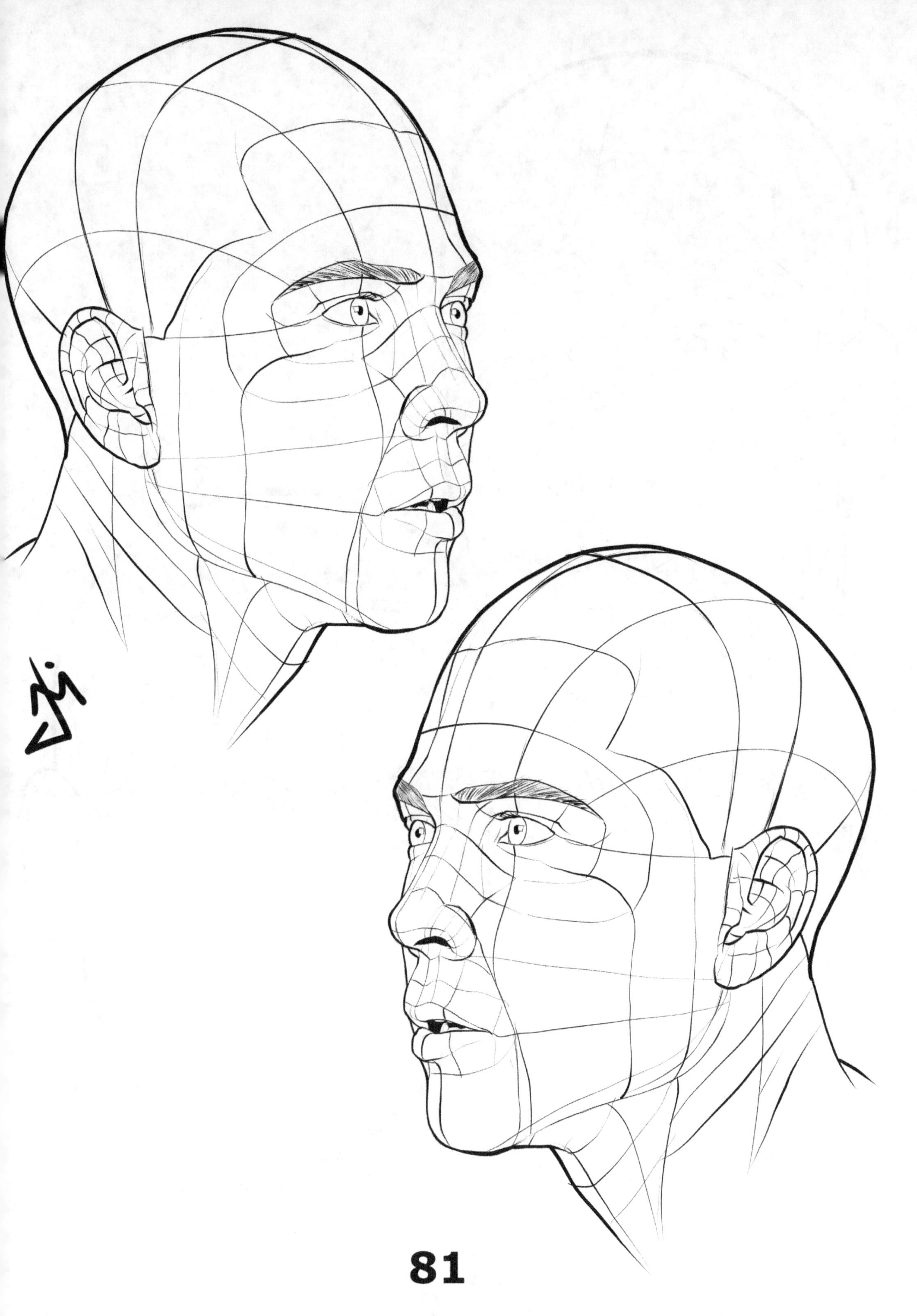

81

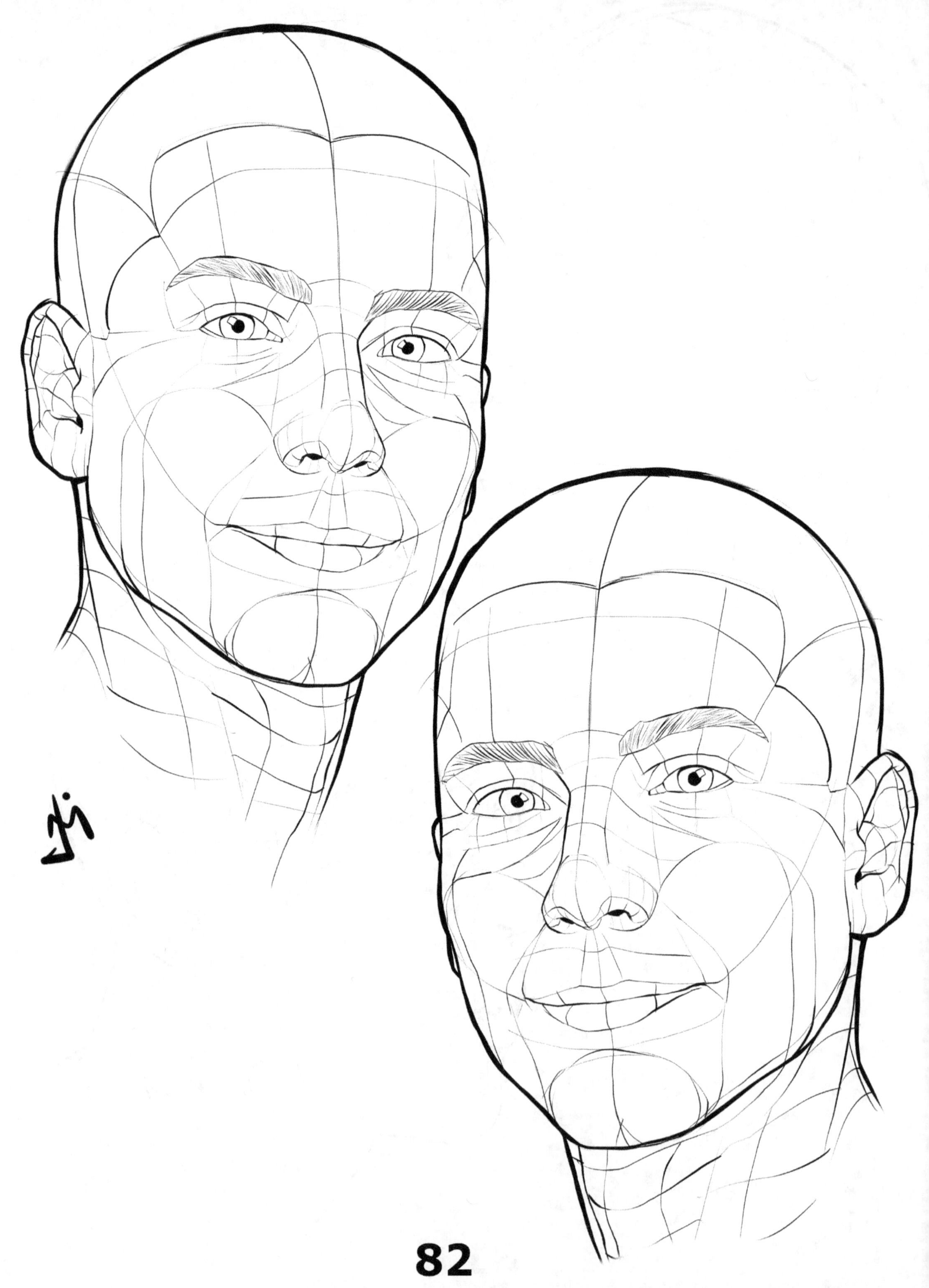

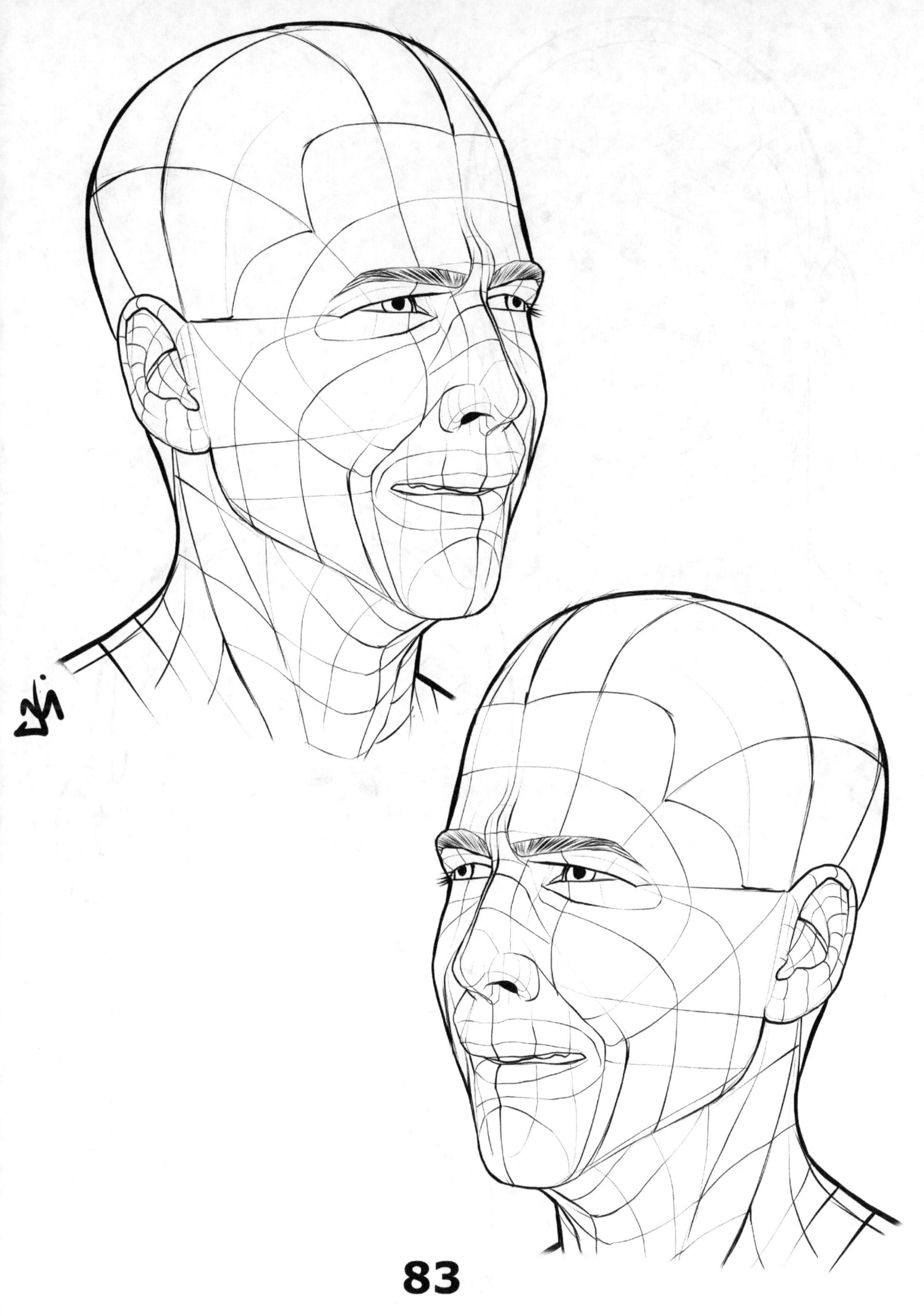

83

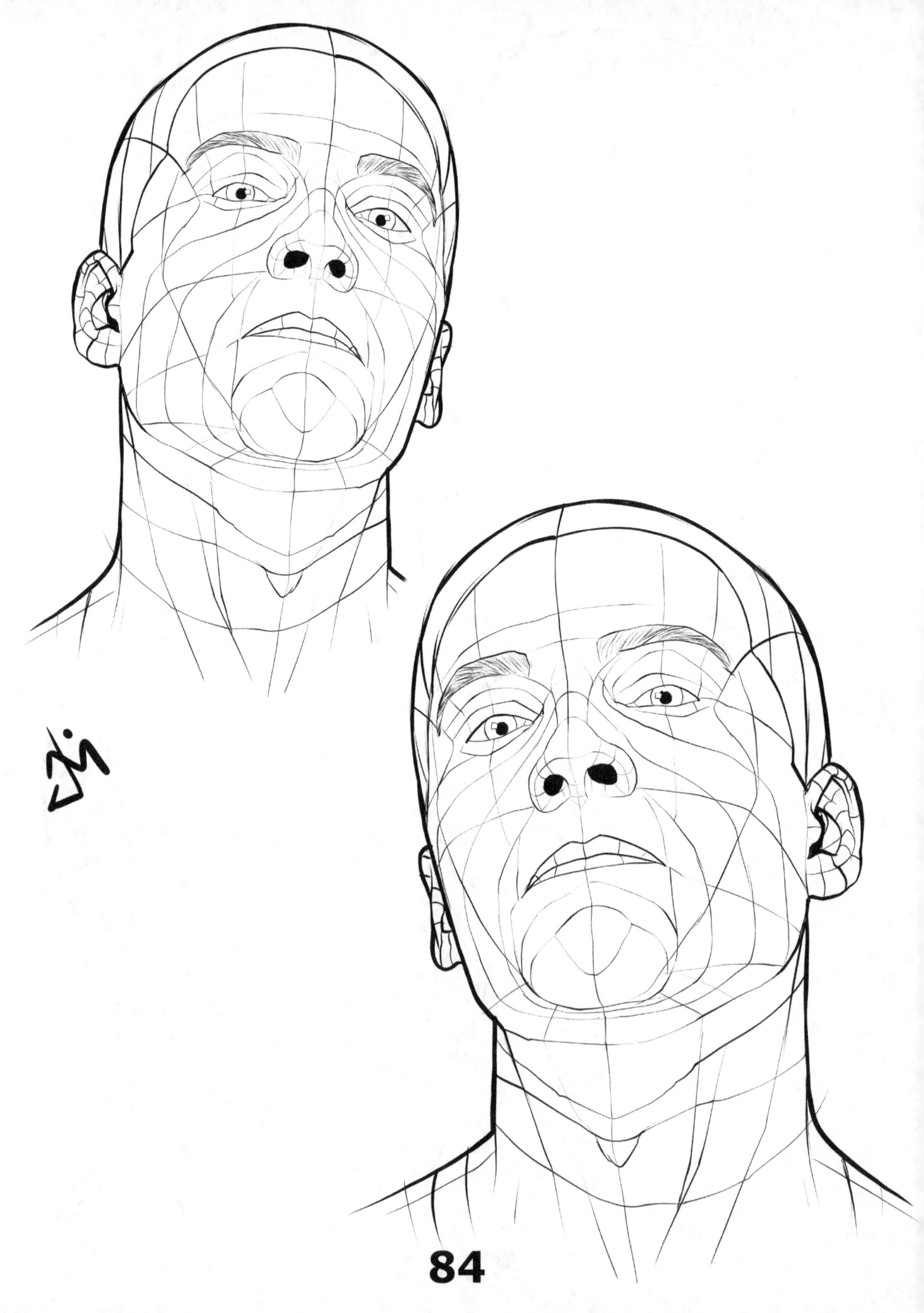

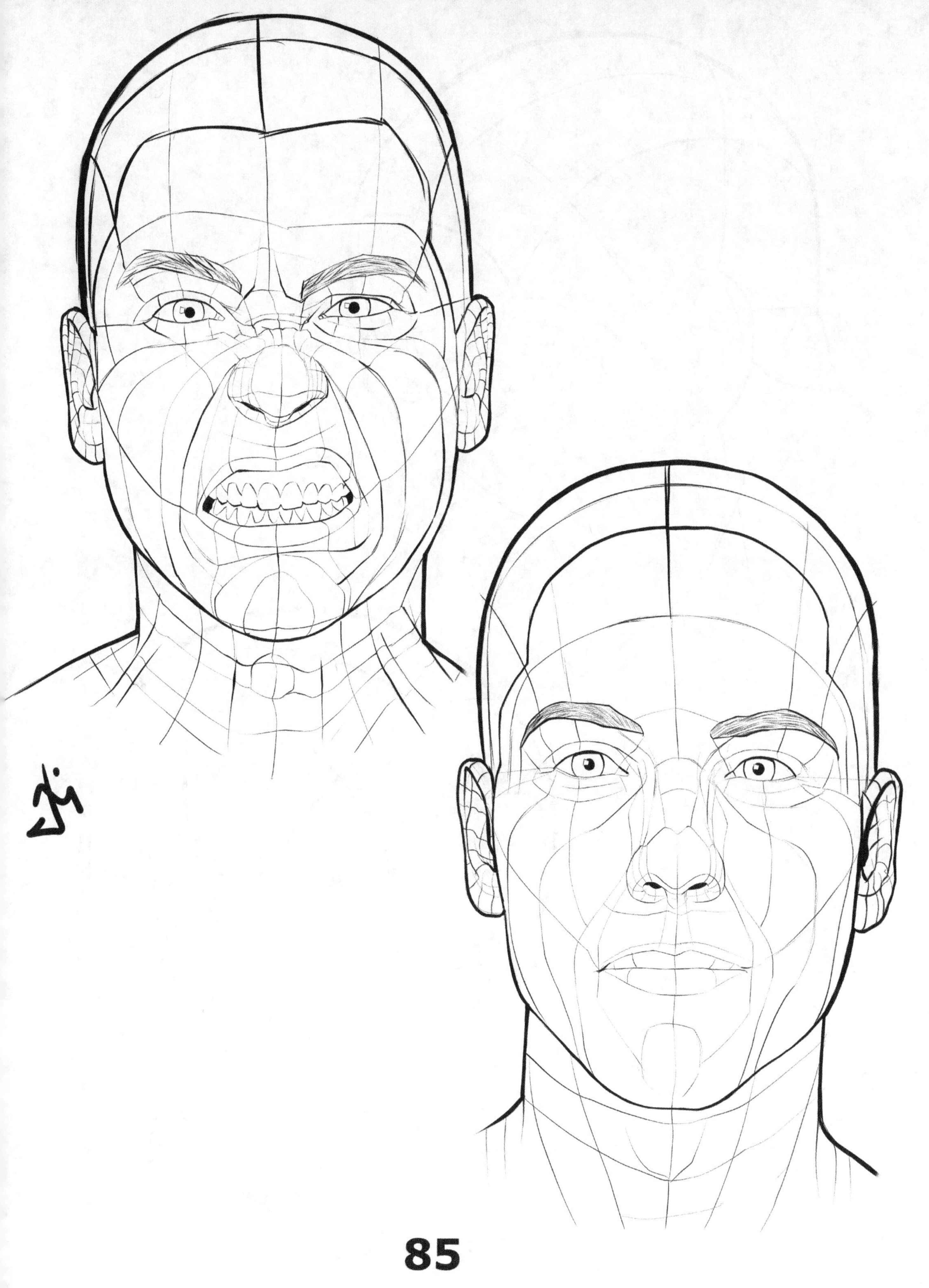

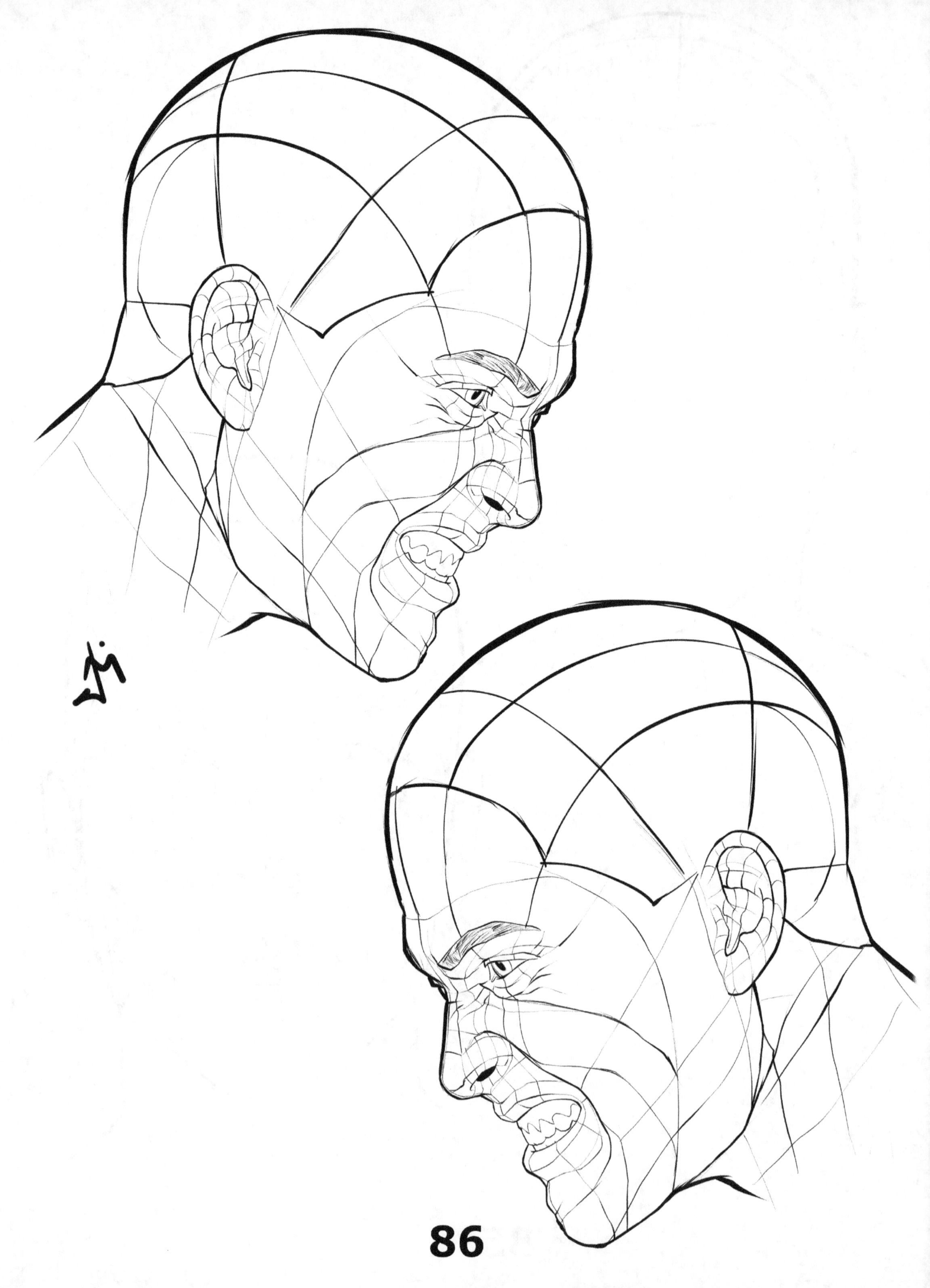

86

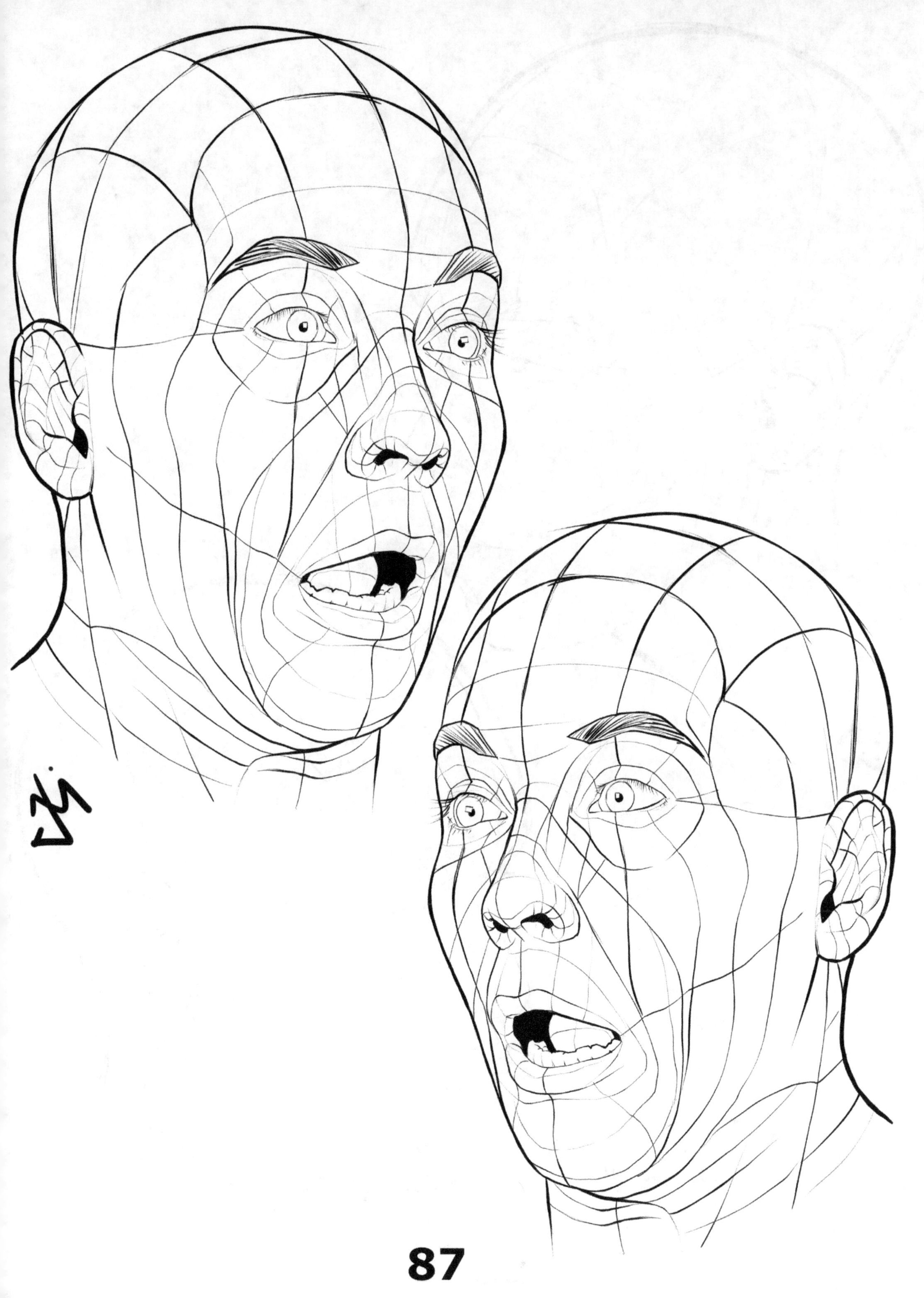

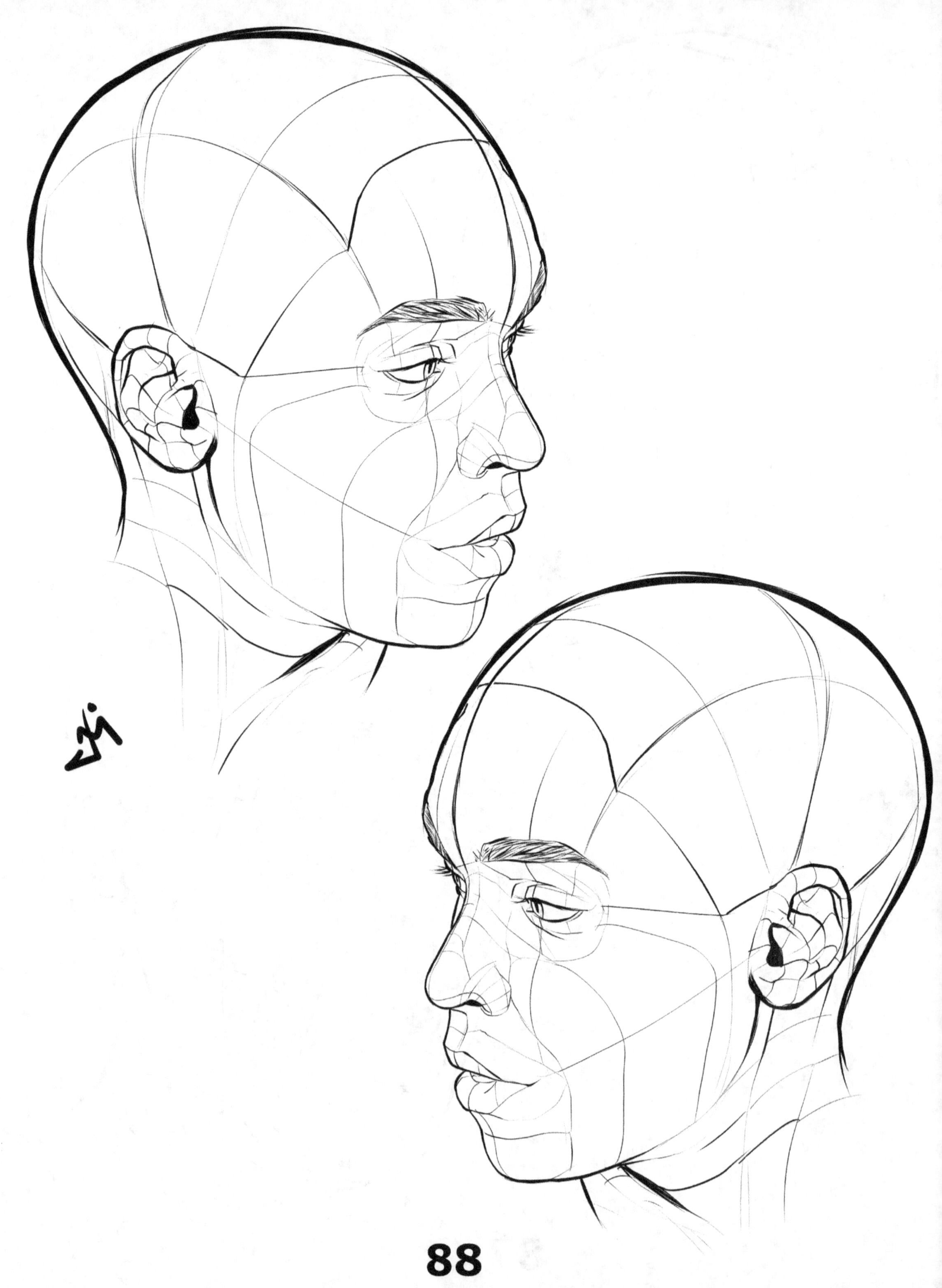

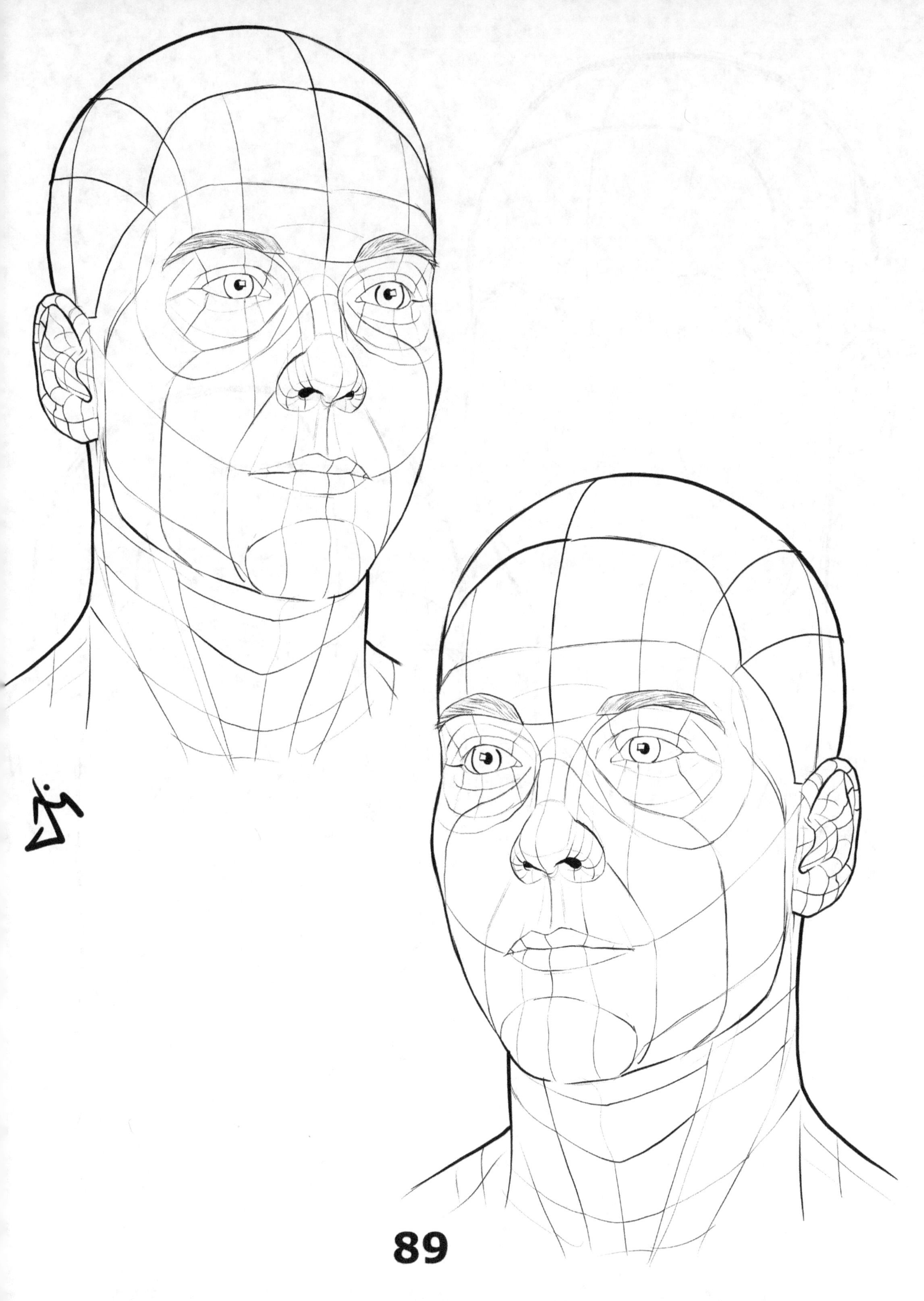

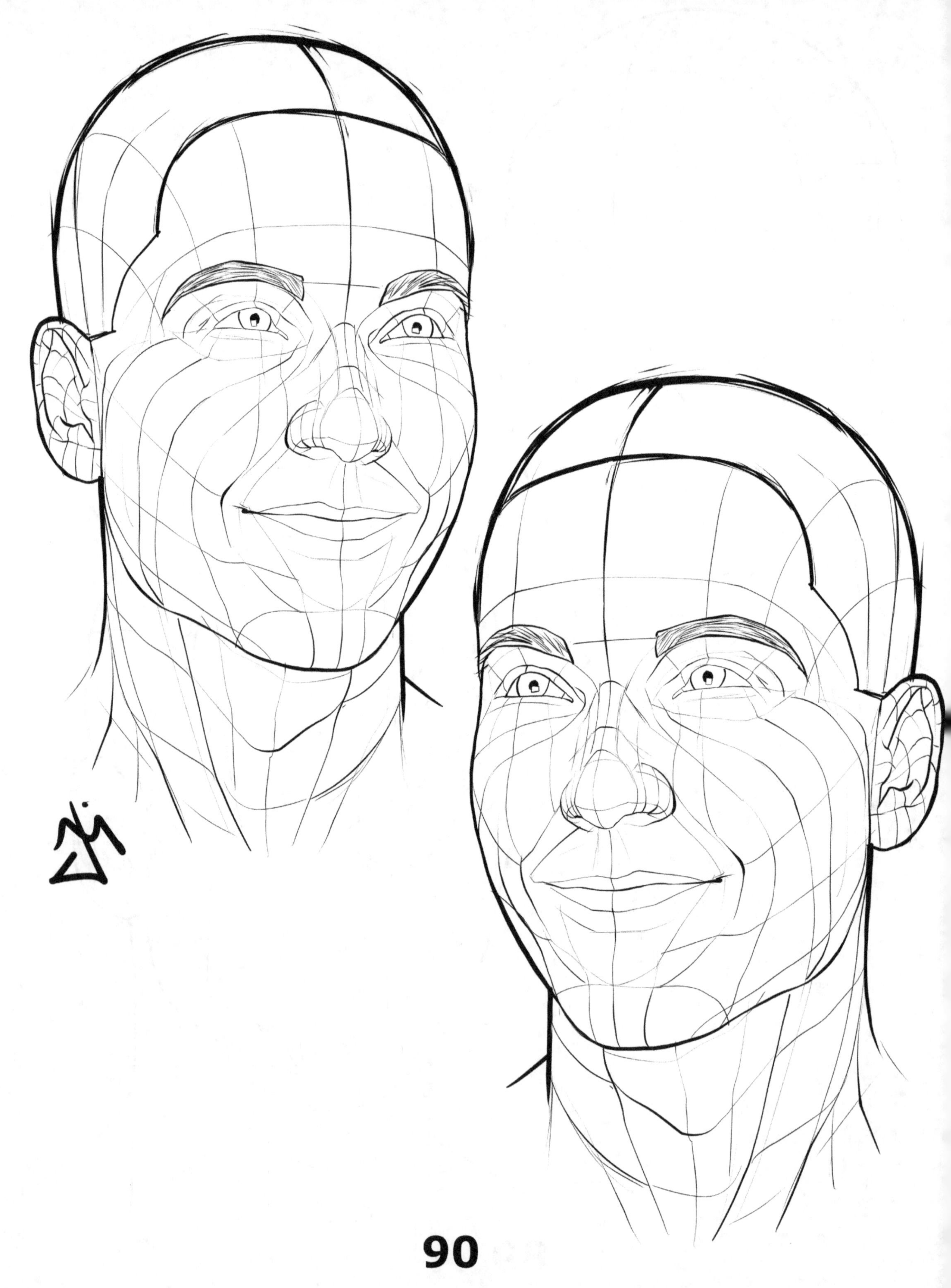

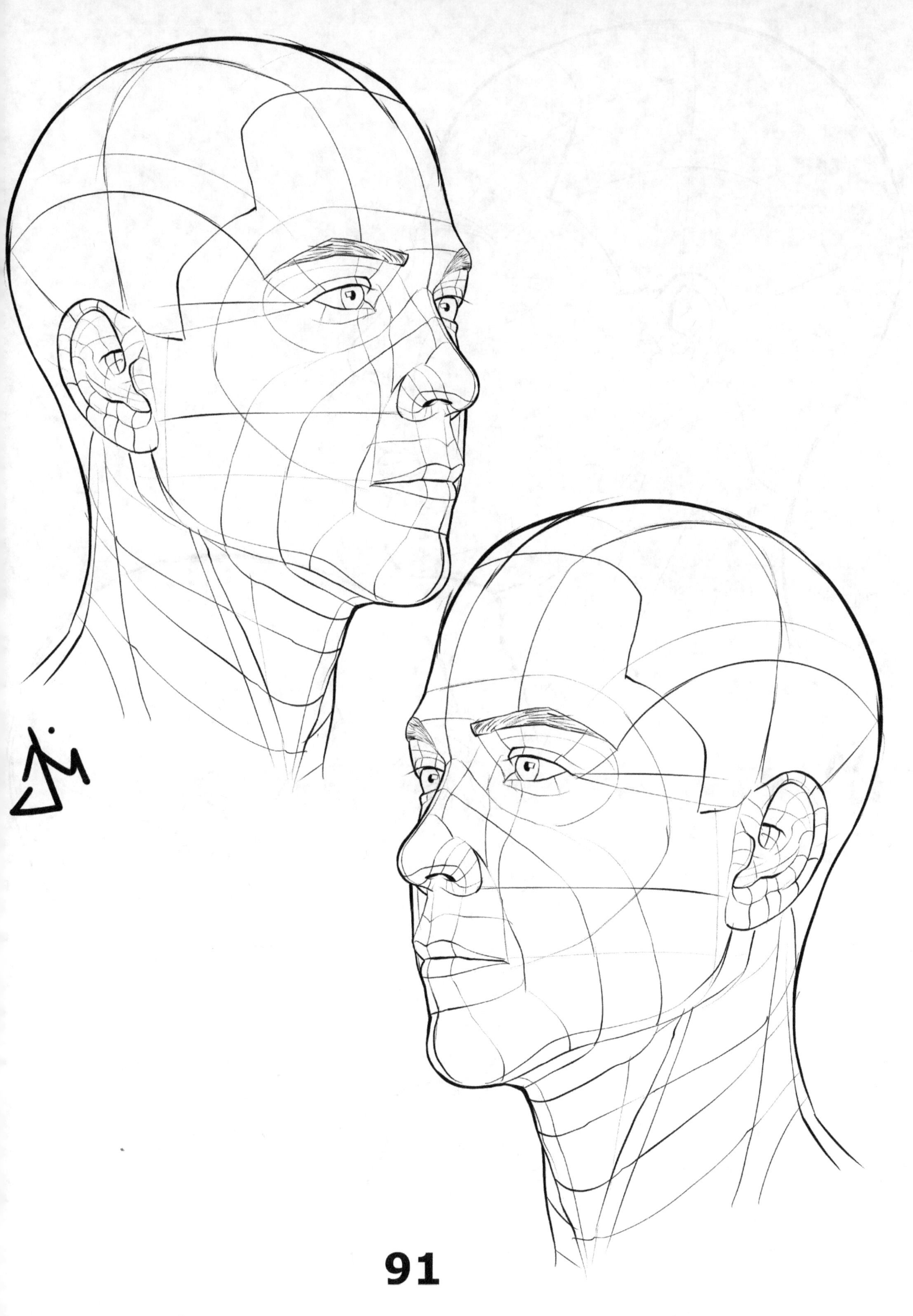

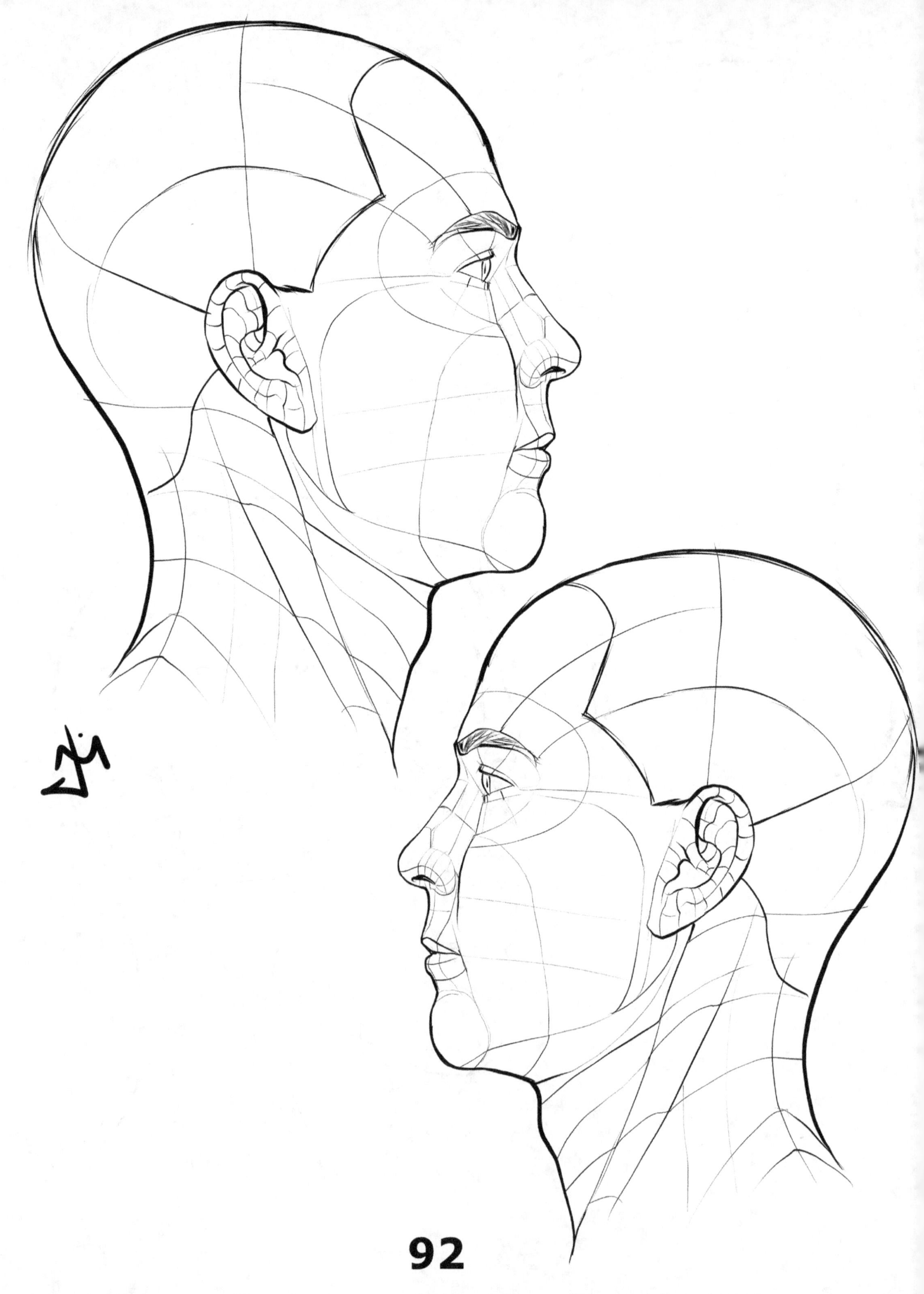

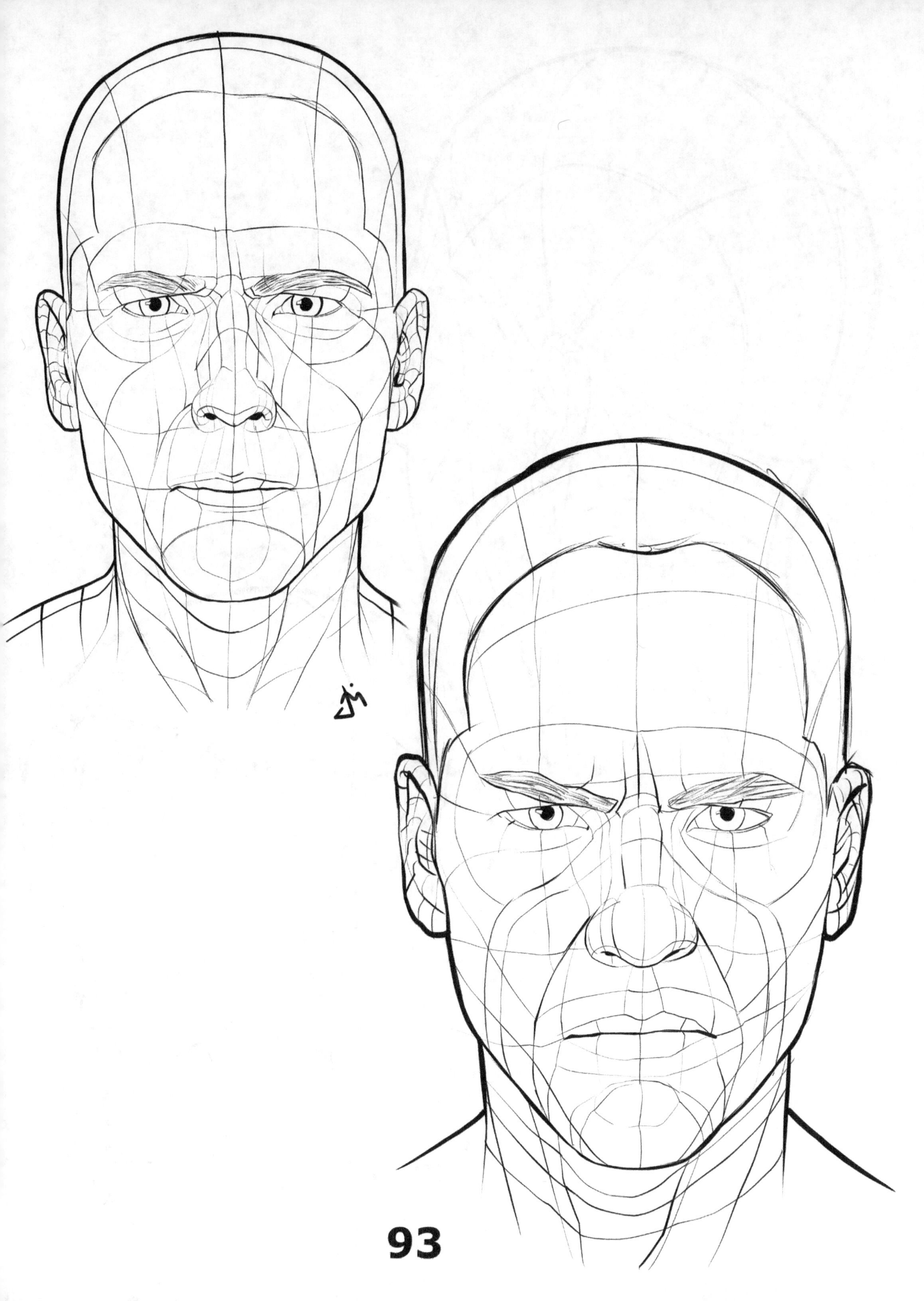

93

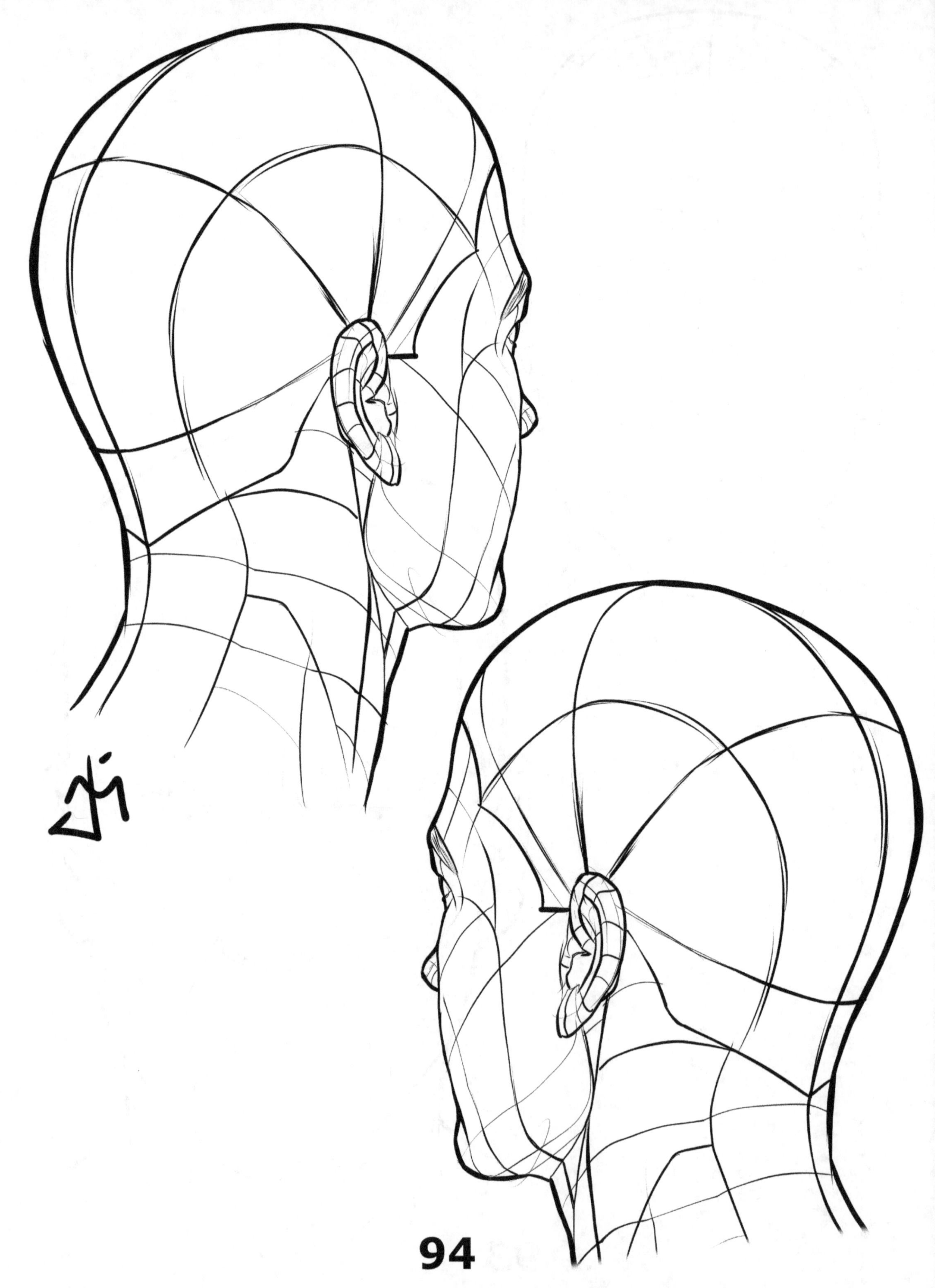

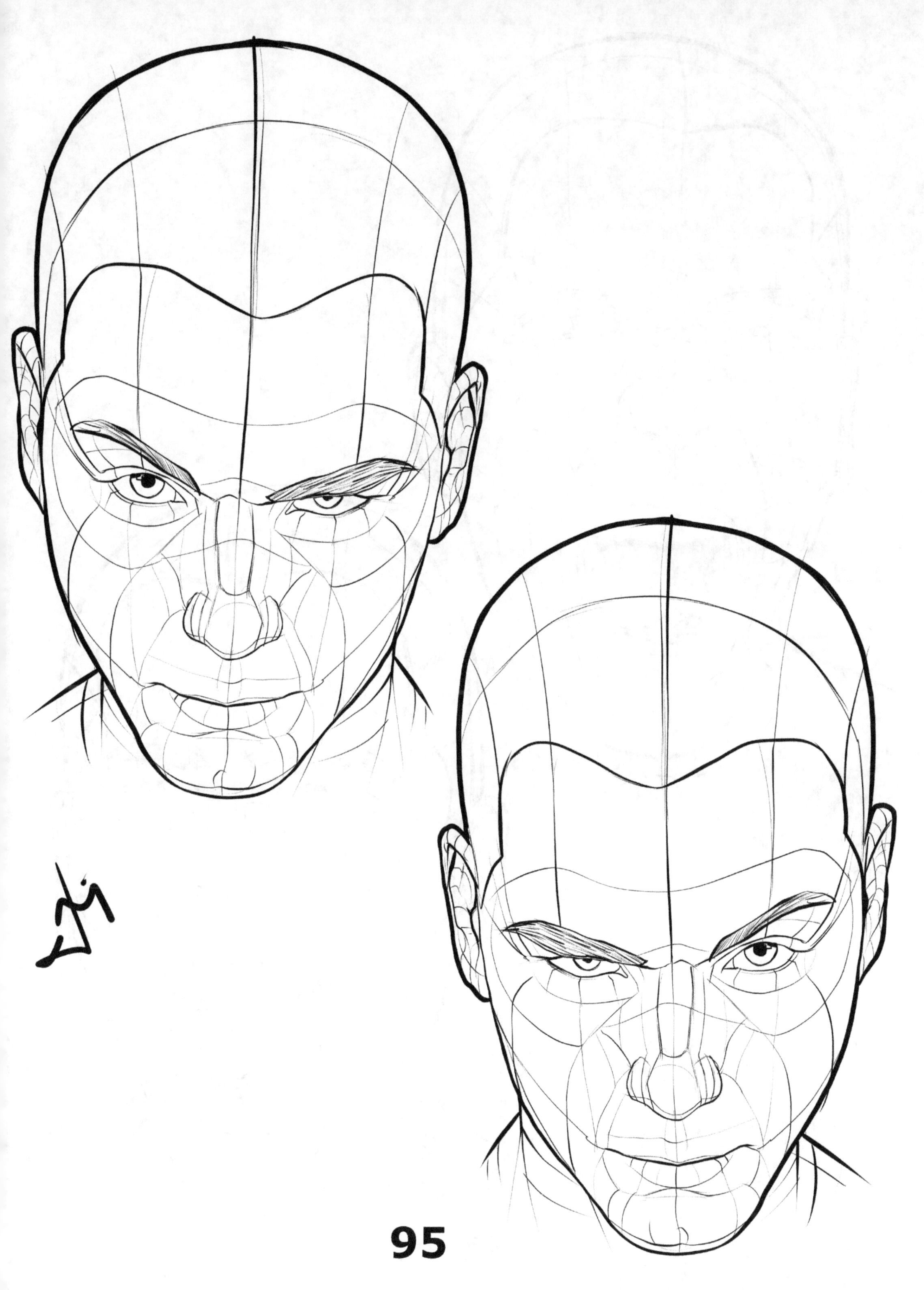

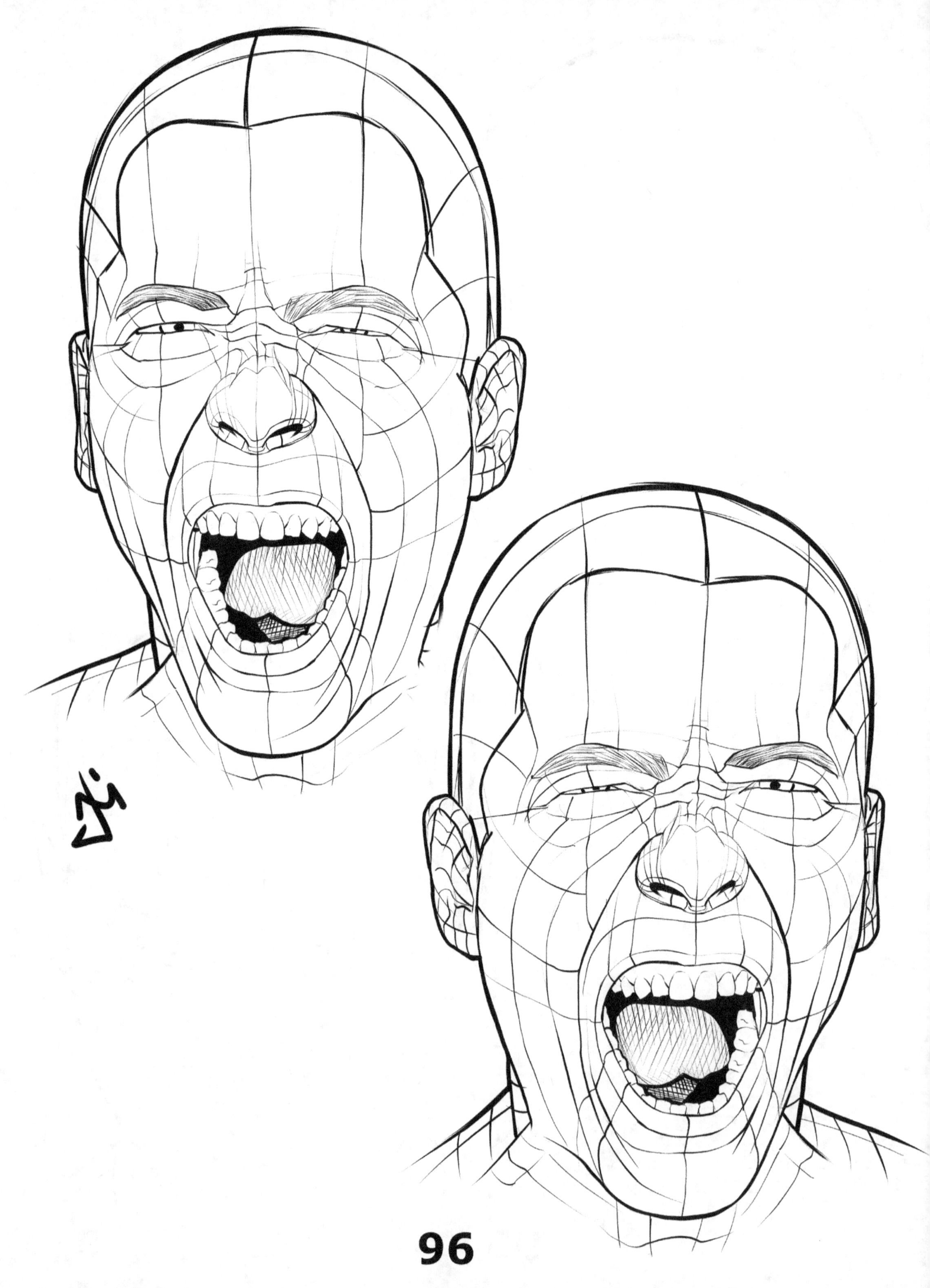

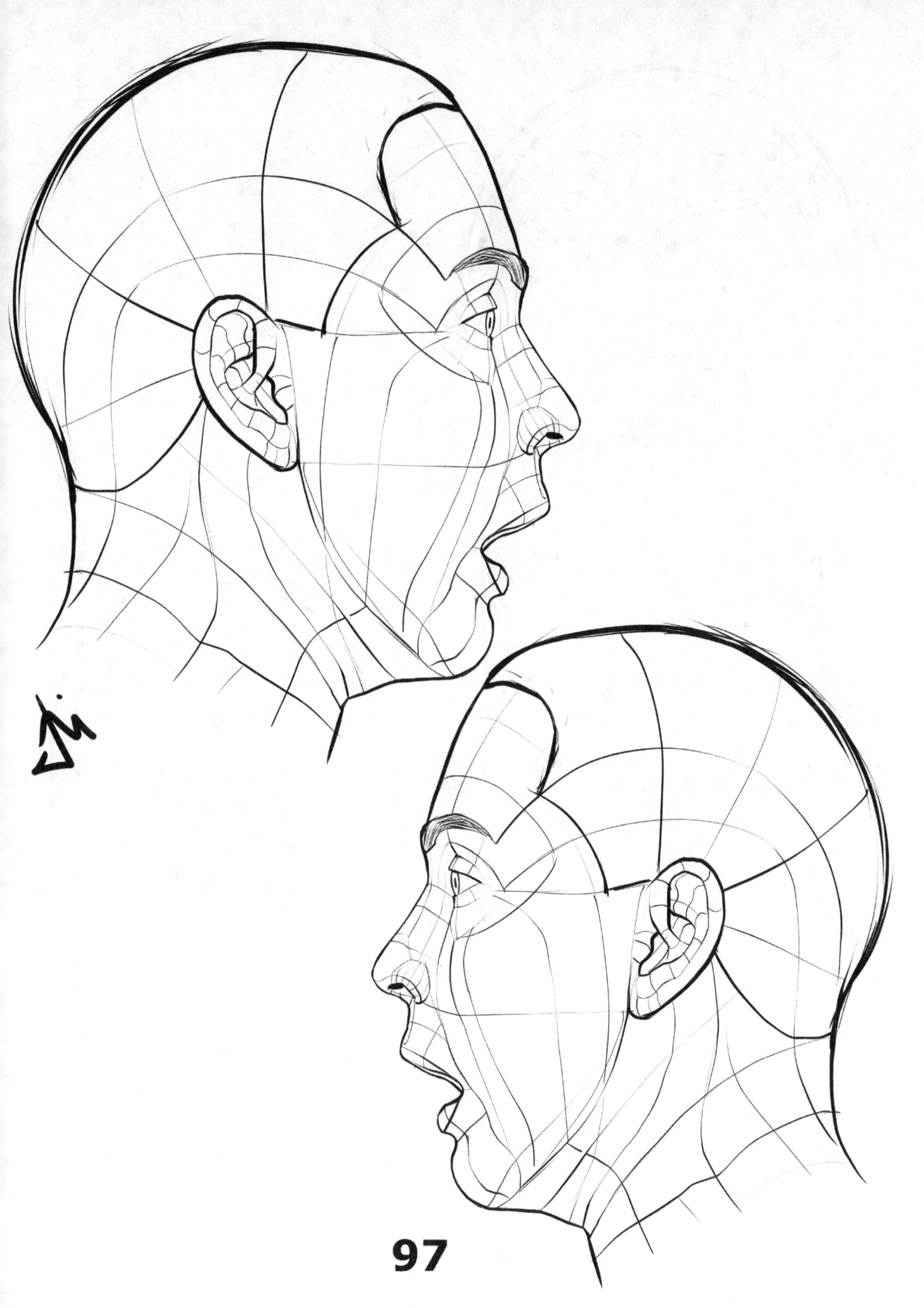

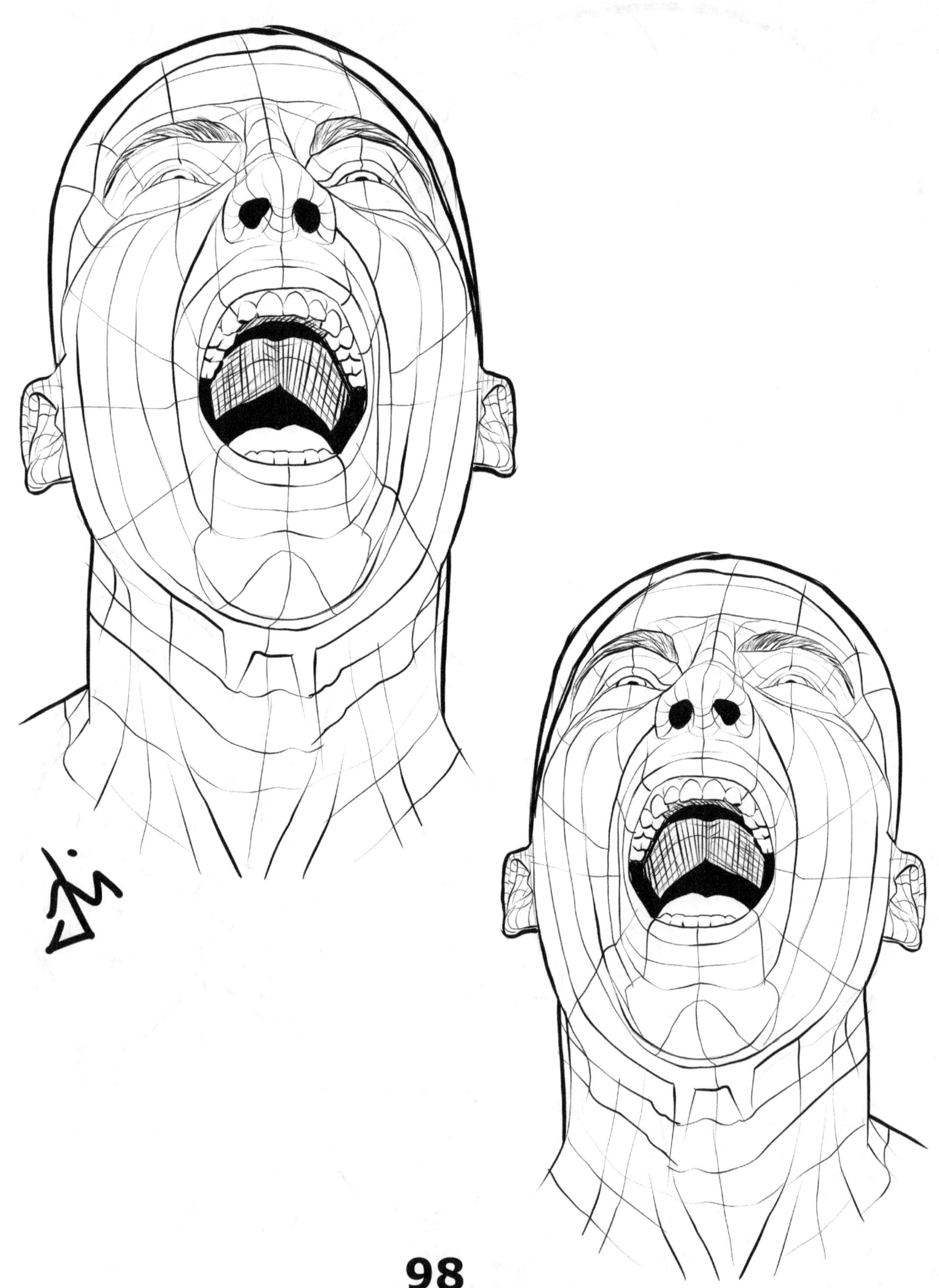

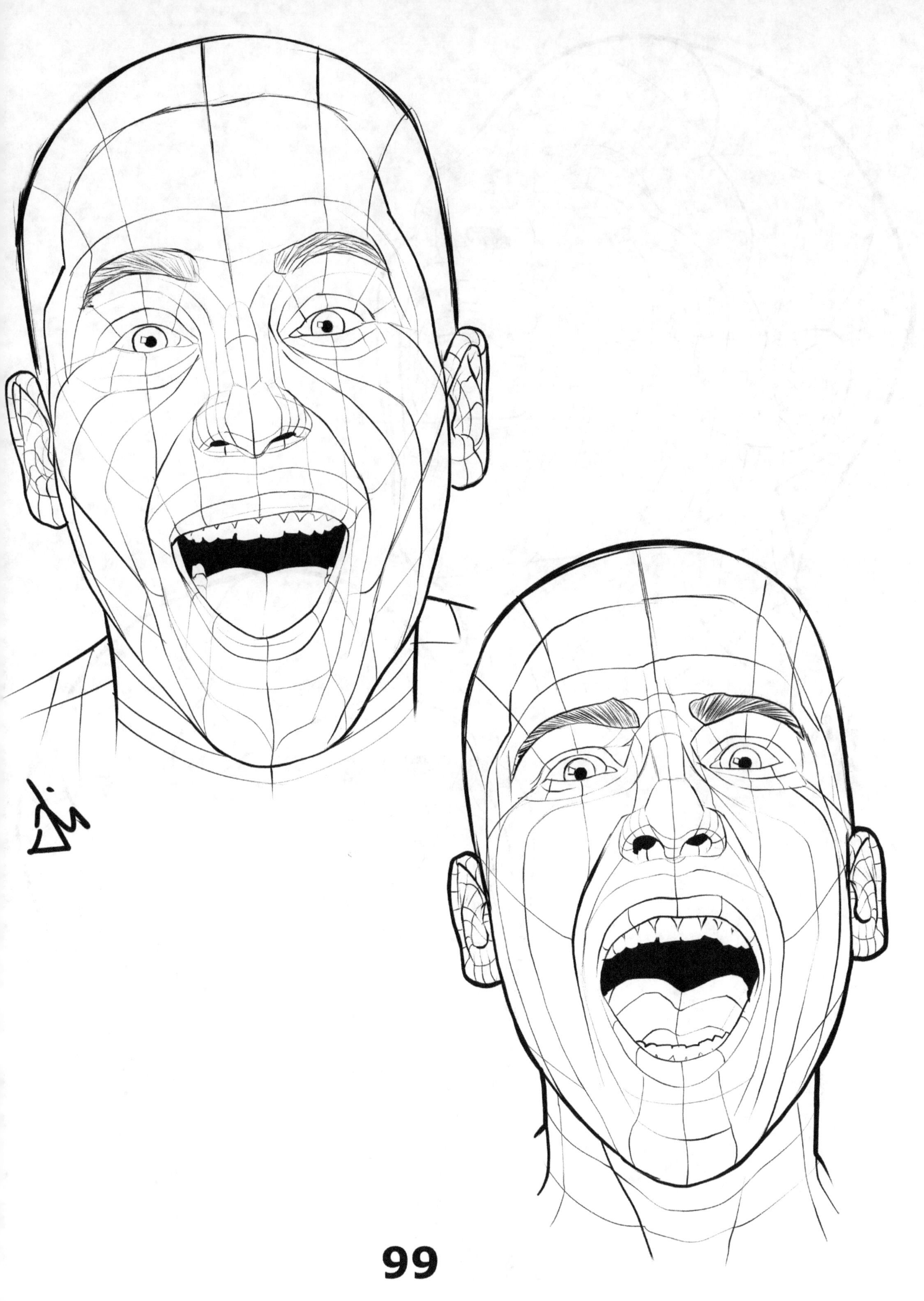

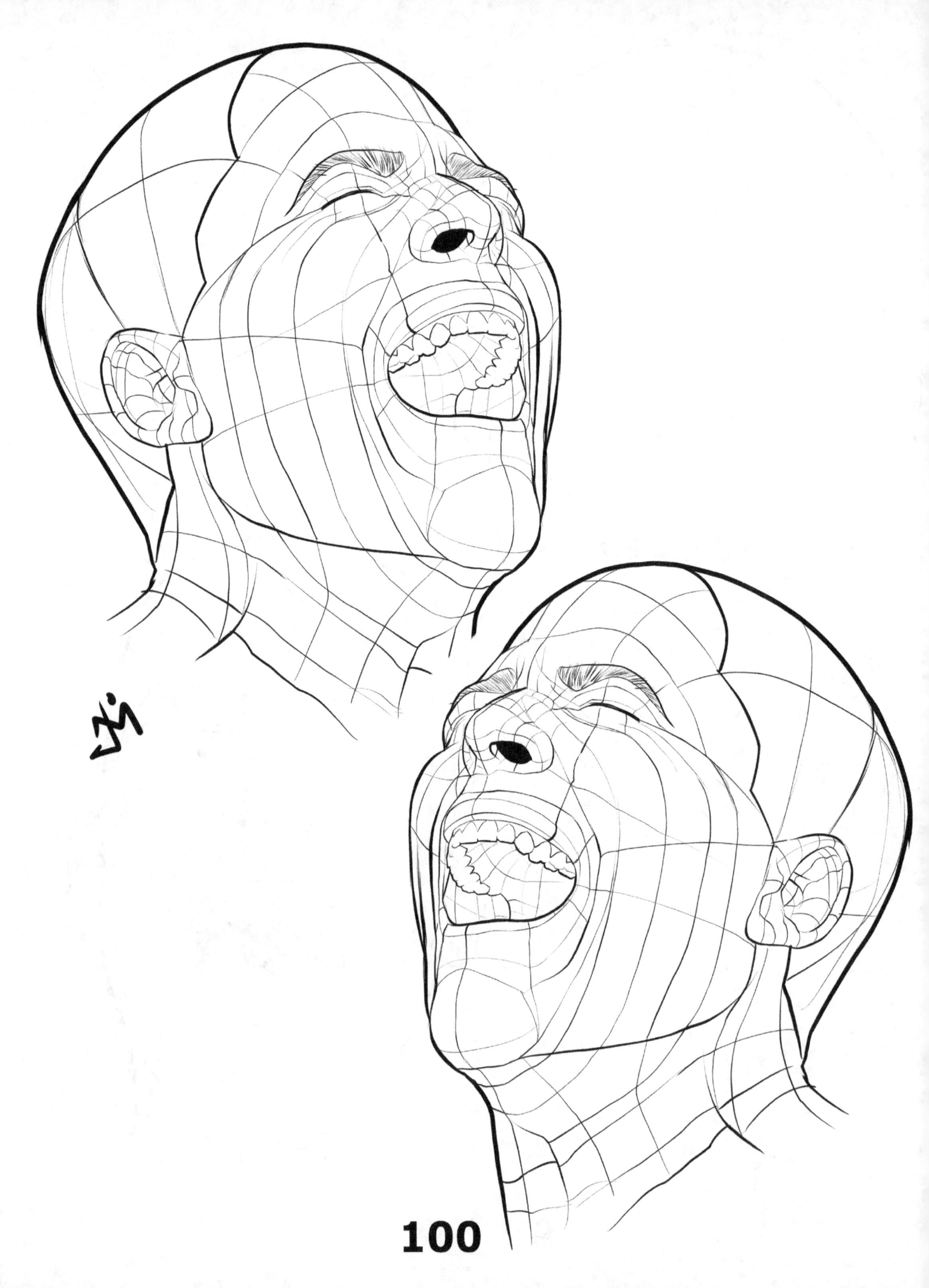

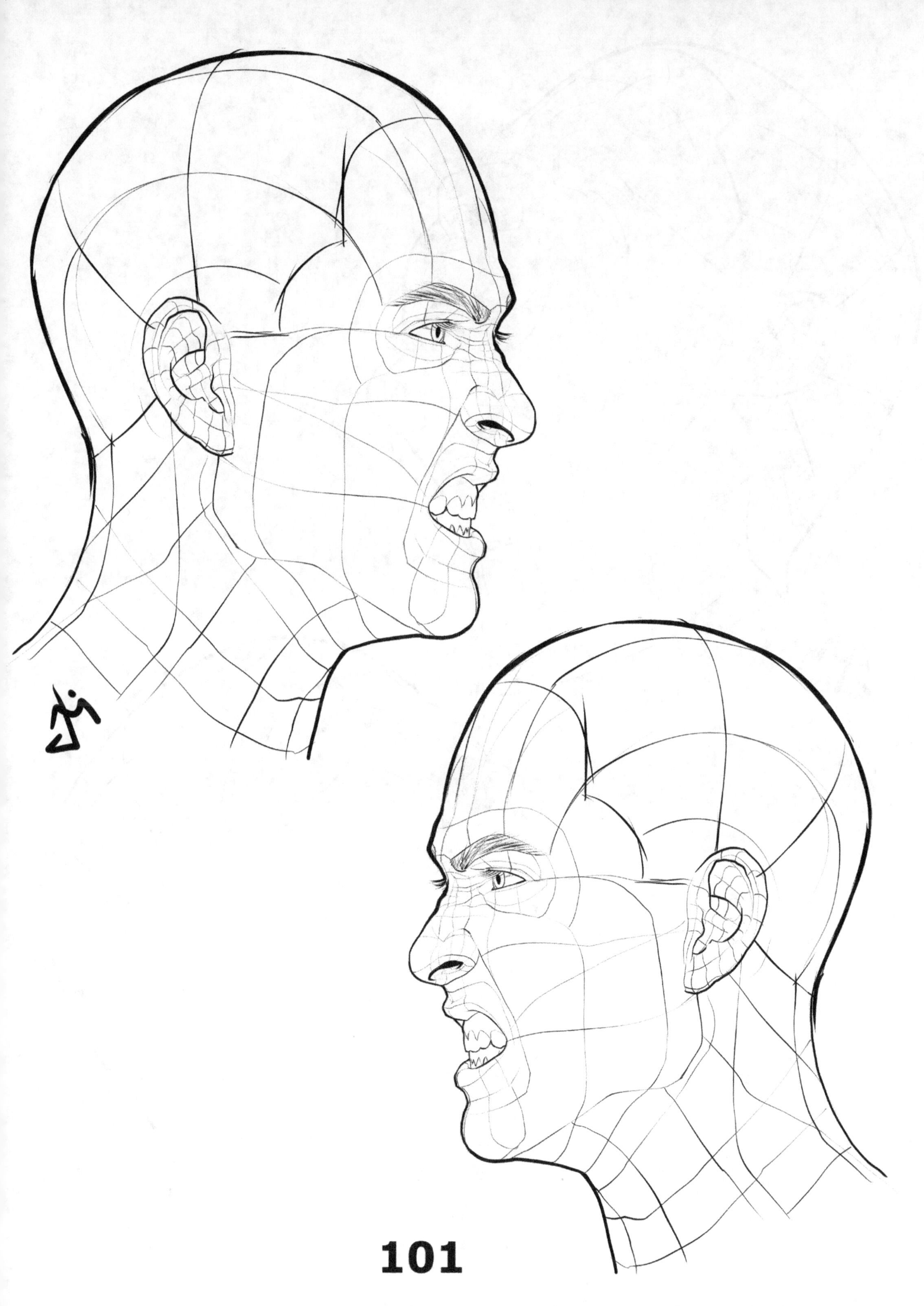

101

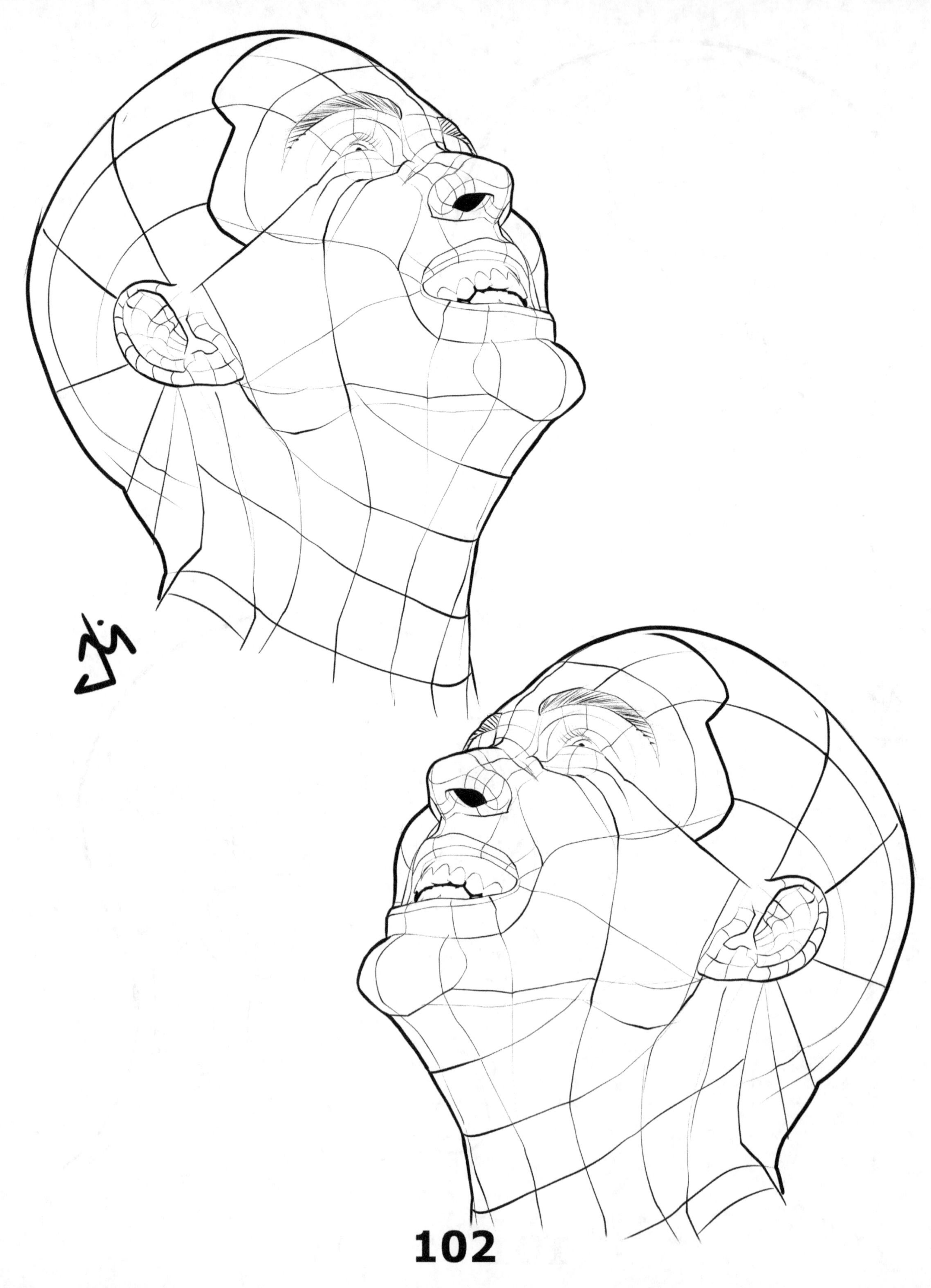

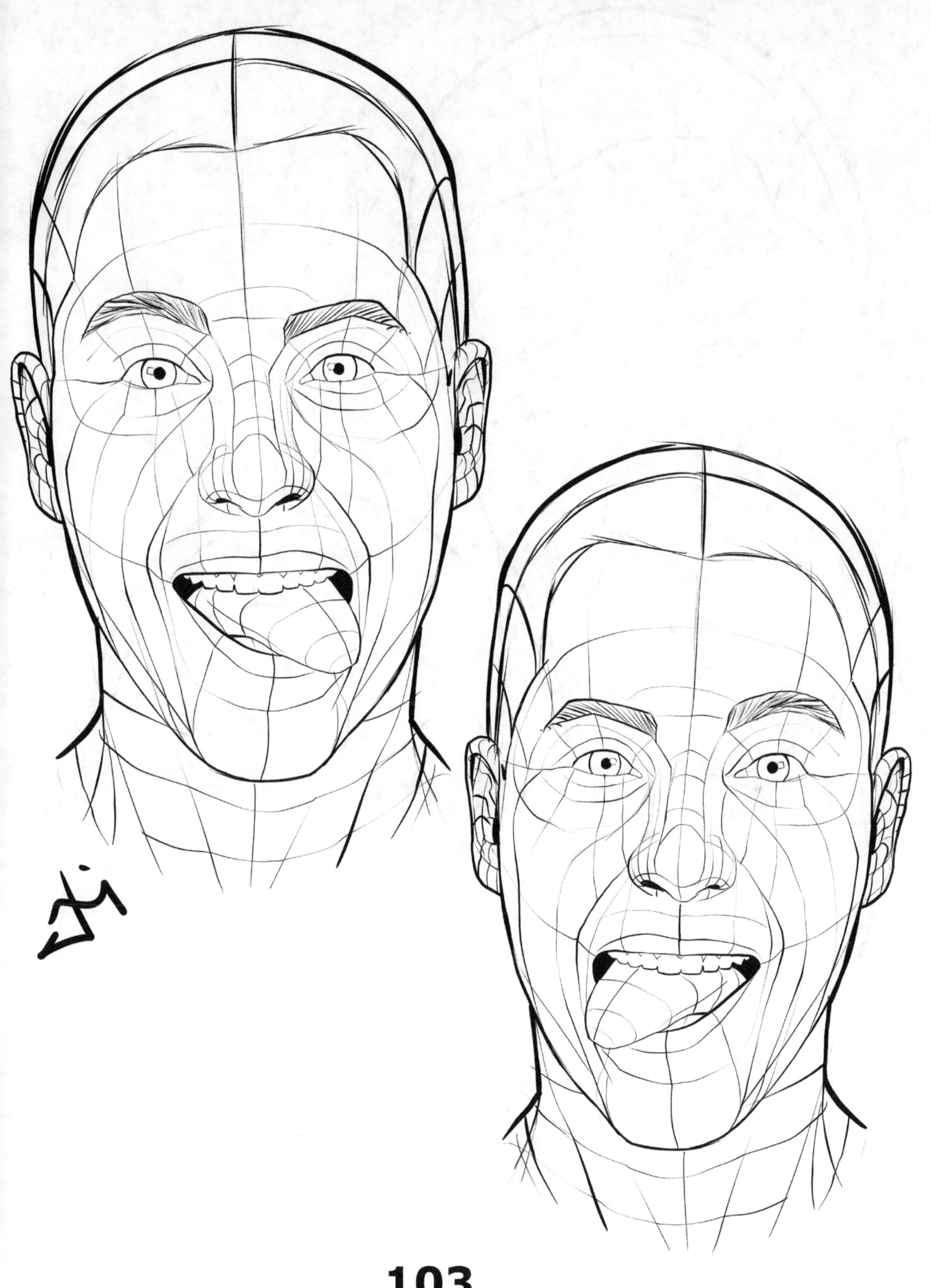

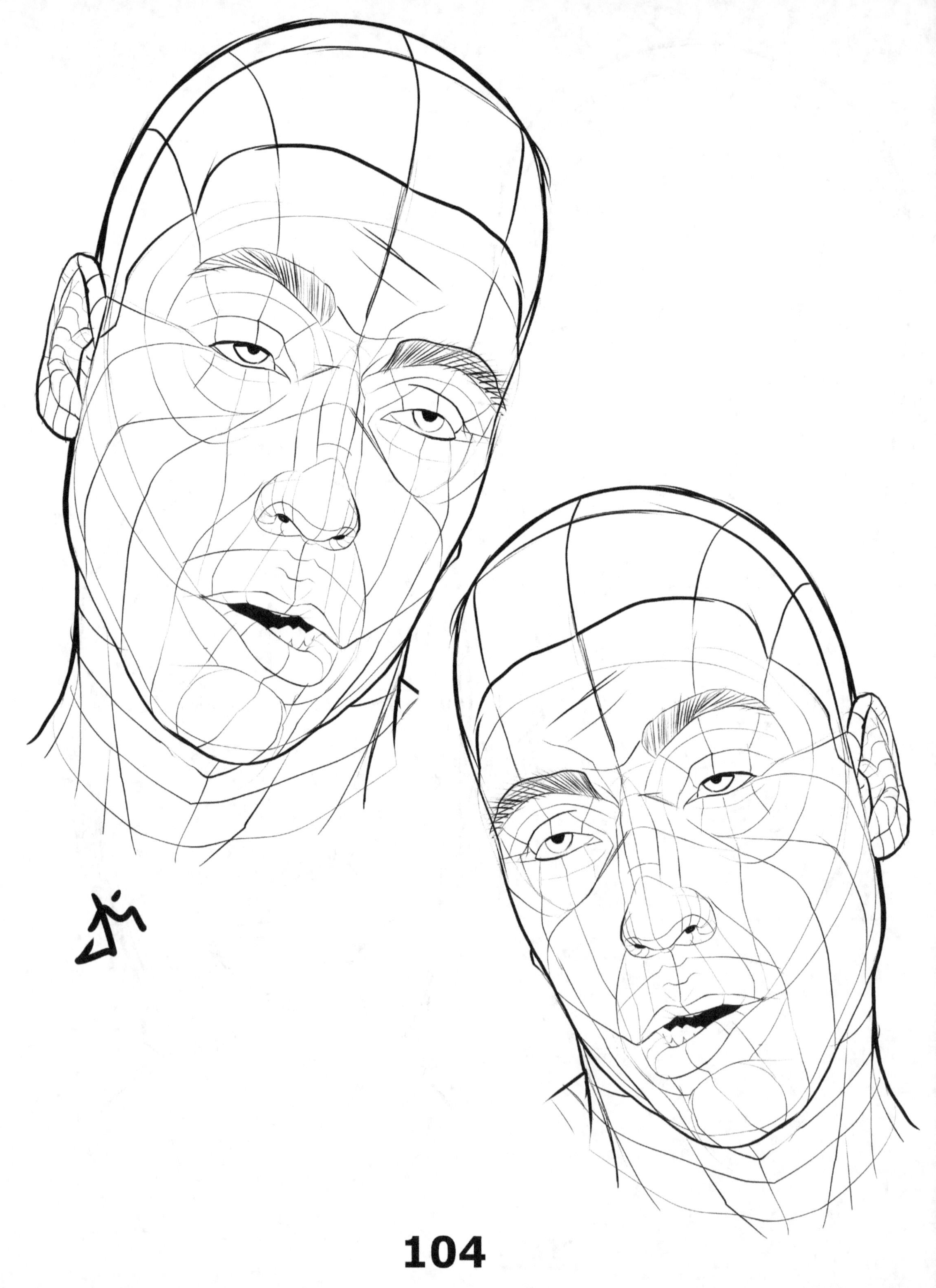

104

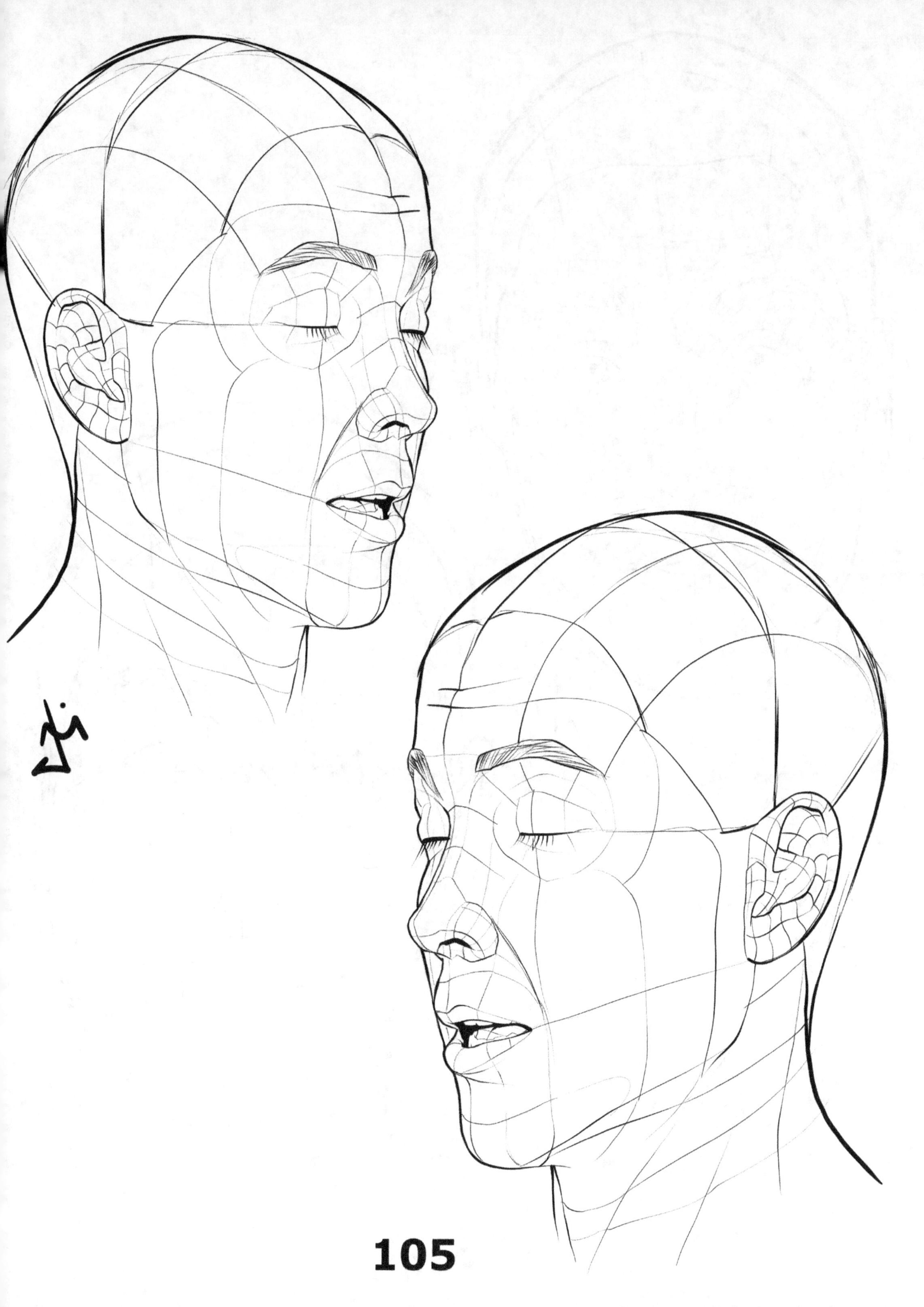

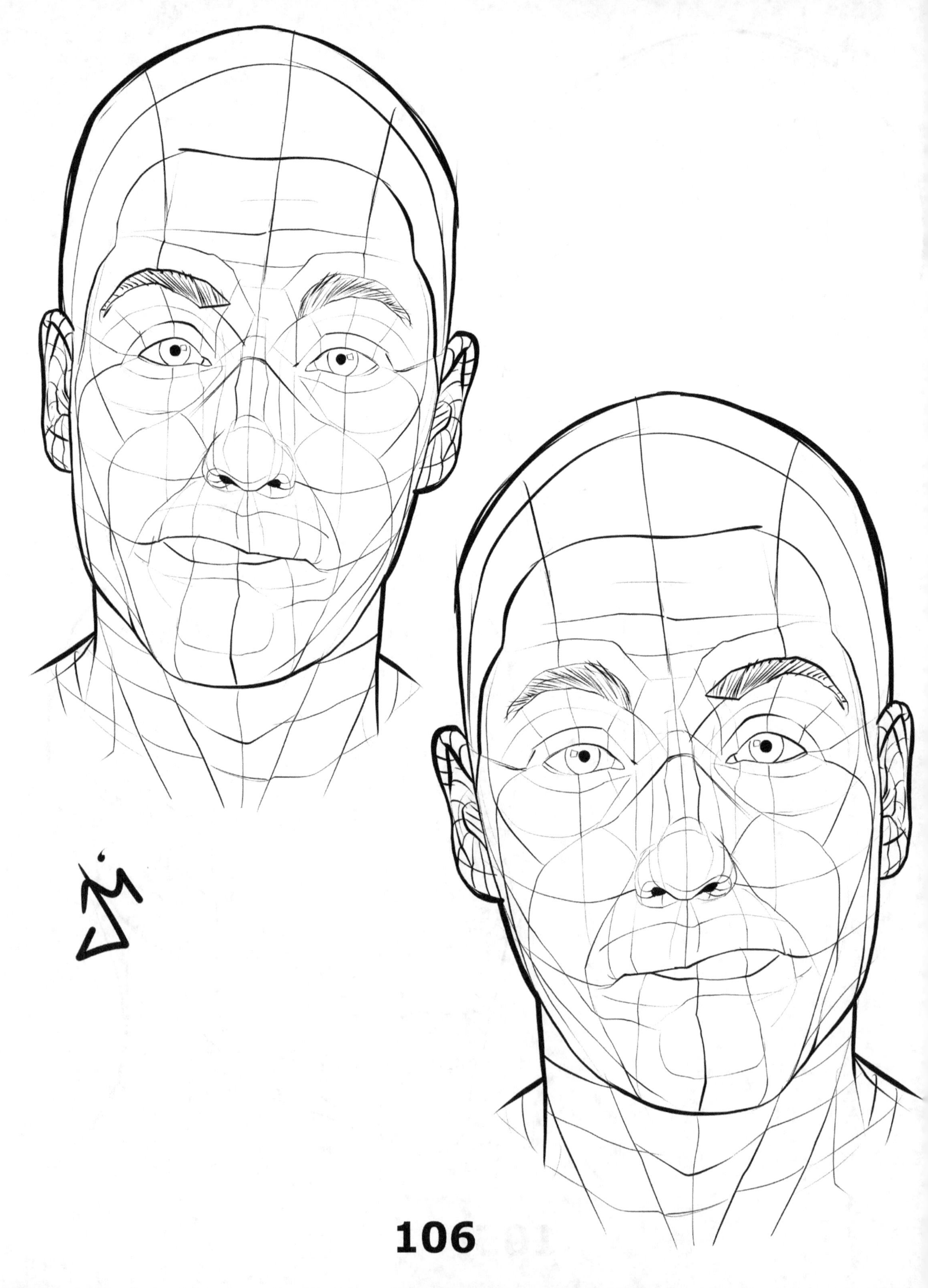

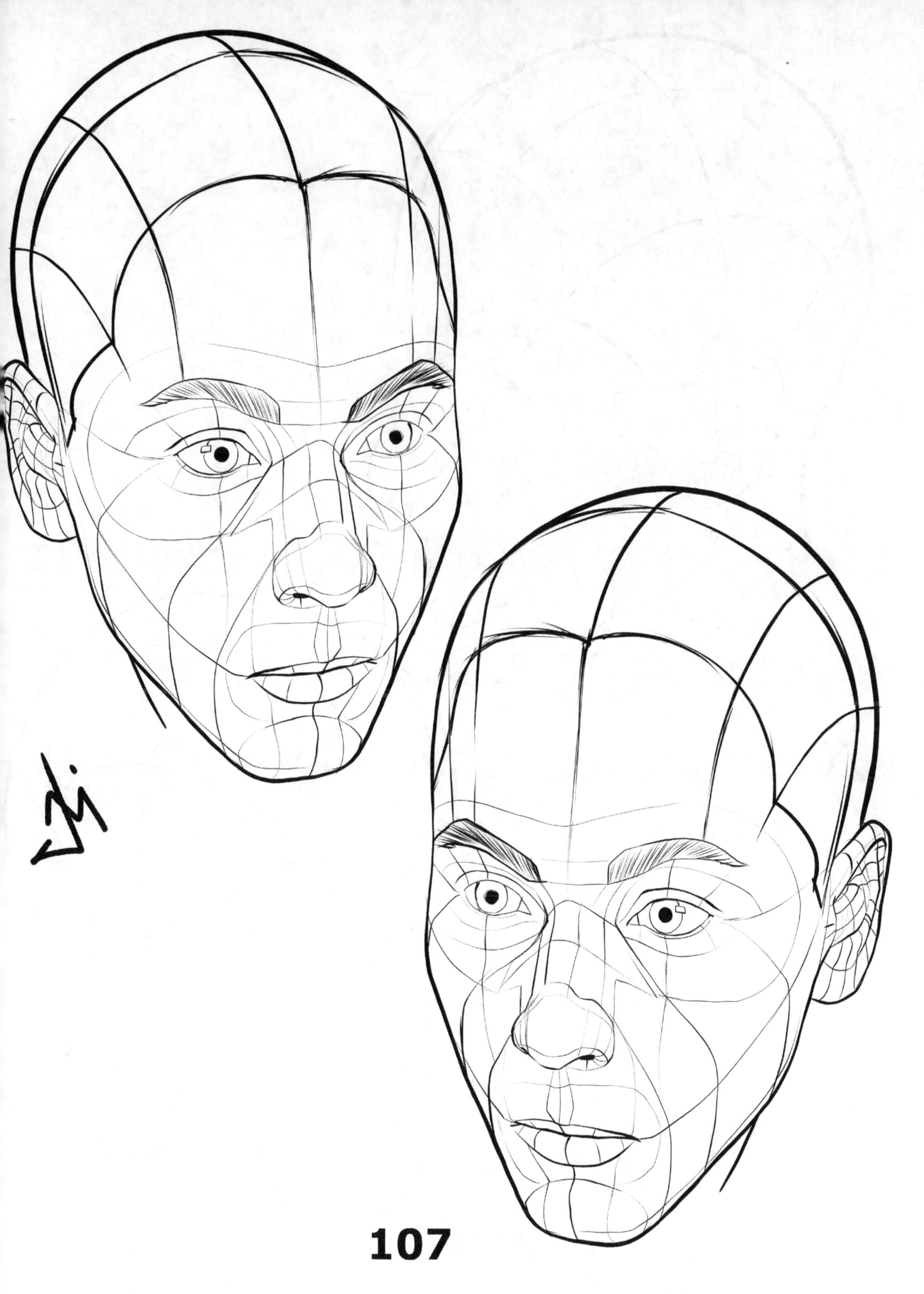

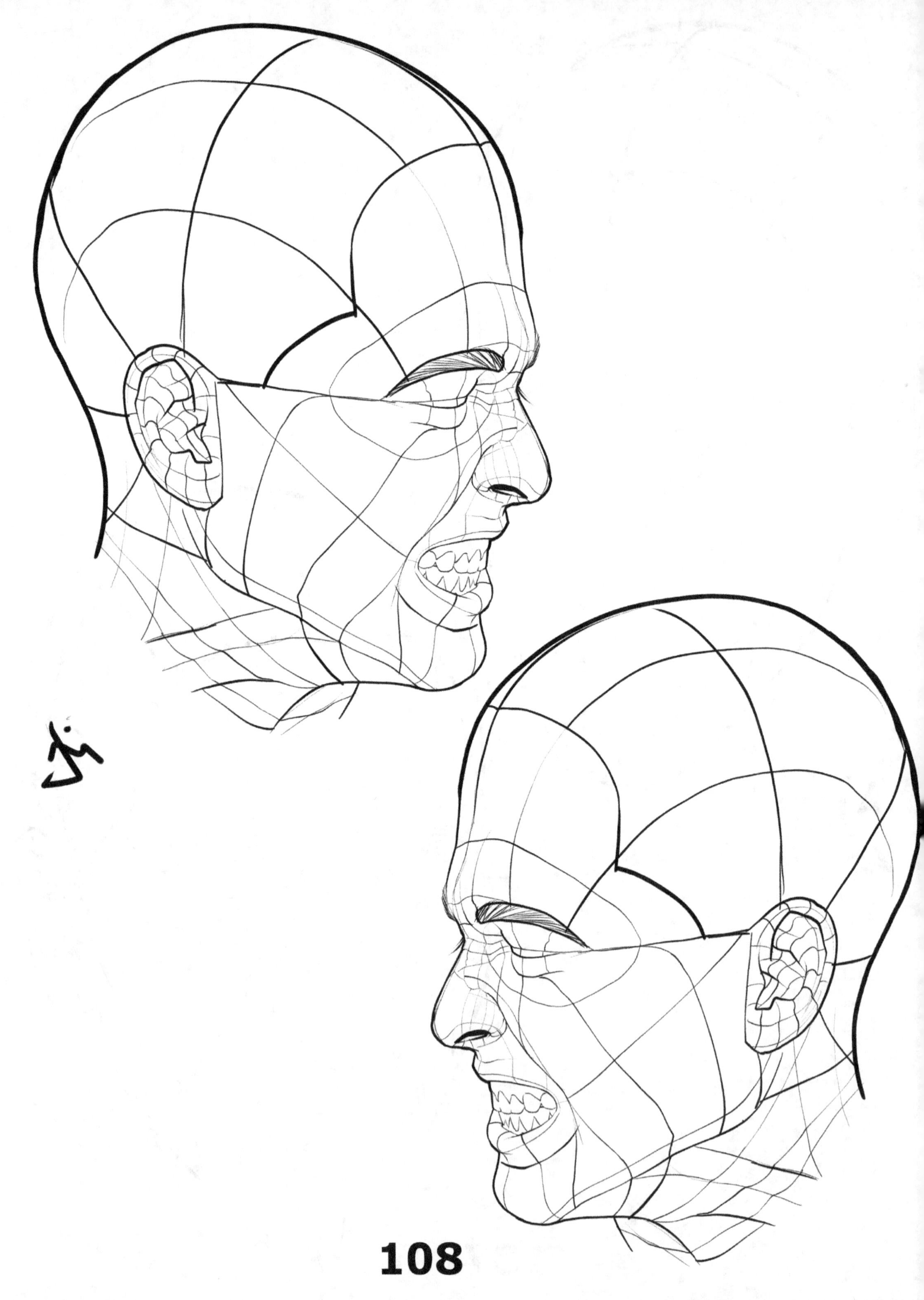

108

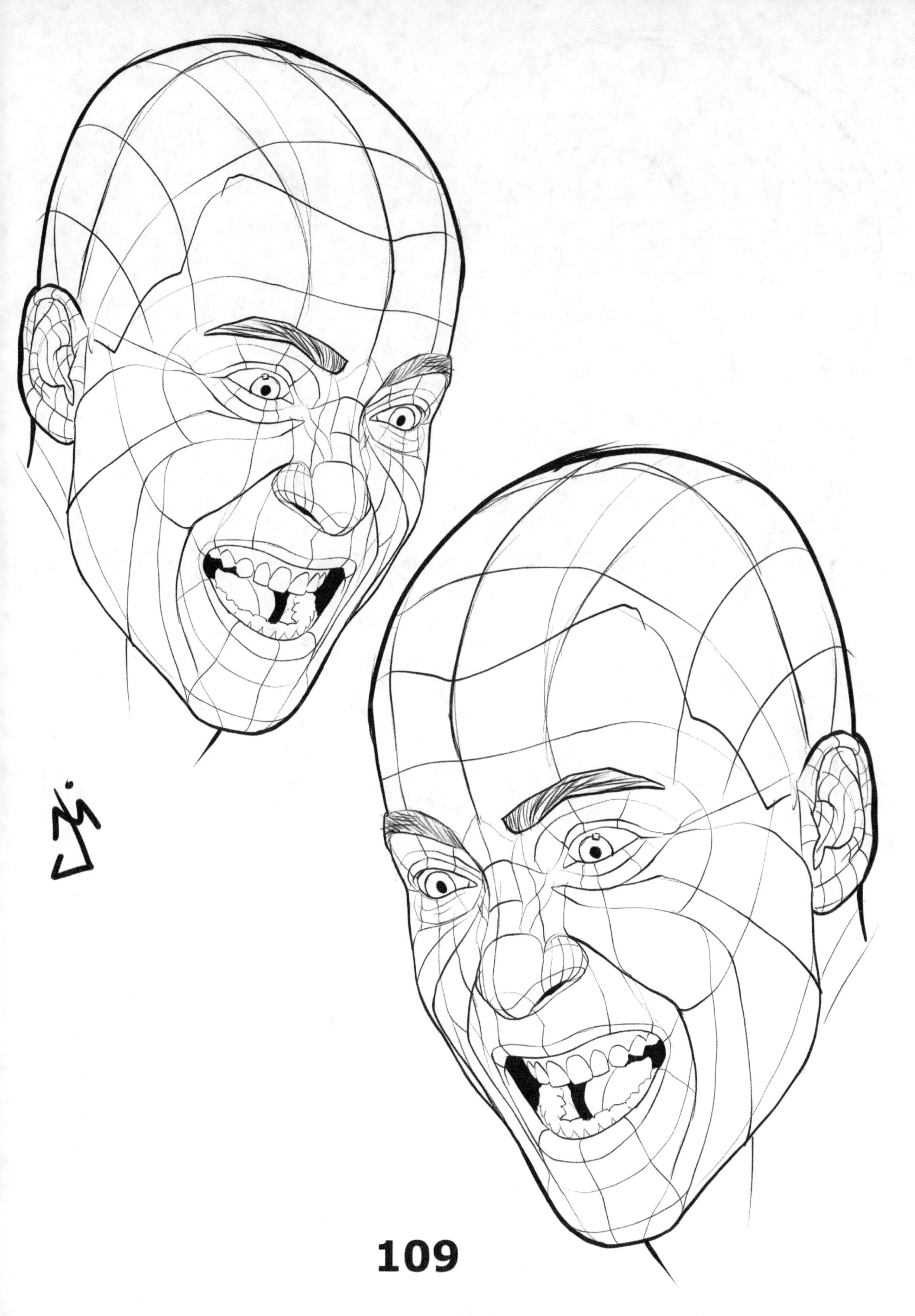

109

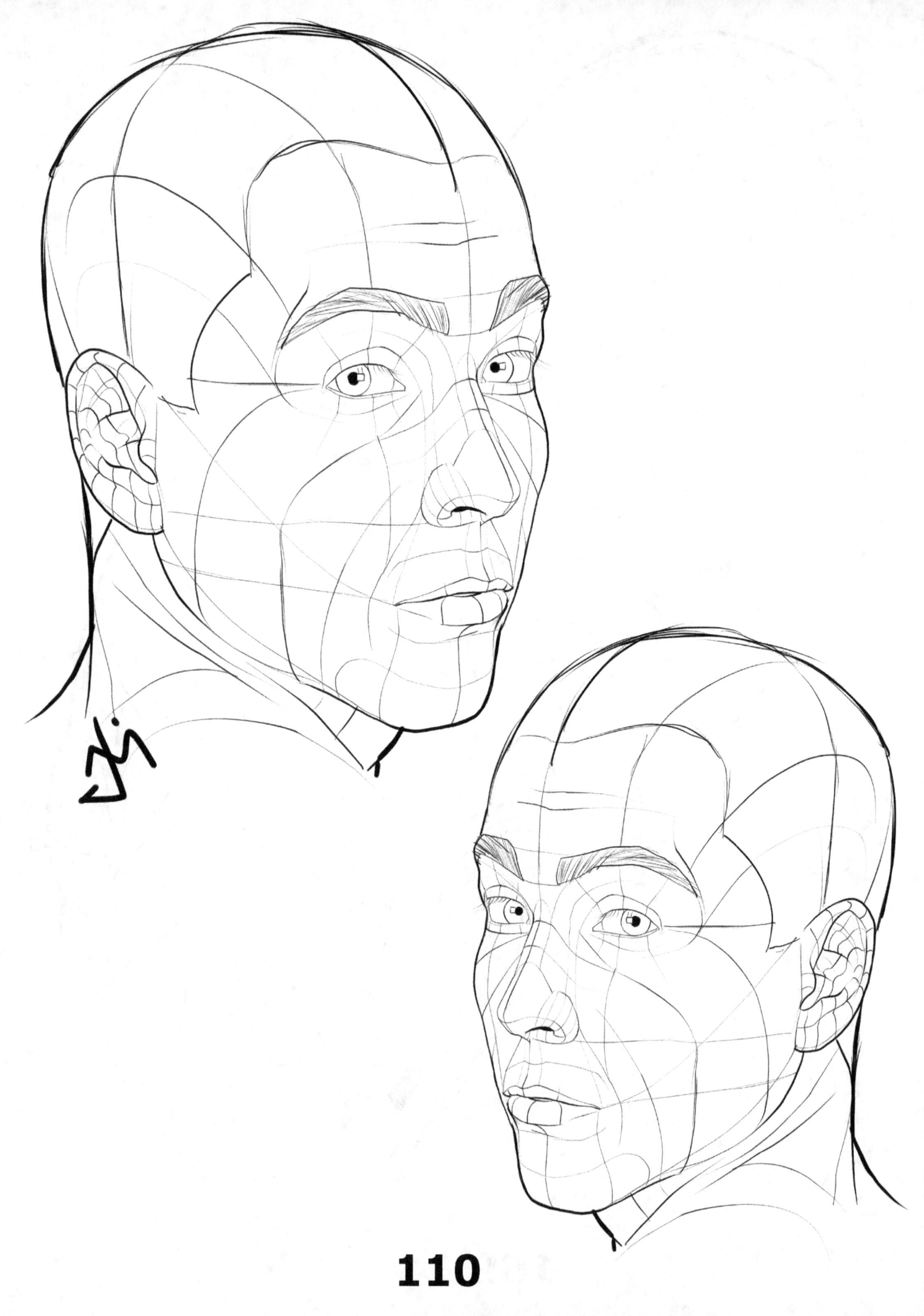

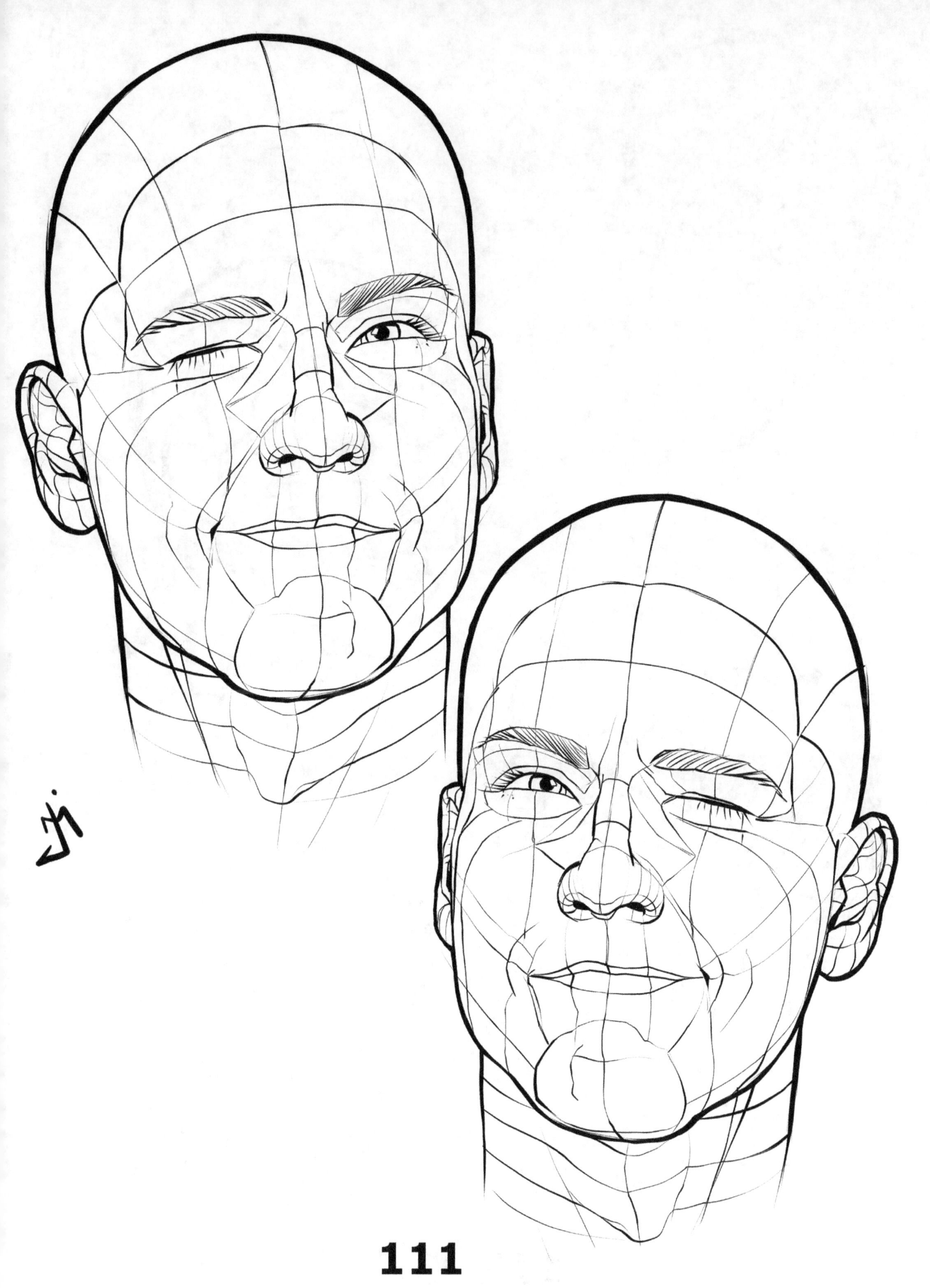

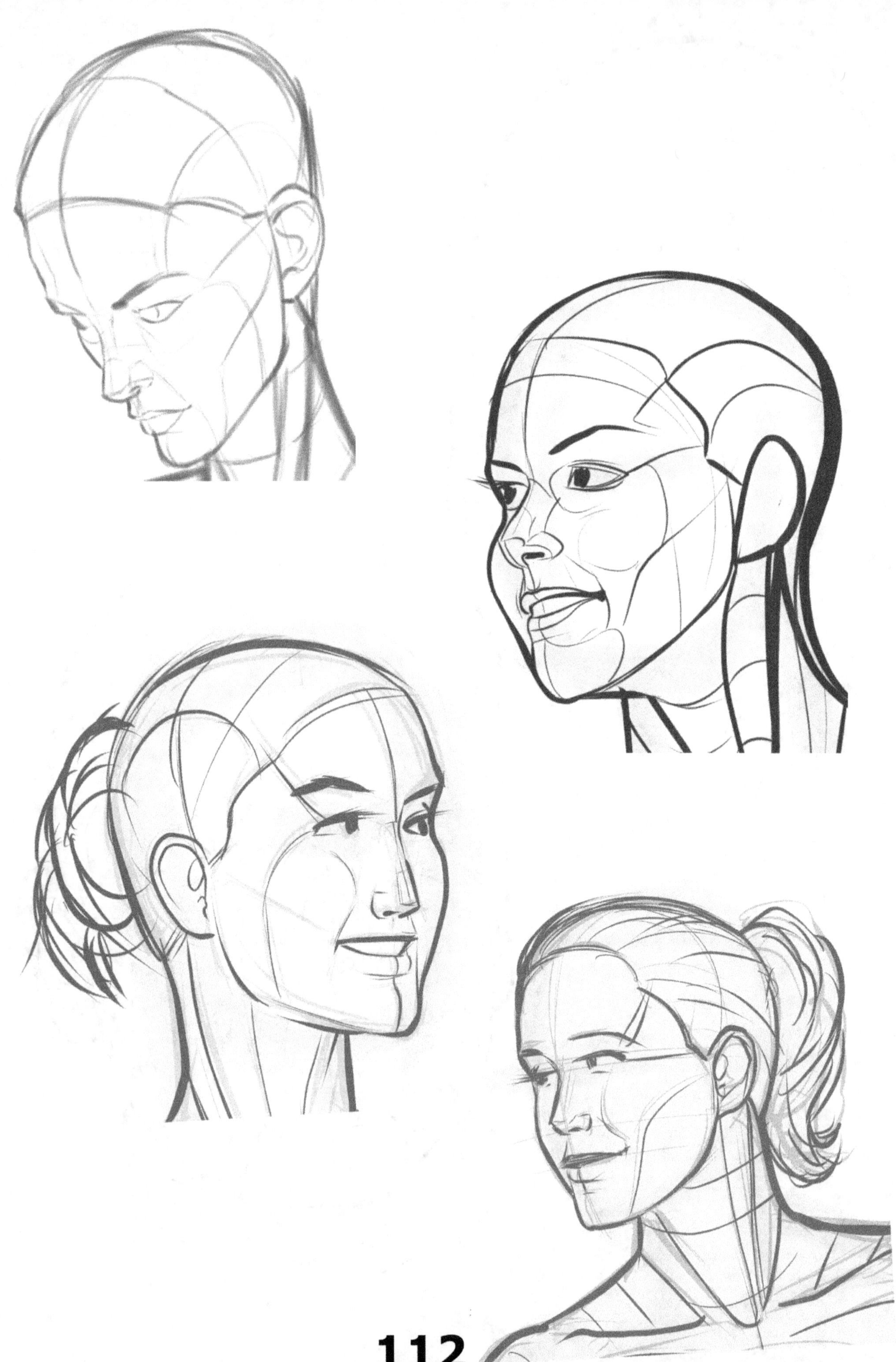

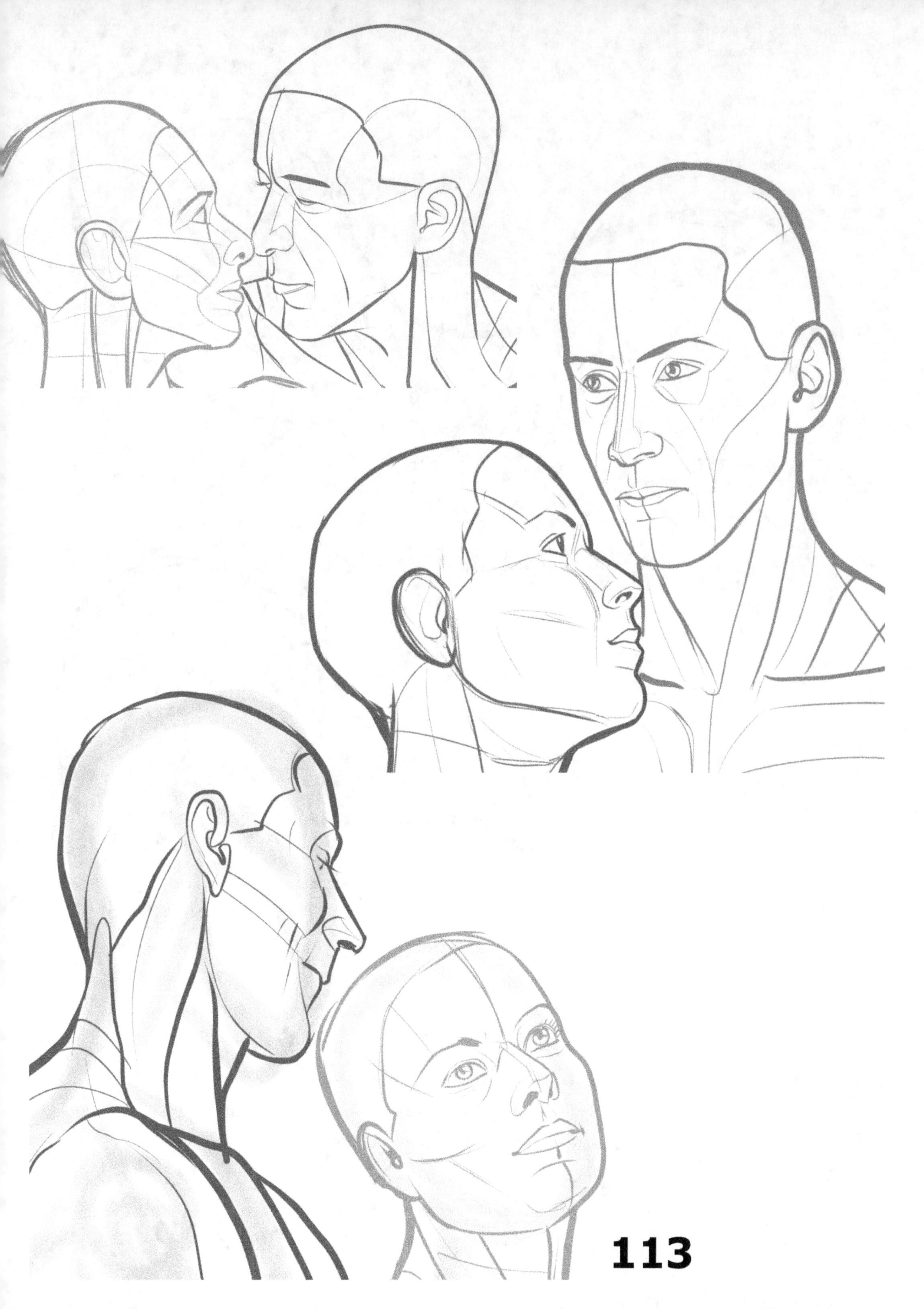

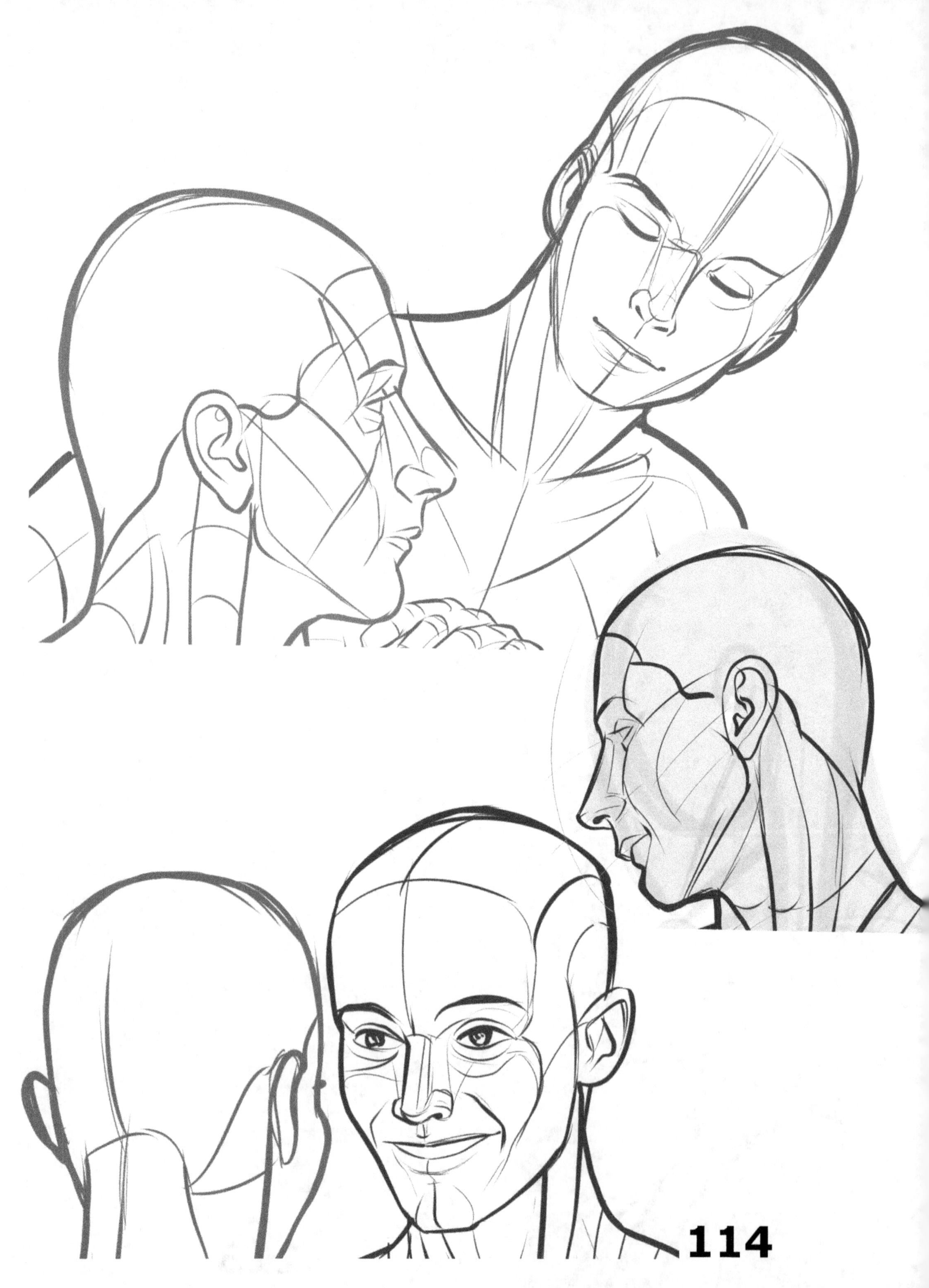

114

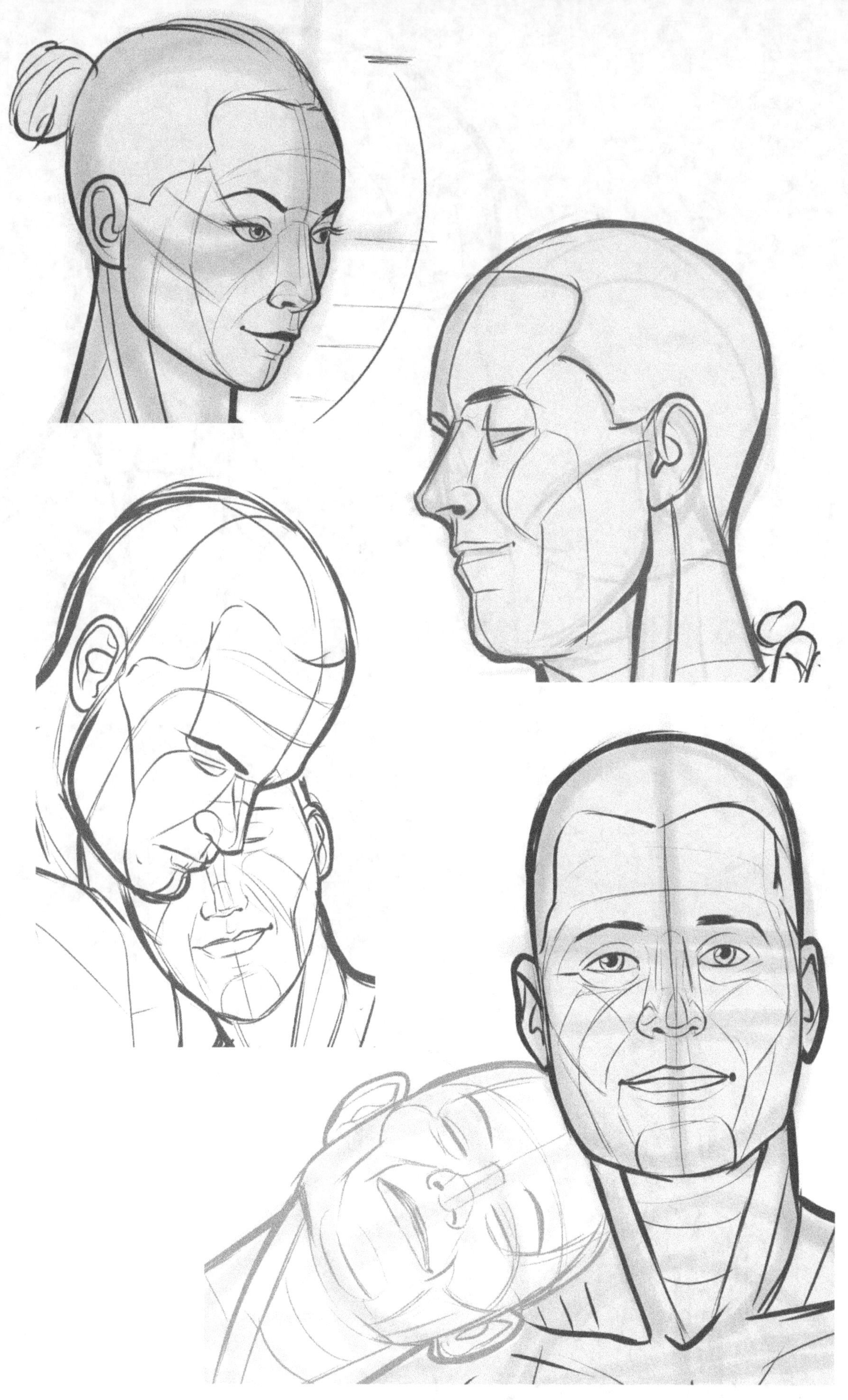

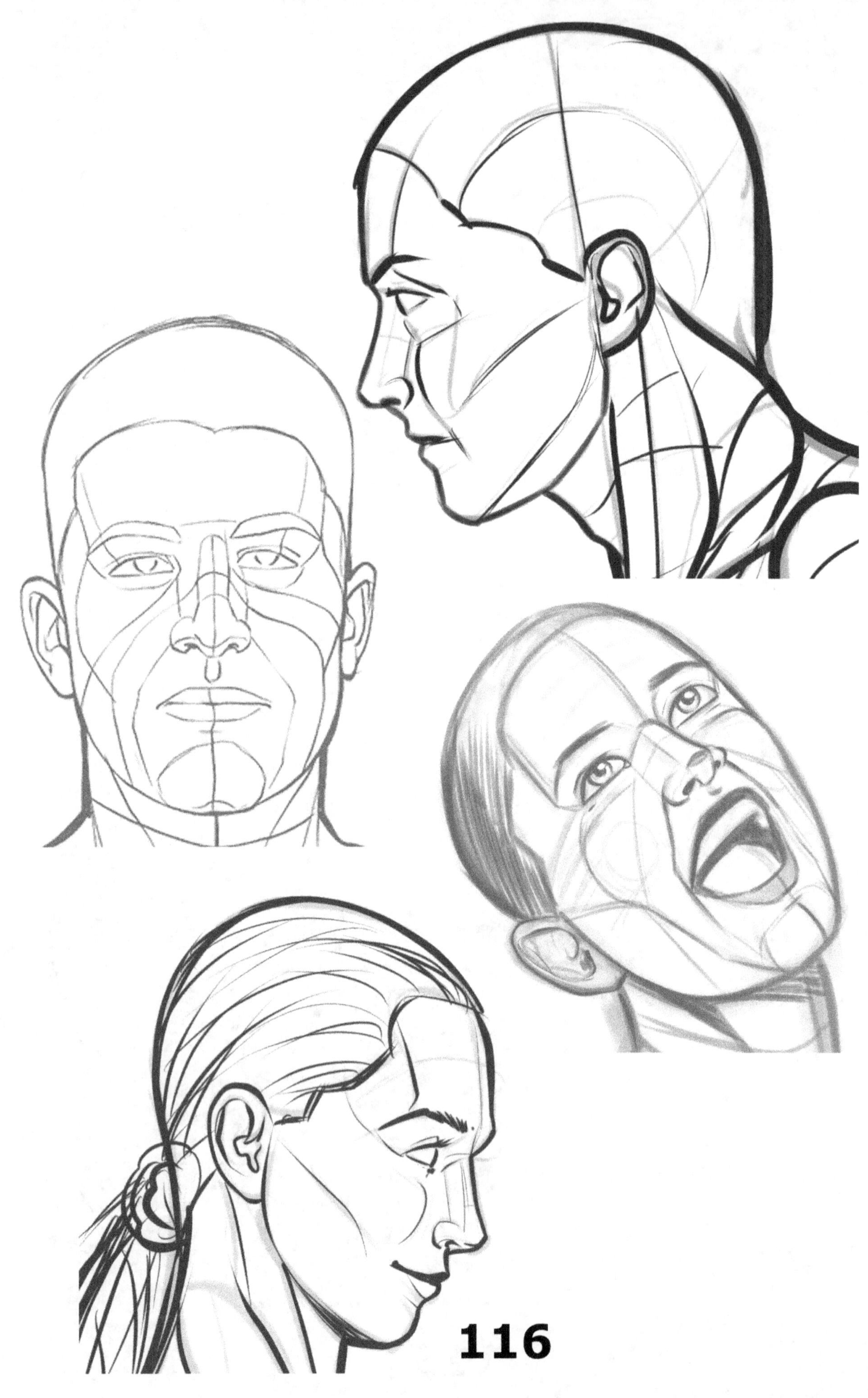

116

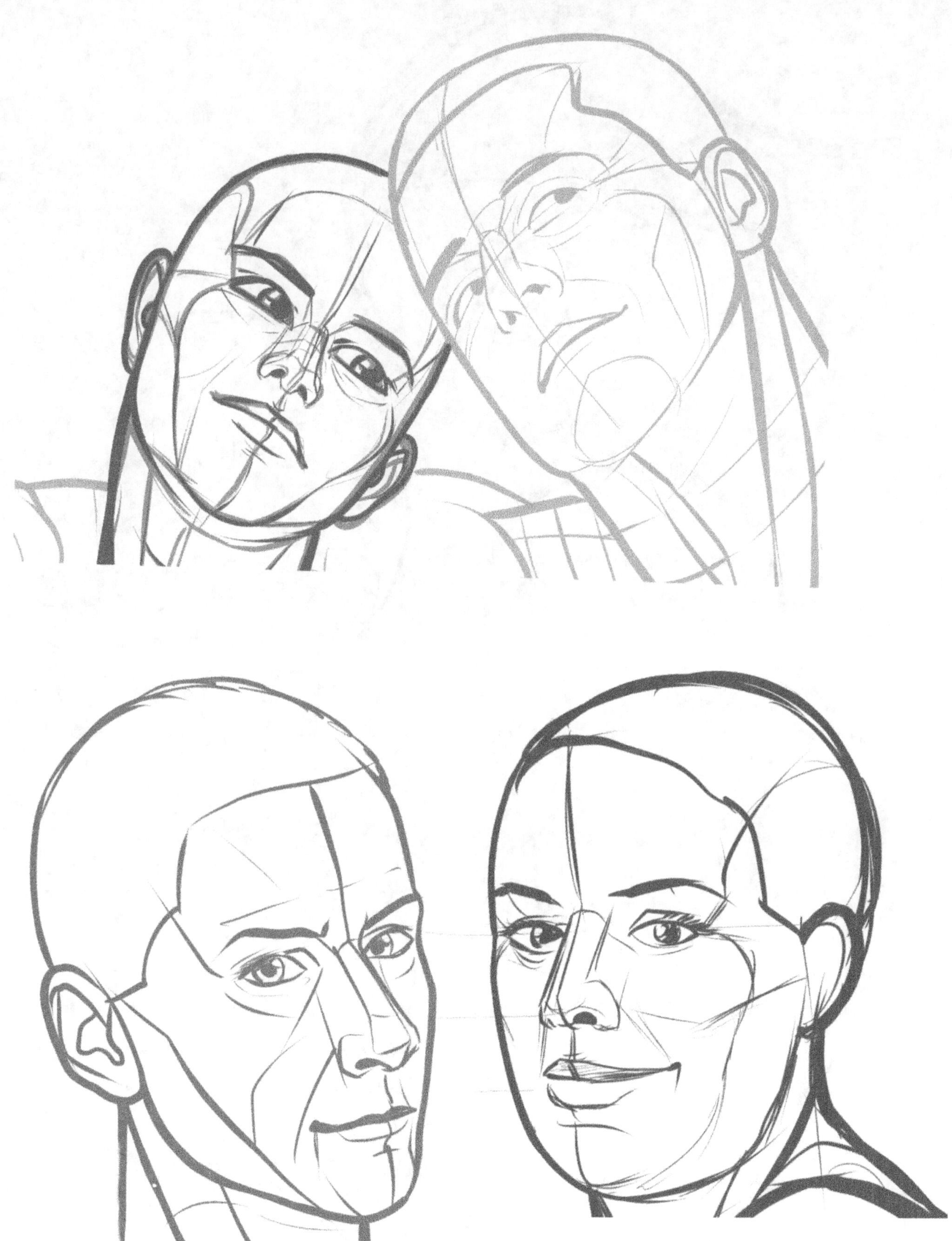

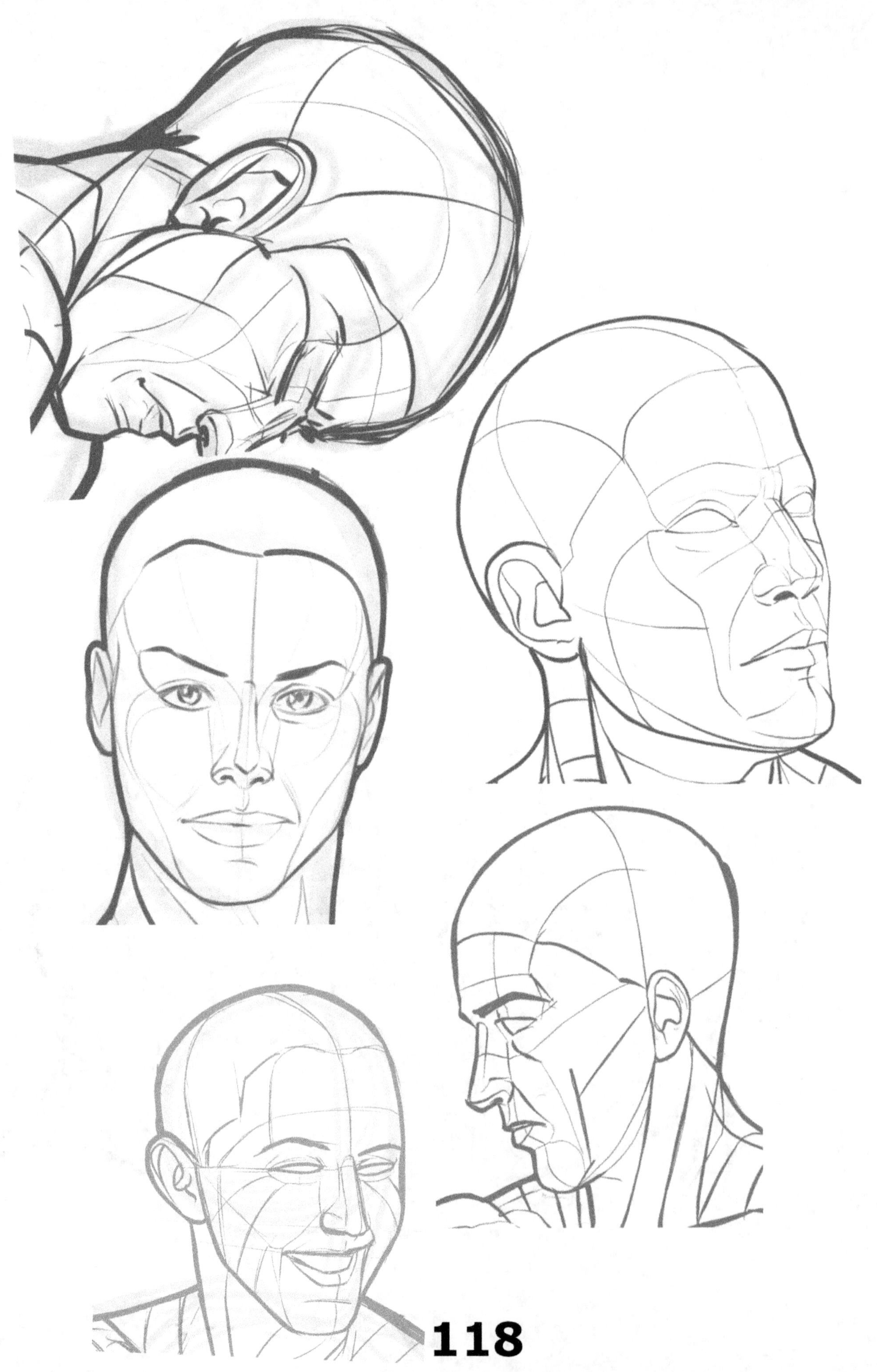

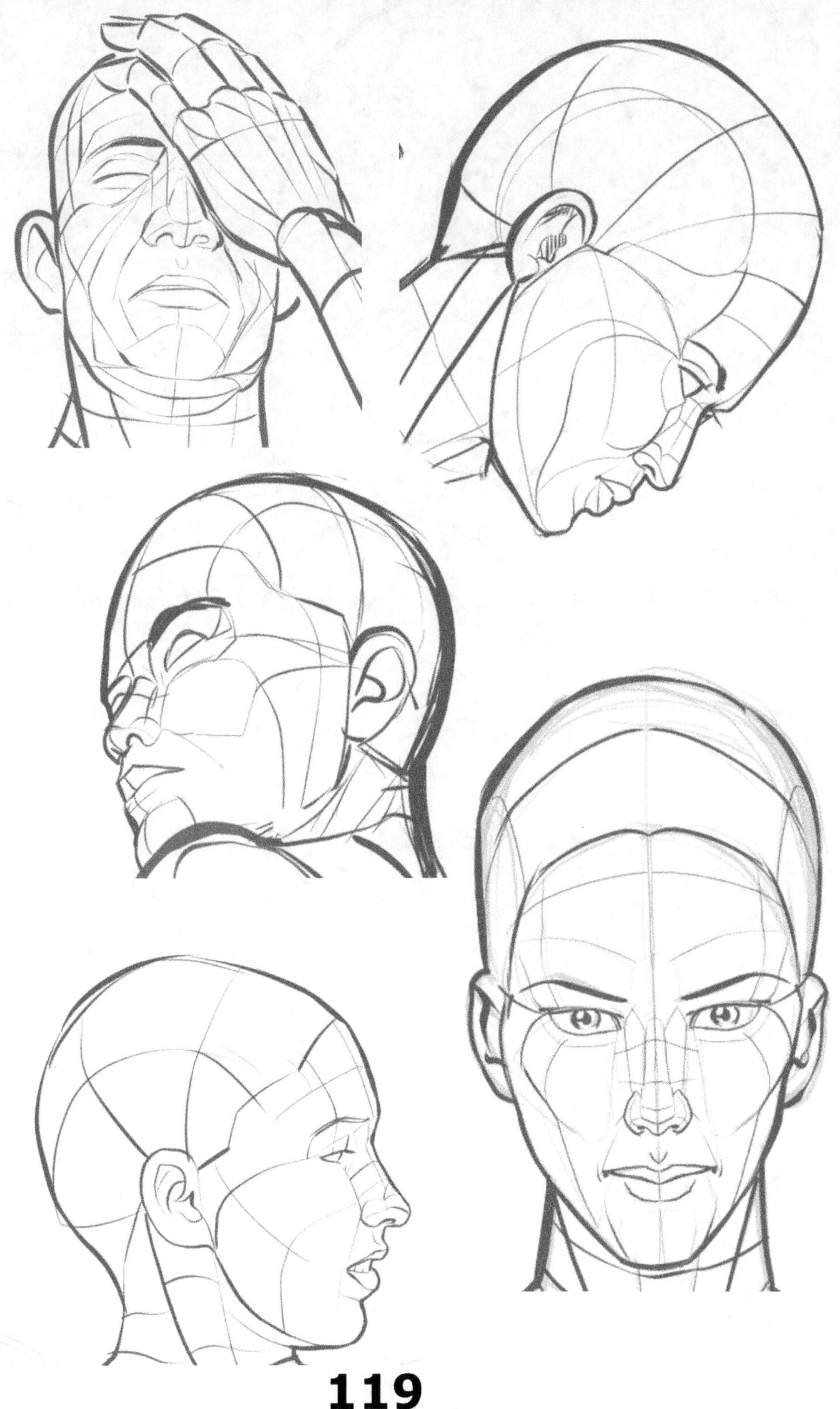

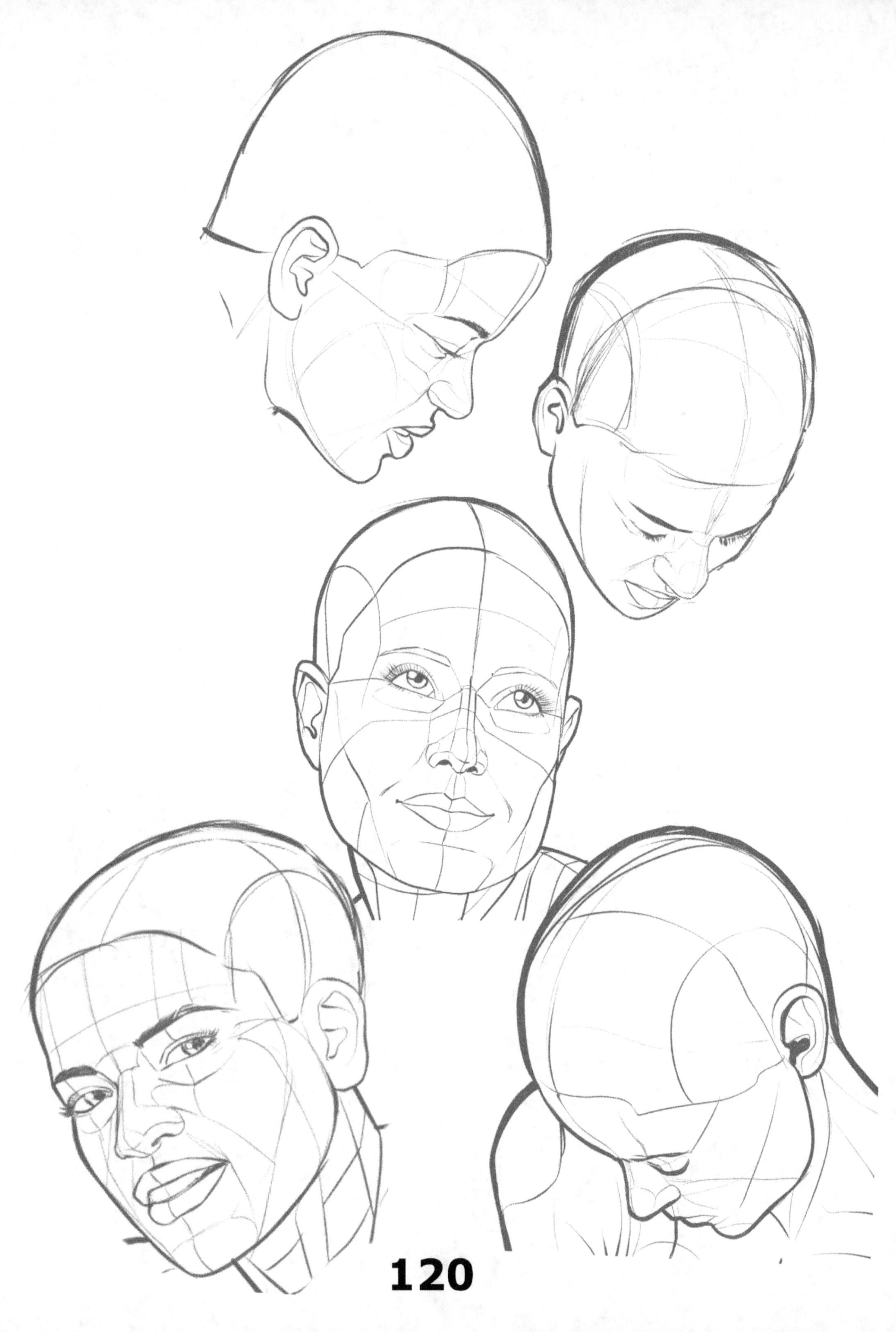

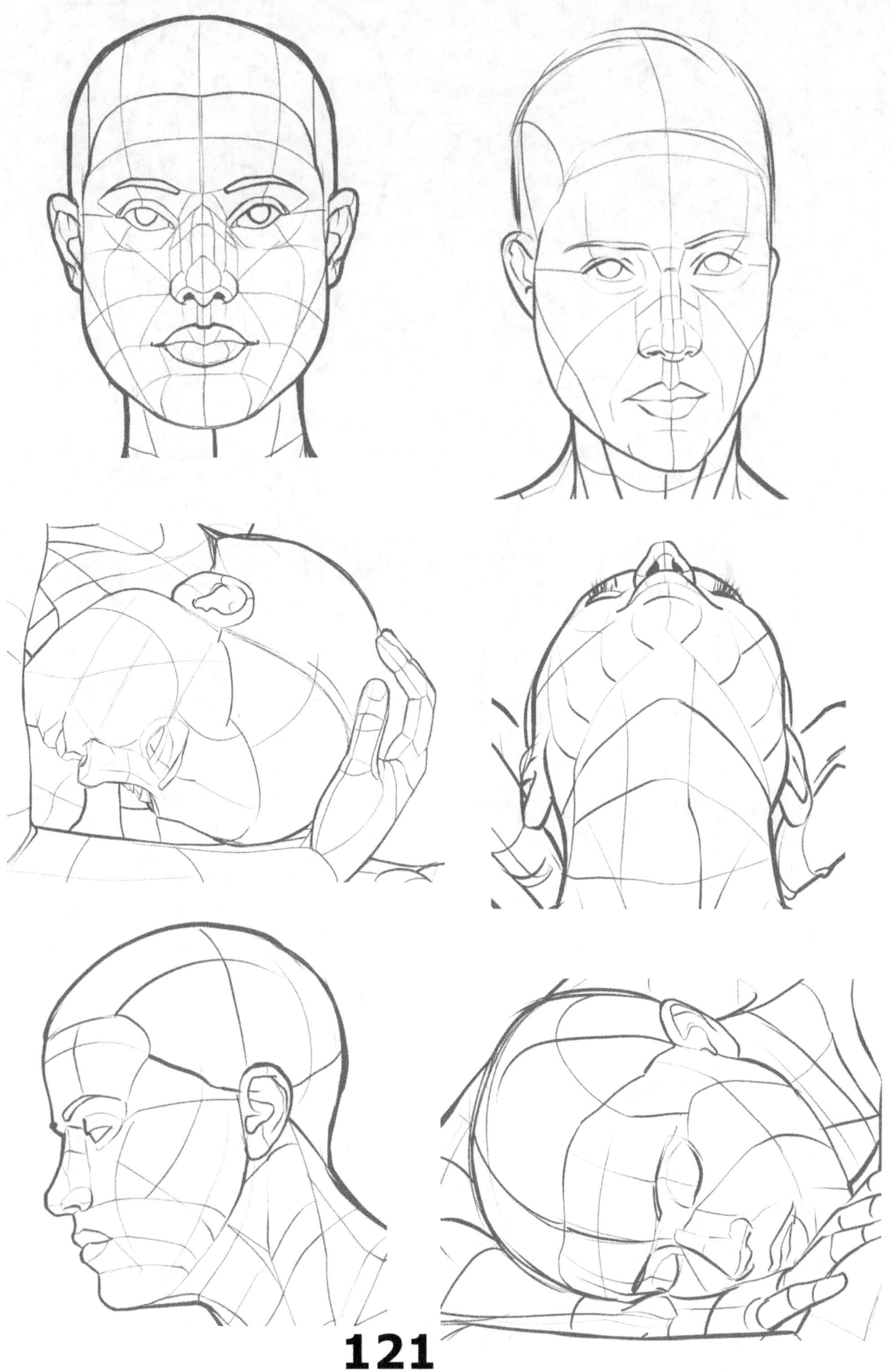

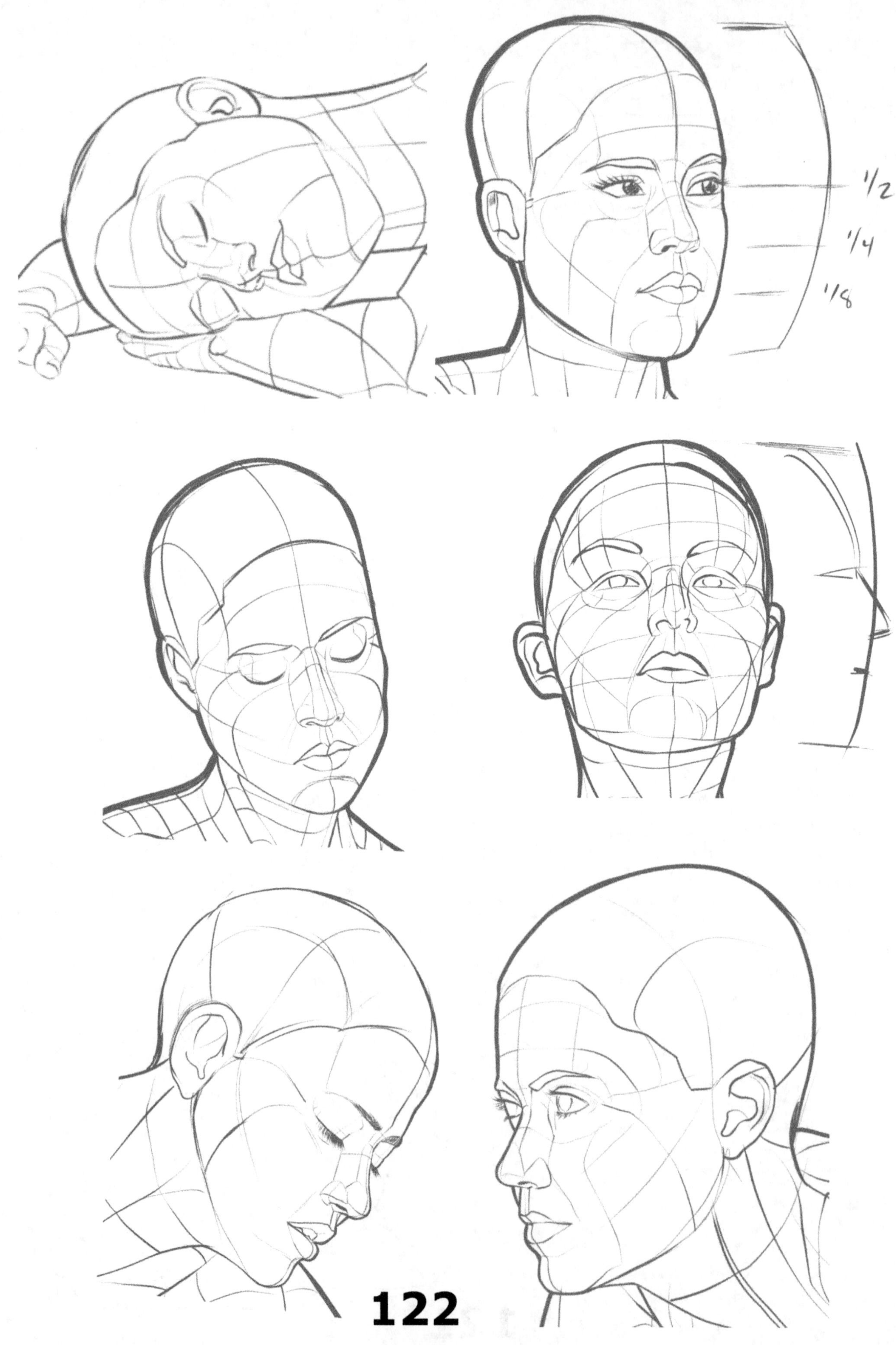

1/2
1/4
1/8

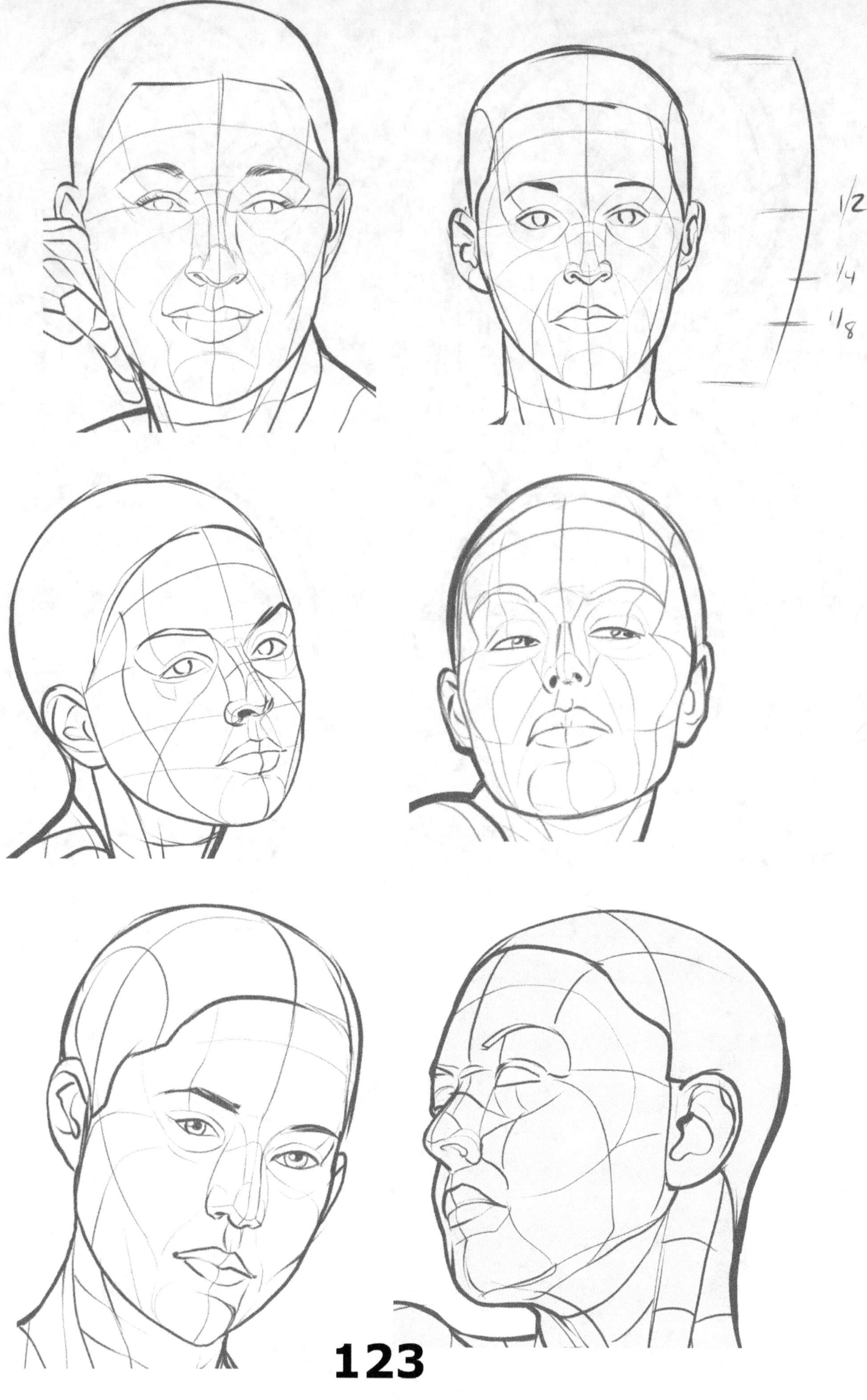

123

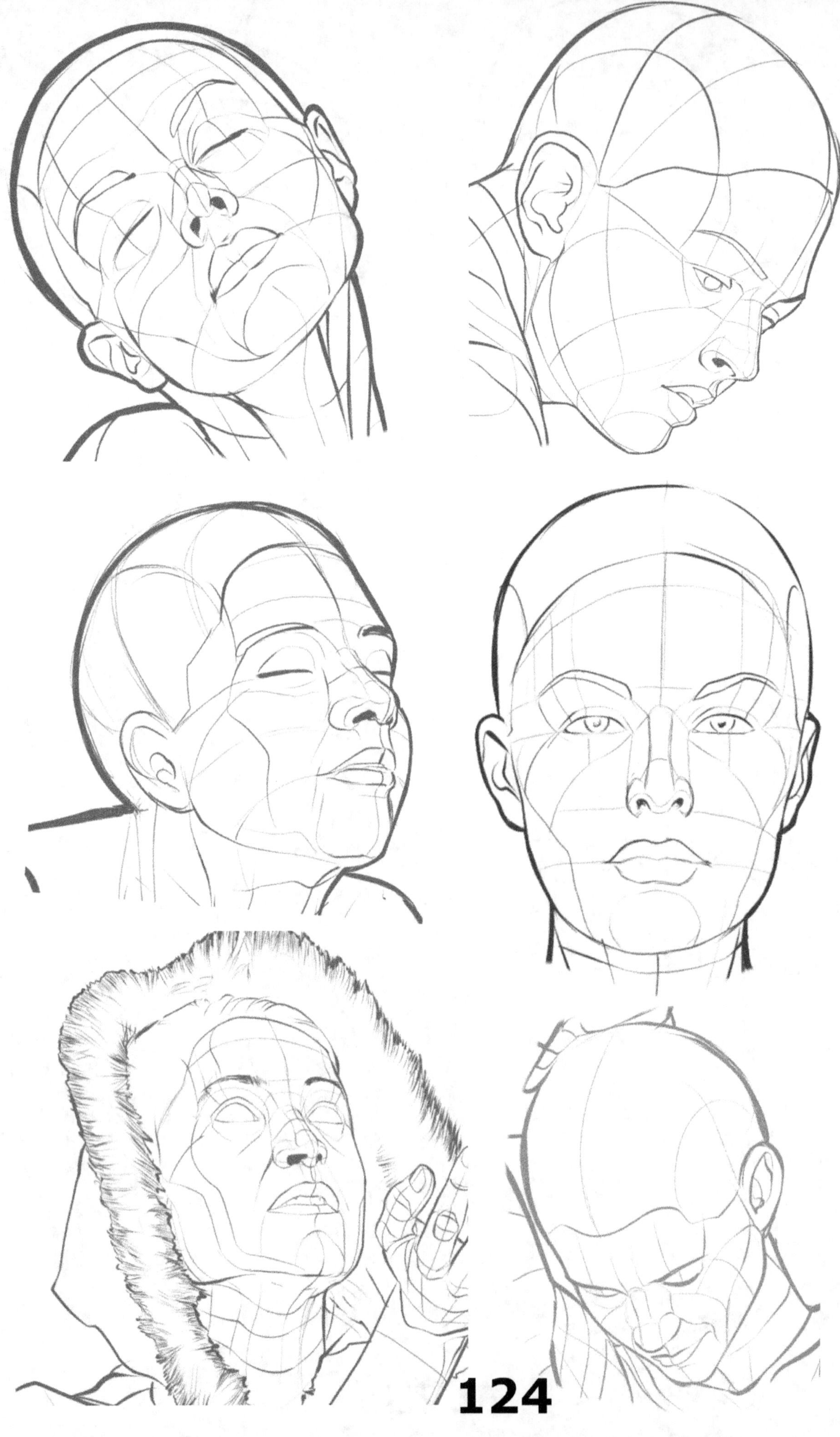

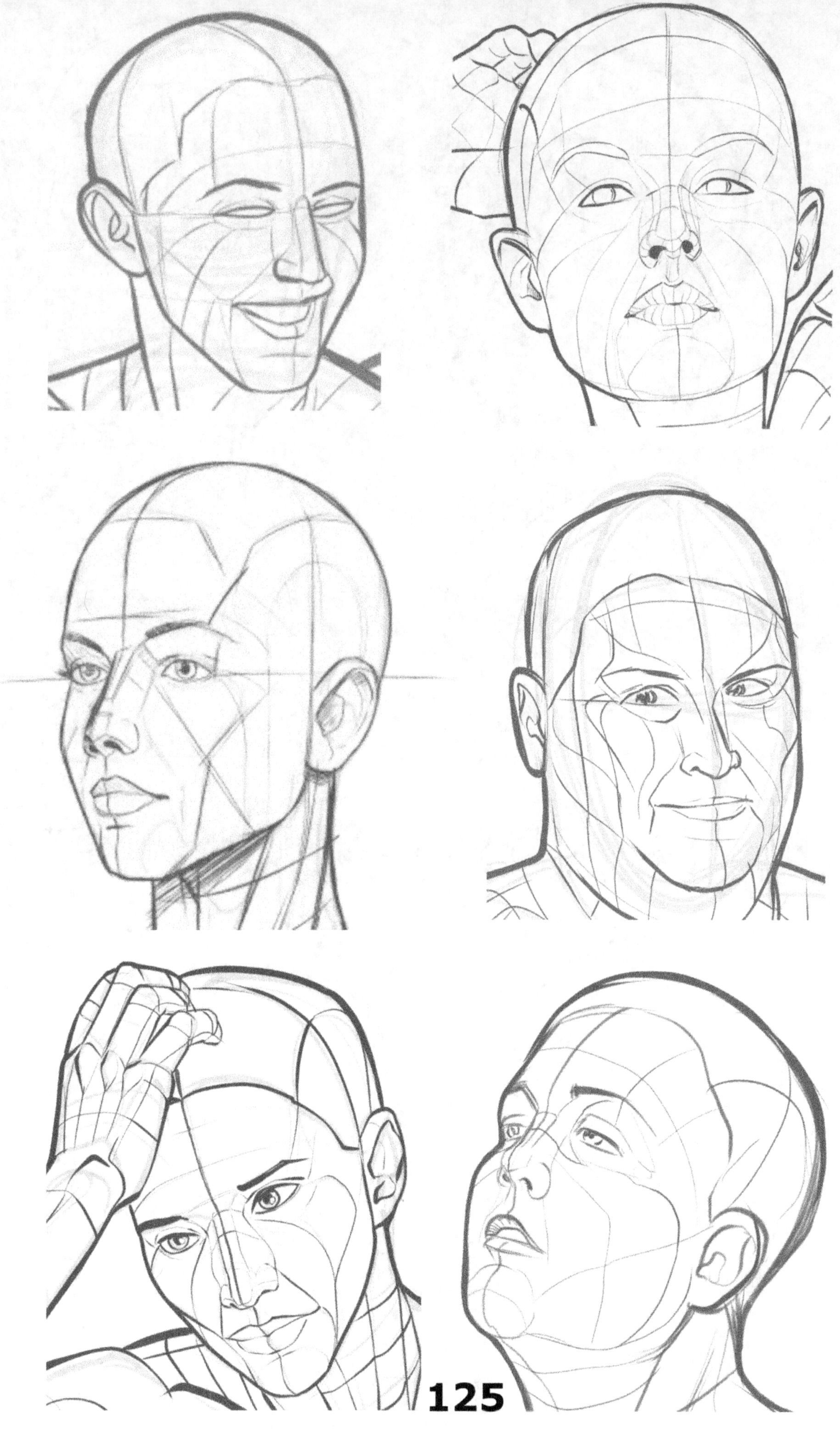

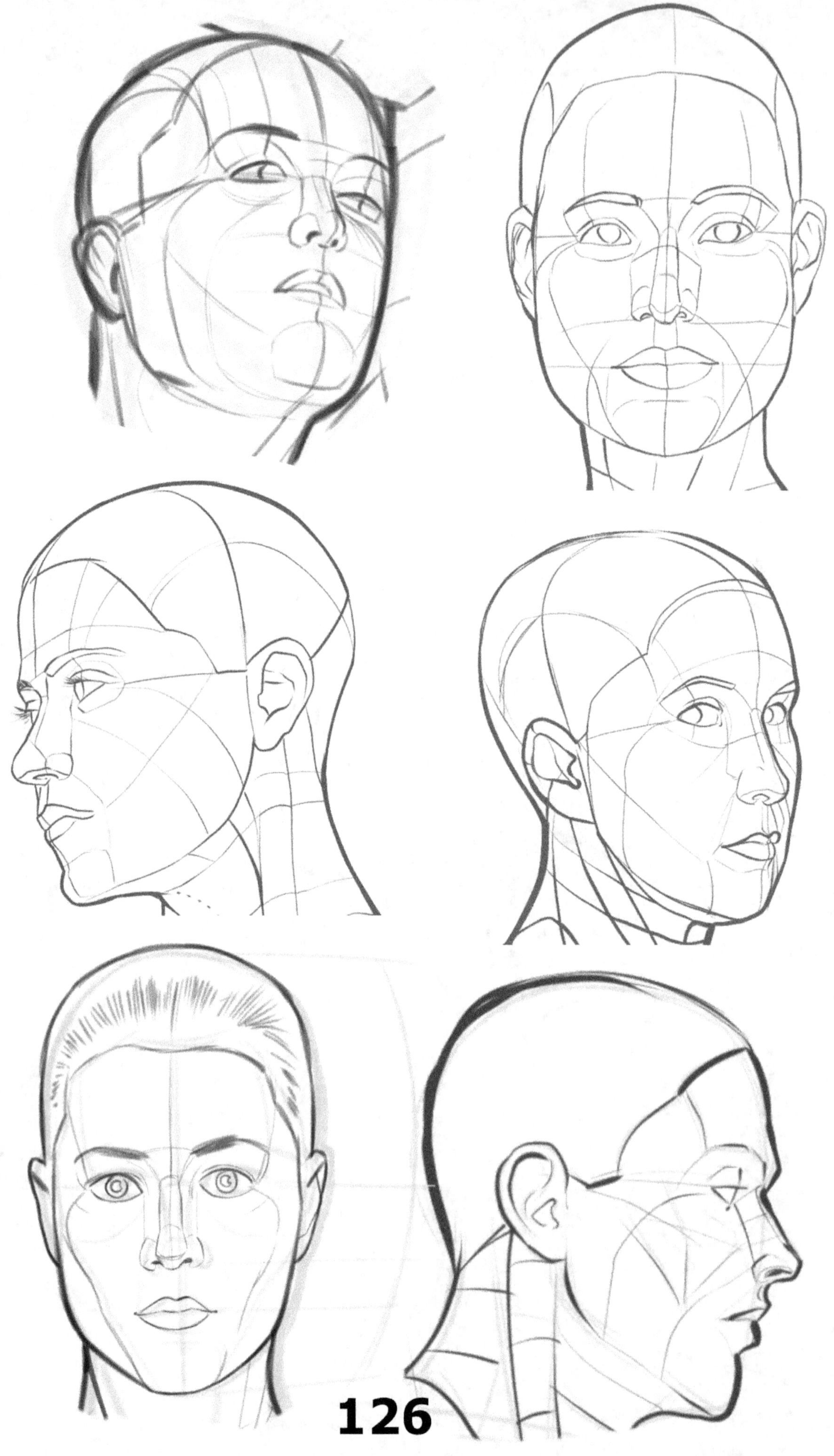

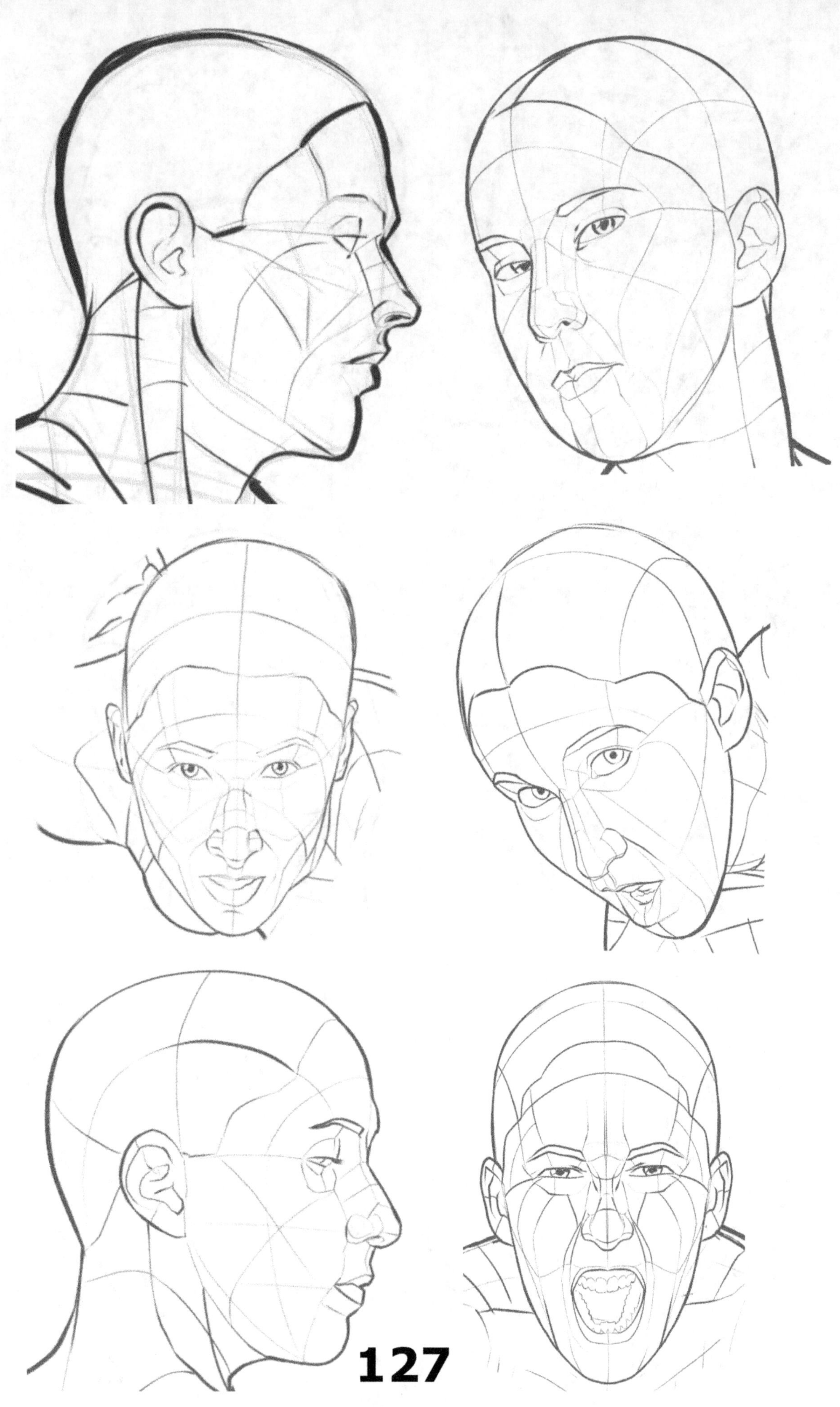

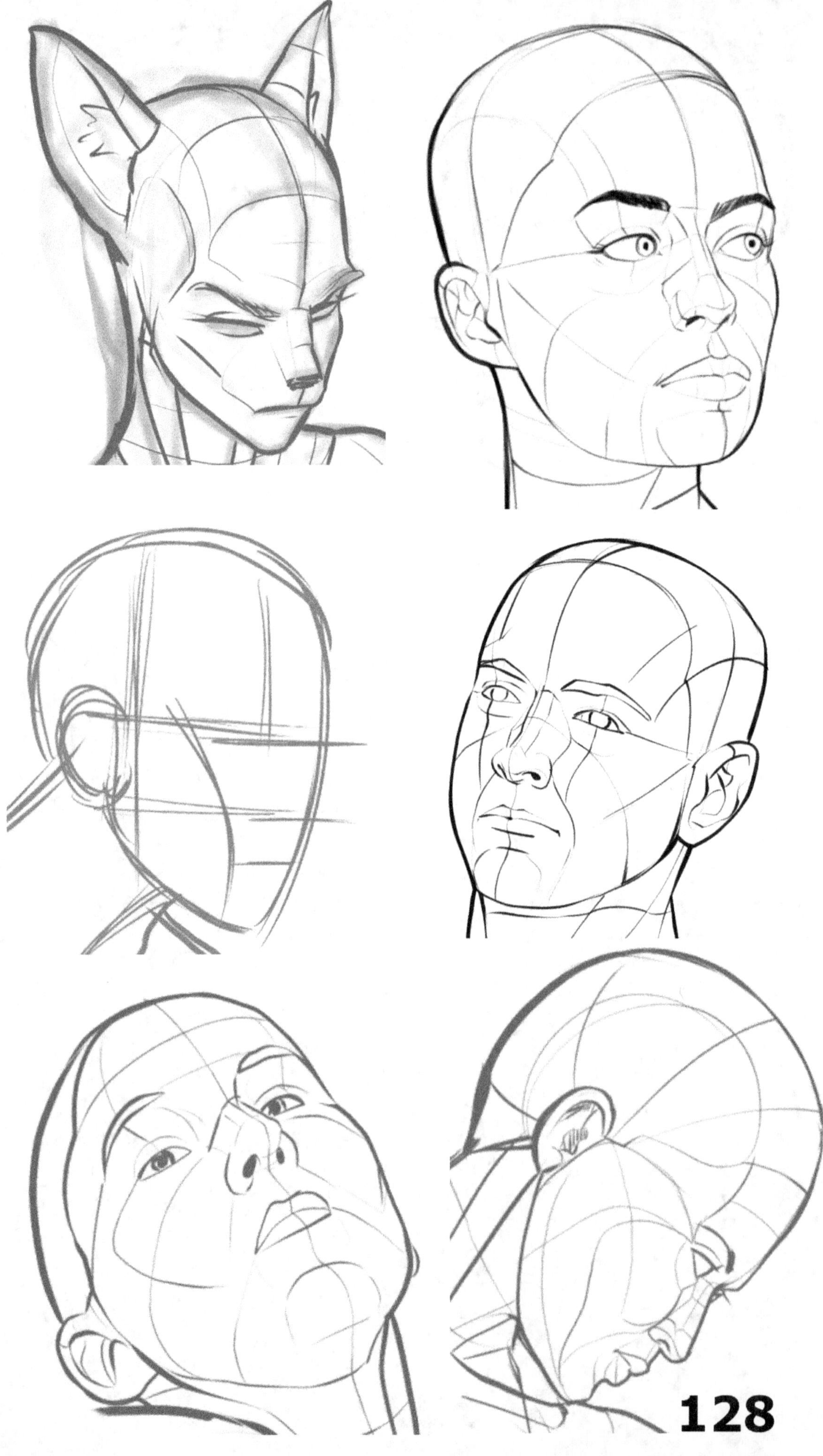

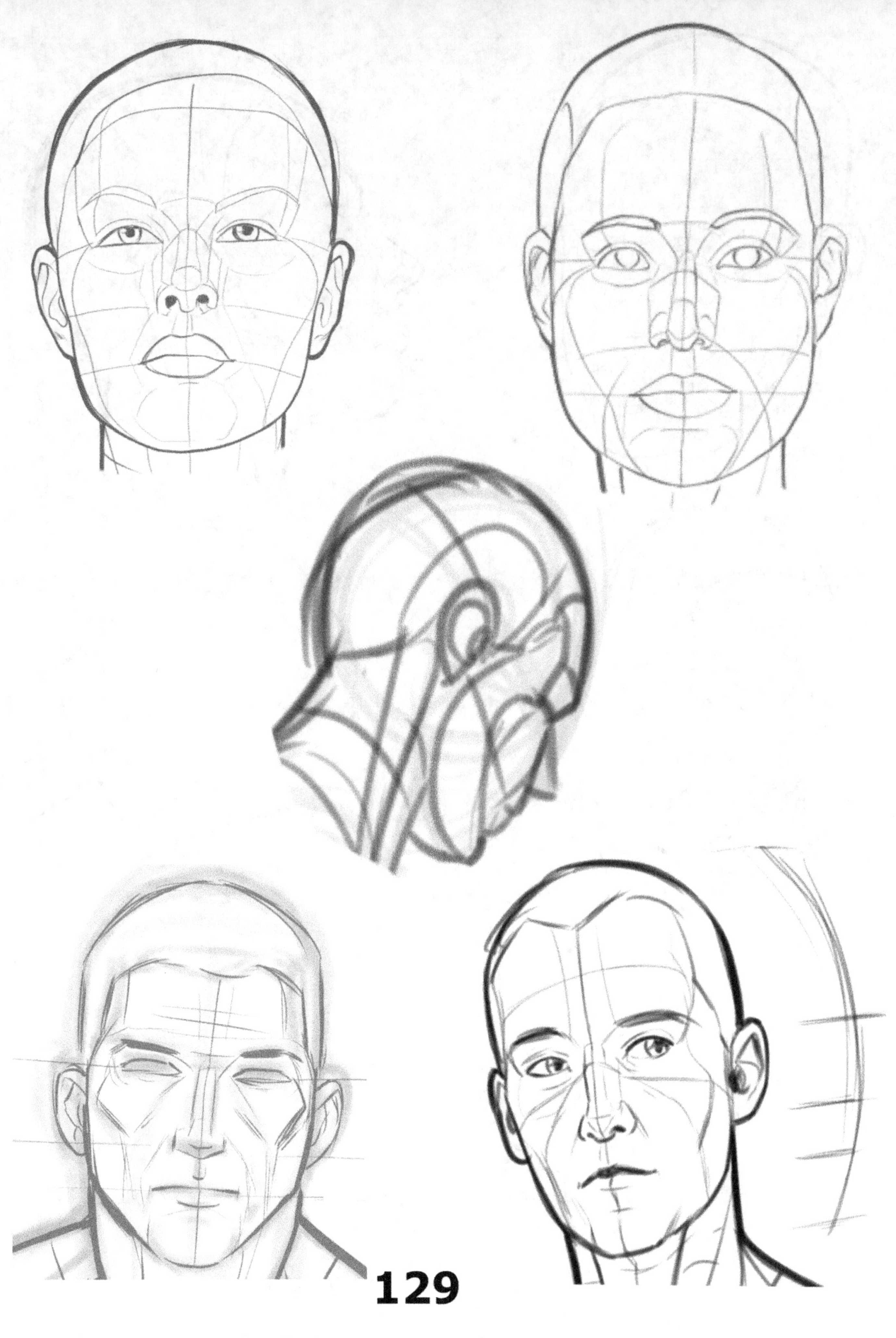

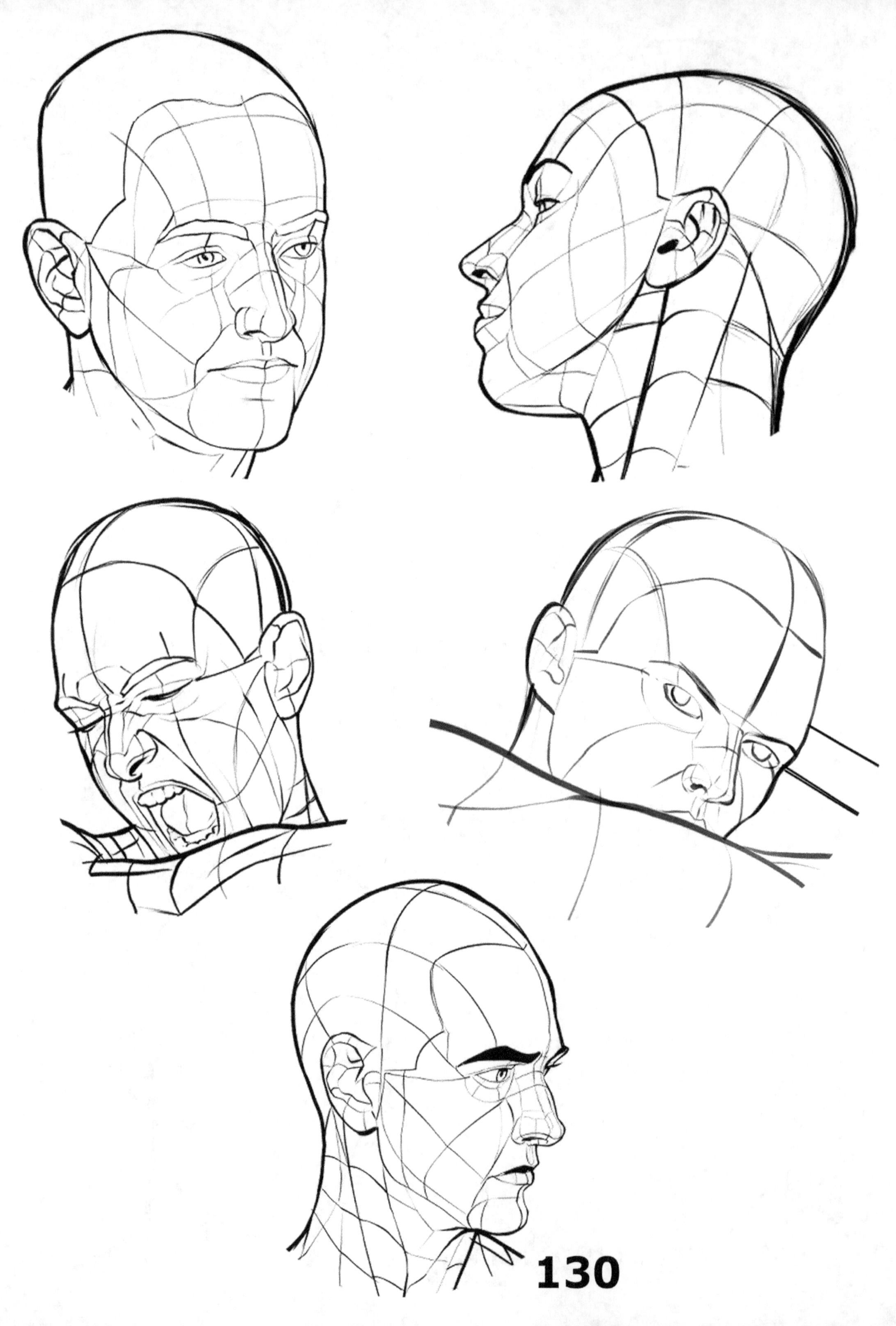

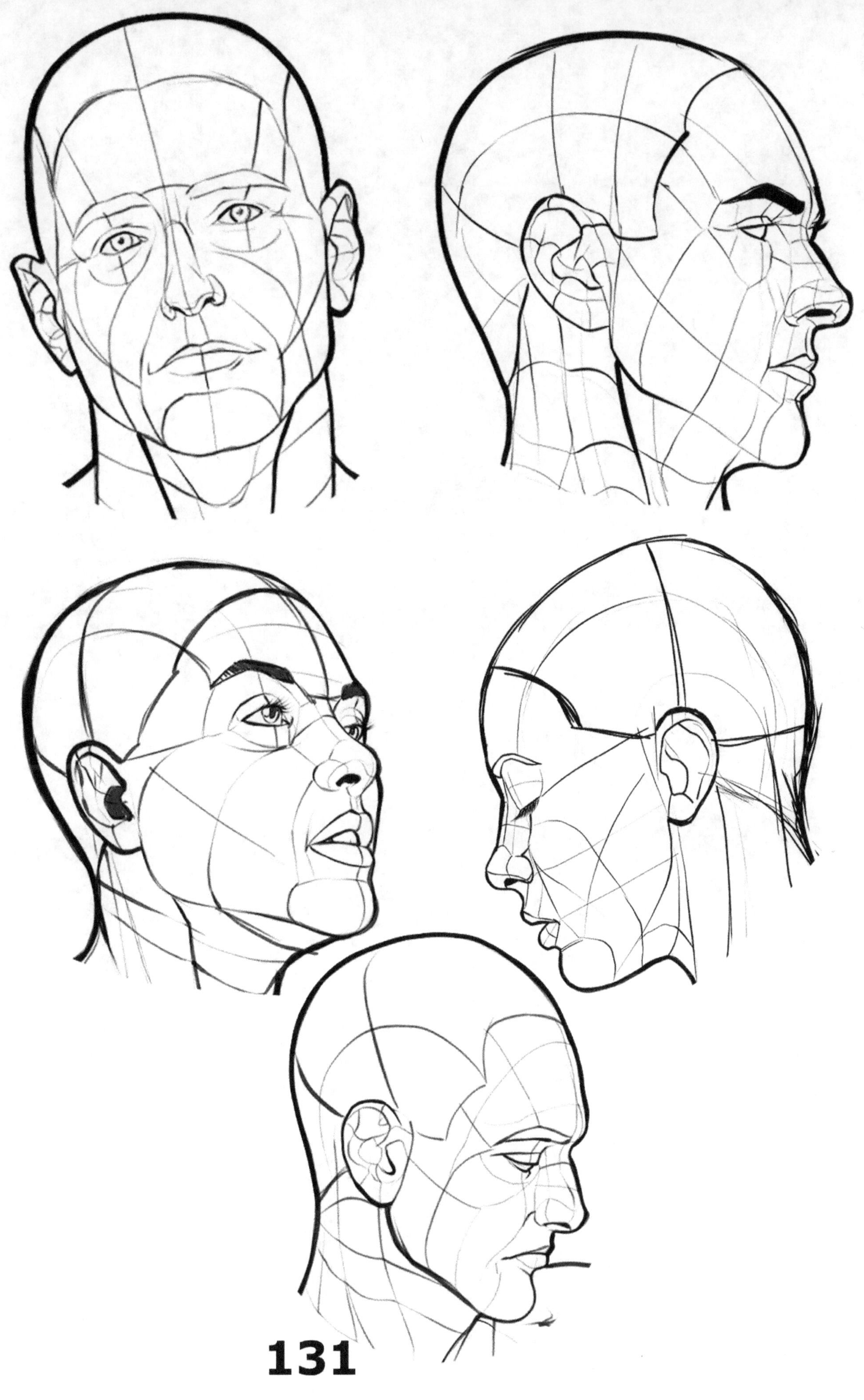

www.ingramcontent.com/pod-product-compliance
Lightning Source LLC
Chambersburg PA
CBHW081617250726
48657CB00009B/2598